FREDERICK BARBAROSSA

FREDERICK
BARBAROSSA

MARCEL PACAUT

Professor in the Faculty of
Letters and Human Sciences,
University of Lyons

Translated by
A. J. POMERANS

COLLINS
ST JAMES'S PLACE, LONDON
1970

SBN 00 211268 X

© Marcel Pacaut 1967
© in the English translation William Collins Sons & Co. Ltd.
and Charles Scribner's Sons 1970

Printed in Great Britain
Collins Clear-Type Press; London and Glasgow

Publisher's Note

The first three chapters describing the Empire
and its setting in the middle of the twelfth
century have been abridged from the original
French edition. The work has otherwise been
translated in its entirety.

Contents

PREFACE *page* 9

1 The Empire in 1152   11
2 Germany in the middle of the twelfth century   19
3 Italy in 1150. The Kingdom of Burgundy   30
4 The man and his aims   41
5 First steps and early setbacks   57
6 Breach of the Treaty of Constance and Italian
    expedition (Summer 1156 - Summer 1159)   73
7 Hopes and disappointments   93
8 A time for courage and resolution
    (1164 - 1168)   114
9 A time for reflection (1168 - 1174)   130
10 War and diplomacy (1174 - 1177). The
    Peace of Venice   147
11 The new policy (1177 - 1184)   167
12 Success (1184 - 1188)   182
13 The tragic apotheosis (1188 - 1190)   195

CONCLUSION   209

BIBLIOGRAPHY   213

INDEX   216

Preface

MANY historians, and some of the best among them, hold that biography makes bad history, since it blames or credits a single man for deeds that involve the co-operation of many, and for circumstances that are beyond any one individual's control. True history, according to this view, is the history of men in society, their behaviour "conditioned" by a whole set of economic, intellectual, spiritual and political factors.

This interpretation of history is perfectly correct if it is not applied too dogmatically or so excessively as to render the "conditioning factors", and quite particularly the economic ones among them, the only subjects worthy of discussion. For to do this is to leave men themselves out of the picture, or to imagine that only inasmuch as they can be converted into statistics or graphs are they of the slightest importance. Human activity cannot be reduced to the satisfaction of material needs or to attempts at pseudo-mathematical reconstruction of the past. Man the digestive apparatus, the vending machine or the serial number is an abstraction and as such utterly fails to reflect the full reality.

History, and this is the crux of the matter, is a form of "universal" analysis of economic circumstances, spiritual aspirations, intellectual attitudes, beliefs, dreams, doctrines, passions, ambitions and myths: it looks at the many material facts, attitudes and feelings that, in every age, fashion man's thoughts and determine his actions. Hence it is extremely complex. To be grasped, it must be examined as a pathologist examines a patient: each of its tissues must be dissected and studied separately under the specialist's microscope. Now,

9

while all are agreed that the economic and structural are among the most important of these sections, they are by no means the only ones worthy of consideration.

Thus a political examination, coupled to economic and sociological studies, may yield extremely valuable information. It has the advantage of being broader, if less deep, and of lending itself to the construction of a synthetic view. The incidents of which it is made up help us to shade in the overall "structural" picture, and this remark applies equally well to biography, which by entering into the skin of one individual may give us some glimpse of the mentality of an entire age— particularly if this individual achieved renown in his own day.

It is for all these reasons that an account of the life and achievements of Frederick Barbarossa, that outstanding representative of German courtly society in the twelfth century, is of considerable historical interest. Frederick I, better than anyone else, expressed the imperial ideal, and his personal achievements highlight the predicament of a great statesman forced to breast the currents of history.

This work does not pretend to be a minute and painstaking analysis of the archives, as were, for instance, my earlier studies of Alexander III and Louis VII. More modest in scope, it is based on general background knowledge of the period and an analysis of German texts dealing with Barbarossa, the Hohenstaufen dynasty and the medieval empire. However, I could scarcely have embarked upon, let alone completed, this brief work without constant recourse to what, to my mind, is the best history of German Emperors in the twelfth and thirteenth centuries: C. E. Perrin's Sorbonne lectures, published by the Centre de Documentation Universitaire.

My own is an unashamed work of popularisation and has no pretensions other than to interest the educated reader in the most stirring pages of German and Italian history in the Middle Ages. It may also be of interest to university students and, who knows, perhaps to their professors as well.

CHAPTER ONE

The Empire in 1152

ON 4 March 1152, the princes of Germany assembled in Frankfort to elect a successor to Conrad III, King of Germany, who had died on 15 February. They chose Conrad's nephew, Frederick of Hohenstaufen, Duke of Swabia, better known as Frederick I or Barbarossa. Upon his election, Frederick automatically became Holy Roman Emperor, although it was not until 1155 that Pope Hadrian IV bestowed this title upon him officially, after a solemn coronation.

What precisely do we know about the Holy Roman Empire, that medieval institution which survived until 6 August 1806, when Napoleon I saw fit to dismember it? The name itself needs a word of explanation. In its historical setting, the term "Holy Roman Empire" expressed both an idea and an ideal.

The idea was to unite in a single political organization all peoples sharing the same aspirations. Much as Alexander's Empire had been based on the spirit of Hellenism and the Roman Empire had tried to share out the cherished benefits of Roman civilization, so the Carolingian Empire was inspired by Christianity. Nearer to our own day, the Napoleonic Empire was similarly based on the philosophical theories of the French Revolution and, later still, the great Colonial empires tried to spread the language and rich cultural traditions of the British monarchy and French Republic to all corners of the earth.

The ideal was thus contained in the idea, indeed it was its very mainspring, for it is the goal of every empire to spread its message to the hearts and minds of all its own people, no less than to the stranger beyond its gates. Thus while the *idea* of Empire leads to territorial expansion and conquest, the *ideal* demands that all subjects, old and new, must strictly abide by its laws and never question its sovereign authority. Attempts to build and preserve a monolithic empire call, at the very least, for the strong and lasting arm of a powerful state.

This need was fully recognized in the Medieval Empire. True, the basic ideal was not always clear, but the princes were all agreed on the absolute necessity of unity and strength, a conviction in which myth and reality often went hand in hand, in which ambitions were confused with dreams, and religion with mysticism.

When Charlemagne restored the Empire in the eighth century, his purpose was to revive the glory of Rome, the memory of which was still very much alive. In practice, the Empire embraced Western Christendom: France, Northern and Central Italy, Northern Spain and Germany, thus covering the whole of the Catholic West with the exception of a few islands. Wherever it spread outwards, for example into Saxony, the Empire immediately made efforts to convert the vanquished to Christianity, thus spreading the faith as well as the authority of the Emperor.

There is no doubt that under the prevailing economic conditions, and what with the immense difficulty of exercising physical control over such vast territories, Charlemagne failed to achieve his objectives. But at the very least, he did succeed in implanting the idea that the West, despite all dissensions, formed an indivisible counterpart to the Byzantine Empire, which had recast the Roman *pars orientalis* in a distinctly Greek mould.

However, Charlemagne's creation was relatively short-lived: the empire he had created split up in the wake of personal disagreements, the emergence of a landed aristocracy, the widening gap between the ideal and the reality, and the Norman and Saracen invasions. By 888 it had virtually ceased to exist;

Germany in about 1150

1. Duchy of Saxony	8. Northern March
2. Duchy of Bohemia	9. Lusatian March
3. Duchy of Swabia	10. Misnian March
4. Duchy of Bavaria	11. Austrian March
5. Duchy of Upper Lorraine	12. County of Holstein
6. Lower Lorraine	13. Landgraviate of Thuringia
7. Duchy of Carinthia	14. Franconia (several counties)

13

in 924, the last emperor of Charlemagne's line died without a successor.

Still, the idea survived, and in 962, Otto the Great having re-established the power of the monarchy in Germany, used the great prestige of his victory over the Huns on the Lechfeld (955)—where he had freed the West from a threat that had hung over it for many years—no less than the renown his arbitrations in Italy had earned him, to have himself crowned Roman Emperor by the Pope.

From 962 to 1152, the Empire had ten successive monarchs. During these 190 years, the Empire embraced the Kingdom of Germany which, at the time, stretched roughly from the Scheldt and the Meuse to the Slav countries beyond the Elbe and the Saale, and from the North Sea, the Eider and the Baltic to the Alps; and the Kingdom of Italy which covered the north and centre of the Italian peninsula to the borders of the Papal States. Since 1038, it also included the Kingdom of Burgundy (Western Switzerland, Franche-Comté). Finally it sought, on various occasions, to impose its authority over the rest of Italy.

And all the time the Empire was advancing and retreating upon the map, its ambitions and dreams kept waxing and waning as well. The first of these ambitions reflected the actual political and territorial situation, and myth had no place in it. The Empire was Germanic and the term *Imperium teutonicorum* first arose during, and was a fit description of, the reign of Frederick Barbarossa. Most of the eleventh and twelfth-century emperors had the same pan-Germanic vision. Imperial power, according to them, rested basically upon the strength of the German crown and should be used first and foremost for her profit. This did not imply, by any means, that the Empire could be reduced to Germany, it must needs include the Kingdom of Italy if not the entire peninsula, and to that end the emperors were prepared to sacrifice all Germany's resources and reserves.

It is quite possible that this conception of Empire reflected a desire to follow in Charlemagne's footsteps and to encompass all of Western Christendom. This implicit ambition was no doubt the reason for the annexation in 1038 of the Kingdom of Burgundy, the third sceptre wielded by Charlemagne. As for the fourth, the sceptre of France, who can say that no German emperor dreamed of seizing it as well? Thus Otto the Great may well have intervened in the dynastic quarrel between the Carolingians and Robertians in the hope of gaining control over the French kingdom, even though he did not lay claim to the French crown himself. In any case, the idea of a united Christian West—no doubt kept alive by legends round, and memories of, the person of Charlemagne—was never completely forgotten. This would explain the somewhat contemptuous way of referring to other rulers as *reguli*, petty kings, as did, for instance, Benzo, Bishop of Alba and a steadfast champion of Henry IV. A contemporary of Barbarossa, Stephen of Rouen, a Norman monk, called Frederick the legitimate heir of Charlemagne, and the Capetian a mere usurper.

For a long time, however, the idea of Western Empire remained rather confused, and the name of Charlemagne was invoked not so much to resurrect the great past as to glorify the exalted role of Germany in the present. For, it was claimed, the German Emperor was Charlemagne's legitimate successor. In about 1150, the *Kaiserkronik*, a work written in the Bavarian dialect, gave the continuous line of emperors from Augustus to Conrad III. It insisted on the fact that the Romans renounced the title of emperor, first in favour of the Franks, and then of the Germans. And according to Otto of Freising, whose work appeared soon afterwards, all this had been decreed by Providence. But none of these texts went on to call explicitly for German domination over the entire West, and in particular over the Kingdom of France—they merely served to tell all the world that the German Emperor was the most renowned and powerful of sovereigns, the prince of western princes.

If more tangible ambitions made themselves felt, it was chiefly thanks to the great and persistent dream of universal empire. If the only emperor before Frederick Barbarossa to express this universal aspiration was Otto III, who reigned not from Germany but from Rome, most of the others must have felt the same call deep in their hearts.

Their dream, for it was never more than that, was to re-unite all Christendom under a single crown. This is what Otto III (983–1002), the son of a German emperor and the grandson, through his mother, of a Byzantine ruler, hoped to achieve when, in a moment of great political and spiritual fervour, he laid claim to the empires of both West and East. The salutation to Otto, recorded by Odo, Abbot of Cluny, fully endorsed this claim:

"May the *Slavs* growl and the *Hungarians* gnash their teeth; may the *Greeks* be struck dumb and the *Saracens* be troubled and take flight; may the *Africans* pay tribute and the *Spaniards* solicit help; may *Burgundy* venerate and cherish the emperor, and *Aquitaine* joyously greet him. May all *Gaul* proclaim: 'Who has heard of the like?' And may the *Italian* people, their arms upraised, cry out: 'By the Lord, this is the only true son of Caesar, Otto the Great'."

But Otto's ambition was never fulfilled—even Italy offered him strong opposition. His end came prematurely; his failure was patent. Yet his ambitions outlived him, and led some of his German successors to look down upon all Byzantine emperors with contempt.

The universal idea, as we have said, was based not only on the burning desire for Christian unity but also on memories of the Roman Empire, which Charlemagne was widely believed to have restored. This was precisely why Otto III established his court at Rome, and proclaimed her the "capital of the world" by a charter of 1001. Most of his successors, too, looked

upon Rome as their capital, even if their court was in Germany.
This is not to say that they were invariably moved by his idea
of the universal kingdom; some, in fact, used Rome solely as a
base for dominating the peninsula. In short, Rome was the
meeting point of the German and universal dreams of empire,
two of the prime influences in medieval politics, and it is not
always easy to say which was predominant at a given point in
time.

Thus, though universalism often appeared as the wish to
bring all people into a common fold in which no one nation
was supreme, in practice it often meant strengthening the
heavy hand of Germany, so much so that it is difficult to
determine how far the ideal was used as a mere cover for
German expansionism.

All in all, we may say that idealism and political strategy
were inextricably intertwined in imperial theory. In practice,
however, German Emperors throughout the tenth, eleventh
and twelfth centuries, except for Otto III, were content to
govern over Germany, Italy and the Kingdom of Burgundy,
even though many may have dreamed of extending their
authority further afield.

As a result of the revival of a vigorous electoral system, in-
cessant interference by the Holy See, divisions within Germany,
and the demand for emancipation in Italy, the empire was
shaken to its very foundations. Thus, by 1152, while the
Emperor still wielded nominal power over his possessions in
Germany and Italy, he lacked the means to enforce his authority
or to administer his provinces. His chief counsellor, the
Imperial Chancellor, was invariably a churchman, and saw to
the drafting of and implementation of his orders, but for the
rest he could rely on no one. The Imperial Diet (*Reichstag*),
which was attended by all princes, was supposed to assist him
with advice but was often more of a hindrance than a help—
prolonged negotiations were invariably needed to enlist the

support of the most powerful nobles for any major project. Moreover, the *Reichstag* was far more concerned with local than with imperial problems.

The strength of the Empire, then, depended largely upon the Emperor's position in Germany, a subject we shall now examine in some greater detail.

CHAPTER TWO

Germany in the Middle of
the Twelfth Century

In 1152, Germany was deeply divided, as the Houses of
Hohenstaufen and Welf kept pressing their respective claims
to the royal and imperial crown. It is a striking fact that, in the
Middle Ages, as throughout history, national unity so often
dangled just beyond the reach of the German nation, every
advance, every inspired ideal, every heroic exploit being
thwarted by new difficulties and insurmountable obstacles.
In the very people, loyalties have forever been painfully
divided between province and nation.

Even Germany's natural contours do not make for definite
unity or disunity. North of the Alps is a monotonously un-
changing country of plateaus and plains, cut by a range of
ancient massifs; in the south, the character of the landscape is
undulating, and at times even harsh. True, Germany's great
rivers—the Oder and Vistula, and even more important, the
Rhine and the Elbe—with their great valleys, all flowing north
to the sea, have some unifying influence, as have the mountain
barriers of the Rhine and Bohemia in the south, but there is no
natural boundary in the west or in the east, where the vast
plains stretch far into the distance. A far greater unifying
factor is the climate—cold winters and hot, often wet, summers.
Life under such conditions is neither agreeable nor easy; it calls
for courage, toughness and great initiative.

Germany is a country of black forests with scattered clearings harbouring large villages; of populous valleys usually

dominated by a castle or burg. Towards the north, the forests grow thinner and give way to heathland, studded with lakes, lagoons and bogs. In 1150, the countryside had not changed greatly since Carolingian times, and the economy was still based on feudal property ties and on agriculture. The chief crops were cereals and, in a few districts, grapes.

However, signs of economic change had begun to appear everywhere. First, as the population began to grow, the forests were pushed back and new settlements sprang up in the clearings. At the same time, many Germans began to leave their homes, above all to migrate to the newly-conquered Slav territories in the east. Travel along the great waterways also kept increasing, and several of the southern towns, such as Ravensburg and Ratisbon (Regensburg) started to establish commercial contacts with Italy. From 1100 onwards, Norwegian, Frisian and Flemish merchants called regularly at Cologne. Soon afterwards, German merchants began trading from Bardowick on the Elbe, and from Cologne and Bremen, both of which were growing fast at the expense of Tiel, south of Utrecht. They travelled as far afield as Visby on the island of Gotland, with its predominantly German population, Schleswig in Denmark, and even London, trading chiefly in Rhenish and Alsatian wines, and dried fish from Scandinavia. Moreover, they carried cloth from Flanders and Friesland as far south as Enns in Austria, and silver and copper from the Harz mountains along the great east-west trade route from Magdeburg through Goslar, Soest and Dortmund to Cologne. Finally they did a great traffic in salt from the rich Lüneburg deposits.

But none of these activities made specifically for the growth of national unity—Germany was not the only country with a continental climate and growing commerce. Historical rather than economic developments—which may take a host of divergent paths—helped to bring the German people together and to stamp them in a common mould.

The Romans had left little trace of their colonization on

Germany, even in the region between the Rhine and the Meuse which had been an important Roman province with Trèves as its capital, so little, in fact, that it was the Germans, those "invaders from beyond the Rhine", who were instrumental in the destruction of the Roman Empire. True, they were subsequently converted to Christianity and incorporated into Charlemagne's Holy Roman Empire, but when this in turn broke up, they were again cut off from the rest of the world and driven into isolation.

Thus, north of the Alps, a kingdom grew up, bound together by a common language. This factor was the most important single element in the growth of national unity, notwithstanding the persistence of a host of regional dialects, and even of Slavonic pockets in Lusatia, Misnia and Bohemia, and Romance pockets in Rhaetia and Lorraine. The very name *Deutschland* recalls that Germany is the country of the *Diutischiu*, of German-speaking people.

Though the heart of the country was historically the region east of the Rhine and north of the Alps, Germans also spread into, and "Germanized", many neighbouring lands: they invaded the territory between the Rhine and the Meuse; set up Marches (*Marks*) to protect Bavaria against attack from the east and south-east; and in the tenth century entered Austria (*Oesterreich*), Styria, Carinthia, Carniola, together with Tyrol and the ecclesiastical principality of Brixen. The western boundary of Germany came to take in all of what is now Switzerland east of the Reuss, and the south-eastern boundary embraced the Duchy of Bohemia flanked by Moravia. However, there was no definite frontier in the east and north-east. This was continually extended as the Germans consolidated their hold over the Slavs, and although this advance was interrupted towards the end of the eleventh century, by 1125 the frontiers were once more being pushed forward. The County of Holstein sought to gain control of the Baltic coast; the Northern March (*Nordmark*) which, in 1134, had been entrusted to that enterprising Ascanian prince, Albert of Ballenstädt, known as Albert the Bear, was extended into Brandenburg; and Misnia and Lusatia, ruled by the Wettin family, were augmented by the seizure of Silesia from Poland.

Thus Germany in the twelfth century was pulled in two directions: the imperial ideal drew her south into Italy, while the need to expand led her to the east. And this double progress was greatly helped by the absence of strong neighbours. The Slavs were on the defensive, and the Kingdom of Poland was prepared to accept vassal status. The same was true of Denmark to the north. In the south, Italy formed part of the Empire and, as such, was under German control; to the west, France was fighting for her very existence againts Catalonia and England. The absence of separatist movements within, and of any real threat from without, thus combined to allow Germany to develop her own national character, based upon a common language and a common culture.

Yet the path towards German unity was not nearly as smooth as it might have been.

To begin with, the westernmost provinces of Brabant, Hainault and Holland were far more concerned with their own affairs than with Germany's imperial projects. In a sense, they had never been part of Germany—in 843, at the partition treaty of Verdun, they were handed neither to Charles the Bald as part of France nor to Lewis II as part of Germany, but were given, along with Italy, Provence and Burgundy, to Lothar, to form a buffer state on the northern border of Lorraine, and did not become part of Germany until 935. Subsequently, though they did not actively seek independence, they remained self-contained and unconcerned with events in the distant east and south of Germany.

In addition, two special forces, that had evolved within Germany herself, tended to oppose greater cohesion.

The first was the confused and confusing concentration of powers in the hands of the aristocracy. Their authority, like that of the crown, was possibly based on popular support, though it seems more likely that it was built on military strength. The most powerful nobles in the tenth century were those who, as the central authority grew weaker, had strengthened their own principalities, based, as Charles E. Perrin has put it, "on ethnic groups with their own dialect and legal institutions". Such were the five ethnic duchies (*Stammesherzog-tümer*) that made up Germany in the tenth century: Saxony, Bavaria, Swabia, Franconia and Lorraine, each with marked features of its own. Subsequently, the crown fought hard to reduce their particularist claims, and during the eleventh century it did, in fact, succeed in gaining a measure of control over them, and in wresting major concessions from the dukes. In this, the kings were greatly helped by the gradual transformation of the old ethnic duchies into straightforward territorial ones, i.e. into regions united not so much by ties of tradition and law, as for administrative purposes. Nevertheless, in the middle of the twelfth century, the dukes, although they no longer resembled their ancestors in either their titles or their prerogatives, still represented a major power in the land. In particular, the subjects over whom they ruled—nobles and peasants alike—remained outside the king's direct jurisdiction. Moreover, the dukes successfully upheld the idea that power must be shared equally between the king and the aristocracy—an idea that gained considerably in influence once the electoral system came back into favour in 1125.

For all that, it would be wrong to exaggerate the importance of the aristocracy as a force opposing unification. True, the crown had to overcome a great deal of resistance and still more inertia on the part of the dukes, but none of them ever attempted to secede, if only because their idea of government involved allegiance to the crown, and also because, despite the ethnic characteristics and regional traditions of their estates, they considered themselves Germans first and foremost.

Feudalism, the other strong decentralizing force in twelfth-century Germany, tended to produce the same results: it posed a threat to royal authority, to cohesion and national unity but not to the survival of the realm. It was feudalism which, in the middle of the twelfth century, set one prince against another, for instance in the bitter struggle between the Welfs and the Staufens. There is no need to enlarge upon this point. As elsewhere in the west, feudalism established itself in Germany during the ninth and tenth centuries. It was basically a system of dependencies, in which the weaker nobles were forced to seek the protection of their more powerful liege lords, willingly paying them homage in the form of services (financial, legal and military). As a result, the power of the leading nobles was constantly extended, while the power of the crown was correspondingly diminished—a vassal owing allegiance to his immediate master and not to the monarch. Moreover, the public administration tended to become feudalized as well—official posts were granted in fee by the crown and so came under feudal law, which whittled away the power of the sovereign even further. Thus while counts were initially officials appointed by the king to administer a district or a county, they became powerful figures in their own right, and their lands fiefs outside the gift of the king.

However, once again, the results were not as bleak for the king as they might appear at first sight. The concept of the state and of public authority remained far more deeply in-grained in Germany than among her neighbours, thanks chiefly to Otto the Great (Otto I, King of Germany from 936 and Emperor 962–973). In particular, the Germans continued to recognize their king as supreme ruler, and conceded that all local authority was held by his favour, even if, in the accepted political theory, king and nobles were stated to share authority. The king's sovereignty was strengthened further by the fact that, from the reign of Otto I until the Investiture Dispute, he enjoyed the full support of his bishops, whose prerogatives reverted to the crown upon their death. In short, the monarch was and remained sovereign lord, even at a time when the system established by Otto I had already begun to crumble. In theory, at least, his word was law, and what disruptive forces had come to the fore and had begun, actively or passively, to challenge his power, were still too weak to break up his kingdom.

Geographically and administratively, Germany was divided into a number of feudal principalities, the most important of which were the Duchies of Swabia, Bavaria, Carinthia in the south, Saxony in the north, Bohemia in the east and Upper Lorraine in the west. Within these small principalities lay a host of countries—224 all told in 1024—many of which had come into existence by usurpation of royal prerogatives, while others still owed direct allegiance to the king.

The most important of all German cities was Cologne which, in the early twelfth century, extended its town wall for the second time, this time enclosing 483 acres. As a result, Cologne became the largest city in Western Europe. Other fast-developing German cities were Worms, Spires, Mainz and Basle in the Rhineland; Würzburg in the centre; Augsburg in the south; and Soest, Fritzlar, Magdeburg, Goslar (where the new and old towns fused in 1108), Jumne (on the island of Wollin in the Oder estuary), Stettin (with a strong Slavonic element), Bremen, Dortmund and Hildesheim, all of which received their charters at the time, in the north.

Since, as we saw, all these cities came increasingly under the direct authority and protection of their sovereign, they may be said to have acted as a strongly cohesive element in the complex structure of medieval Germany.

How powerful was the king of Germany in practice? And what was the basis of his authority?

Let us repeat, that in theory and with certain minor restrictions, the German, more than any neighbouring king, had full jurisdiction over all his subjects, whether free men or serfs.

Nevertheless, it must be emphasized that this theory, as it has been expounded by many German historians, shows only one side of the picture. In practice, the king was bound to the oath he swore at his coronation, in which he promised to defend the true faith (against heresy and schism), to protect the church and its priests (without whittling away their privileges), and to govern in accordance with the laws of his ancestors (that is, with tradition). In principle again, all dukes and counts held all their powers and prerogatives exclusively by their sovereign's grace, but in fact, the sovereign's rights were frequently challenged by the electors who kept invoking their ancestral rights, while conveniently forgetting that these rights were supposed to be delegated by the reigning monarch. Thus the actual political situation depended upon the balance of forces between kings and nobles, a balance that was influenced by different factors at different times.

Most important, perhaps, the king was generally recognized as having the right and duty to preserve the peace, to protect every man's person and property. Now these rights were no more secure in twelfth-century Germany that they were elsewhere in the west. Private wars between nobles were a permanent feature, and claimed victims from men of all ranks. Moreover lawlessness and banditry were rife throughout the empire. And in Germany—unlike France and other Christian countries which left it to the church to restore God's peace and propose reconciliation—the king himself had, ever since Henry IV, taken it upon himself to outlaw private wars by proclaiming the peace (*Landfrieden*) and forcing all princes to submit.

It was in the name of peace that the German kings exercised their two basic prerogatives: the royal proclamation of banishment which could be used to punish any disobedient subjects; and the king's pardon. It was also in the name of peace that the German king acted as chief judge, and that he reserved the right to deal with all such capital offences as arson, treason, rape, abduction and murder. Furthermore, the royal court was recognized as the highest court of appeal and its jurisdiction extended over the entire kingdom. No one, except the king, had the right to stop, transfer or interfere with trial proceedings, whether at county assizes or the local courts. Whenever the sovereign visited a county, the count's legal prerogatives, however restricted, were suspended; in short, the king was the personification of justice throughout the land. And when we come to look at his other rights, we find that they are restricted exactly at the point where they are no longer necessary to preserve the peace.

Thus in the military field, the royal prerogative extended to such matters as mobilization, conscription, as well as the granting of exemptions (margraves and their subjects not being obliged to contribute towards campaigns waged outside their territory). But in fact, the levying of troops could only be ordered by a council of princes—the king could conscript none but his immediate vassals and had to rely upon the nobles to levy the bulk of his army. The latter was chiefly made up of knights (tactical developments had led to the almost complete disappearance of foot soldiers, so that men who were too poor to afford a knight's armour were generally exempted from military service). In battle, though the king's leadership was never disputed, the various contingents would be drawn up under their own banners. It was all typically feudal; the king ranked first in power, but he could only use his power in conjunction with the nobility, and to gain their support he had first to prove his prowess in the field.

Turning now to economic matters, we find that the list of royal privileges and prerogatives was very long indeed. The sovereign had the right to mint money, to impose and collect dues and tolls and to authorize the establishment of new markets. But as we have seen, except in his own allods and in cities founded by royal charter, most of these rights were farmed out to the nobility.

The crown as such, then, had few private resources, especially since the electoral system prevented the perpetuation of a royal line and hence the concentration of property in the hands of any one royal family. This was the fundamental difference between the German kings and the House of Capet in France, and it was in vain that Henry III and Henry IV strove to establish a hereditary monarchy, or to accumulate sizeable crown lands in the Harz region.

True, besides the rewards that went with the royal office, besides archbishoprics, bishoprics, and some towns, the crown also owned the so-called imperial estates—with their castles and palaces, but these estates were scattered throughout the kingdom, and did not provide a real basis of power or wealth.

A further obstacle to the accumulation of personal wealth was the rudimentary nature of the king's administration. To staff his chancellery, the monarch had to rely on the services of a few clerks of the royal chapel, some of whom were attached to the court for purely ecclesiastical purposes. His administration (a single ministry) was headed by the Chancellor-in-Chief of Germany (generally the Archbishop of Mainz), the Chancellor-in-Chief of Italy (the Archbishop of Cologne) and the Chancellor-in-Chief of Burgundy (usually the Archbishop of Besançon). The king was further assisted by his court, made up of counsellors—relatives, friends and particularly devoted men—and of four court officials: the Seneschal, the Cup-bearer, the Marshal and the Chamberlain, honorary posts that traditionally fell to the Count Palatine of the Rhine, the Duke of Bohemia, the Duke of Saxony and the Duke of Swabia.

Below these men there was nothing. Administration at county level was in the hands of the feudal lords, and the only body to represent both central and local authorities was the Diet (German inasmuch as only German princes were admitted; imperial in name). But even this body gradually turned into a feudal assembly run by the king's vassals.

Now it was this very feudal structure that tied the king's

hands in his attempts to control the nobility. Certainly, following the tradition established by Otto I, the king was possessed of rights far beyond mere suzerainty—all his nobles (dukes, margraves, counts, viscounts and princes of the church) swore him an oath of fidelity, in addition to the customary homage which they paid him for their fiefs. As part of this homage, they promised their counsel, their help in dispensing justice, their financial aid in cases of special need, and the supply of levies for a specified number of days, on pain of losing their titles, offices and estates. However, the nobility insisted that the Diet must be allowed to arbitrate in all cases of dispute with the king, and that whenever a major fief (a duchy, margraviate or county) was escheated or otherwise confiscated, the king should be obliged to appoint a new tenant without delay, lest he benefit personally from the confiscation.

In short, the nobility took a purely feudal view of their duties to state and crown, with the result that the king could only impose his will by dint of his personal authority.

CHAPTER THREE

Italy in 1150
The Kingdom of Burgundy

BUILT up over many centuries, and retaining the individual
character of her several parts, a great peninsula sealed off
in the north by the Alpine chain, strongly moulded by the
influence of the Romans and relatively untouched by successive
waves of Germanic invaders, proud of her ancestry, quick to
rouse but easily discouraged, twelfth-century Italy was torn by
strife, unique but not unified. The climate varied considerably
from north to south, and the landscape ranged from massive
Alpine peaks to the gentle slopes and wide plain of the Po basin,
from the sheer Apennines to sheltered valleys and peaceful
maritime coves and creeks. This natural variety, no less than
the early and marked development of extremes of wealth and
poverty, helped to foster the rise of political schisms. Unlike Germany, Italy was never drawn into foreign adventure
and conquest; rather did her fame and wealth act as a magnet
on her neighbours, and chiefly on her great imperial partner
across the Alps.

Yet beneath all this variety, Italy had many common
features, as we may gather from the picturesque description of
Italy by Barbarossa's uncle, Otto, Bishop of Freising. When he
saw her, doubtless for the first time, in 1154, he recorded the
following impression: "The country is bounded by the
Pyrenees (which are called the Alps) and the Apennines, very
sheer and varied mountains running the entire length of the

country and, as it were, forming its umbilical cord or garden of pleasure. The Apennines stretch from the shores of the Tyrrhenian Sea to the Adriatic. Fed by the river Po, which geographers classify among the three most famous rivers of Europe, Italy is a country that, thanks to the blessing of its sun and the clemency of its skies, is rich in corn, wine and oil, boasting orchards of every conceivable fruit, particularly chestnuts, figs and olives . . .

"This country is divided into cities which, following the custom of the ancient Romans, call themselves republics. Indeed, the Italians so love liberty that they cannot bear the insolence of office, and so are ruled by a government of consuls rather than by kings. The people are divided into three orders, the capitani, the valvassores and the plebs, and so as to prevent dictatorship, their consuls are elected to serve all three orders and are replaced almost every year. As a result, throughout these cities, in which all the inhabitants must live together by law, there is no noble or man of position or ambition who does not acknowledge the sovereignty of his city, or *contado*. As there is no lack of occasion for wishing to extend this *contado* at the expense of neighbours, the cities do not disdain raising to the knighthood and to high office young men of humble birth, or bringing into the liberal professions workmen in some low and mechanical trade, who would be spurned like the plague in any other country. As a result, they are blessed with wealth and power greater than all other countries. In this they are helped not only by their fine craftsmanship, but also by the fact that their princes have taken the habit of absenting themselves from home. Scornful of the old aristocracy, the cities cling to the dregs of their barbaric past, for while extolling the rule of law, they are quite unprepared to submit to it. In effect, rarely, if at all, do they receive their princes with respect, albeit they are in honour bound to show submission and reverence. And never, or hardly ever, do they heed the law unless compelled to do so by force. Thus it frequently happens that their prince, though he come in peace to claim his rights, is received with hostility. This is harmful to the public weal, since on the one hand the prince must needs waste his substance on military efforts directed against his own subjects, and on the other hand the subjects will never submit until their wealth is exhausted."

How pleasant life must have been in this opulent and fertile country! In his German intoxication with the south, Otto of Freising may perhaps have drawn too rosy a picture of its riches, but his description of an urban civilization with a tradition of liberty so strong that it refused obedience to any prince, even the emperor, was not at all exaggerated.

However, our chronicler overlooked one important fact: Italy was not only a country of cities and urban predominance —feudalism, although much altered and weakened, had not yet disappeared, and remained very much a force in Sicily and the many Byzantine enclaves, none of which formed part of the Kingdom of Italy, or of the empire. That kingdom was bounded in the north by the Alpine mountains running from Monaco (which was part of it) to Venice (which was not). In the south, the border was drawn where the Papal States and the Duchy of Spoleto ended and the Kingdom of Sicily began; it ran from the Tyrrhenian coast between Terracina and Gaeta to the Adriatic near Vasto, south of Chieti. These borders had remained unchanged ever since Charlemagne had used the French model to divide Italy into districts administered by a count.

By the tenth century, feudalism had begun to invade the entire system—in Italy as elsewhere. As a result, the power of the throne was whittled away to almost nothing, and when Otto the Great became Emperor, he set out to reverse this trend. The nobles resisted his efforts with all their force, setting up duchies and marquisates (the two terms were synonymous in Italy) by the fusion of several counties or by straightforward usurpation of titles. Consequently, many counties were enfeoffed to the ruling duke or marquis, while just a few remained fiefs of the crown. By the end of the tenth century, moreover, many counties were split up further, either by the counts themselves, or by the king, or again because bishops laid administrative claim to their dioceses.

In the eleventh century, therefore, the kingdom formed a complex feudal mosaic in which the largest pieces were the duchies and marquisates.

Central authority in twelfth-century Italy had grown so weak that any count who succeeded in seizing territory was generally able to hang on to it. But it was the growth of the cities even more than the disintegration of the feudal system that brought about the spirit of independence and lack of respect for authority that so astonished Otto of Freising. Cities had existed in Italy longer than anywhere else—since the beginning of the Middle Ages, in fact. They formed a dense web of commercial centres, and were traditionally the home of Italy's richest and most influential men. In the middle of the eleventh century, Italian merchants began to take full advantage of the great revival in Mediterranean trade, and so skilful and audacious were they that they quickly ousted the Byzantines (whose importance was in any case declining) and the Saracens. First to reap the benefits were some of the southern cities such as Bari, Amalfi and Salerno. Next it was the turn of the principal northern ports: Genoa, Pisa and Venice. Trade with the East had its logical extension in increased commerce with the West, which proved a ready outlet for Oriental wares and a rich source of manufactured goods. At the same time, skilled craftsmen flocked to Italy as new industries sprang up in all the major towns. All this, coupled to the rapid growth of the native population, gave an enormous boost to urban life. Civic administration grew in power and complexity, the merchant class, and particularly its upper strata, became richer and more powerful, and everywhere a new civilization began to flourish.

F.B.   C

All these social changes tended to diminish the authority of the German emperor who, in any case, ruled over Italy in theory rather than in practice. Along with his title "King of Italy" went an official capital in Pavia, a few manors in Lombardy, Piedmont and Tuscany, but no administration except for the arch-chancellery, a purely honorary office. And as the feudal system was moribund, the emperor could not rely on the nobility, but was thrown back on the support of the cities.

In their attitude to the crown, the Italians were torn between the two currents, and this is precisely what Otto of Freising meant when he wrote that "extolling the rule of law they are quite unprepared to submit to it". On the one hand, they looked upon all government as a potential threat to their independence; on the other hand they felt the need for a strong hand to guarantee their freedom, and protect their rights—indeed, to prevent the kingdom from breaking up. In consequence, most Italians accepted the emperor as a necessary evil—in the hope that he would rule with moderation, respect their autonomy, and treat their cities as so many cornerstones of the empire. This is what Otto of Freising failed to grasp when he chided them for their "barbaric" insolence.

In fact, the situation was even more complicated, since for political or economic reasons, the cities were frequently at war among themselves. There were rivalries and deadly feuds, for instance between Milan and Cremona, or Genoa and Pisa, in which each party was ready to call on the emperor for help, thus greatly strengthening his hand.

Rome herself had undergone many changes, not only in the wake of economic expansion but also as a result of the increased prestige and importance that had accrued to the Holy See from the settlement of the Investiture Dispute. Moreover, every year increasing crowds of pilgrims flocked to

Italy in about 1150

1. Kingdom of Italy
2. Kingdom of Sicily
3. Patrimony of St. Peter
   (Papal States)
4. Duchy of Spoleto
5. Duchy of Romagna
6. March of Ancona

35

Rome. In 1143, the merchants, led by the old aristocracy, staged a violent revolt, took over the government and proclaimed a commune, headed by an assembly called the Senate in memory of ancient Rome. This "revolution" was, in fact, directed against the papacy, which tried unsuccessfully to stave it off under Innocent II, Celestine II and Lucius II. In 1145 Eugenius III attempted to negotiate a settlement, but, shortly afterwards, he was forced to flee to France, whence he did not return until the end of 1149—with the help of the King of Sicily.

Meanwhile Arnold of Brescia, an extremely able monk and passionate reformer who had settled in Rome in June 1146, launched a fierce campaign against the wealth and worldly power of the church. Under his influence, the commune was led to take up an even more intransigent position. Arnold, vexed that the Pope should have turned a deaf ear to his complaints, now redoubled his attacks on the Curia, accusing it of opulence, and challenging its temporal authority, on the grounds that the citizens of Rome had a traditional right to run their own affairs. And so, when Eugenius III returned to Rome, he found the position even more difficult than it had been on his departure. Attacked by Arnold, opposed by the commune, and harassed by some of his vassals who were taking advantage of his other troubles, he was forced to call in the emperor's aid (1150–1152), thus greatly weakening his own authority.

This was the more unfortunate for the Holy See, because the question of whether or not the Papal States were part of the Kingdom of Italy had long been the subject of fierce debates, the more so as the legal rights of the matter had never been clearly established by Charlemagne or by Lothar and Lewis II. Thus when Otto the Great and his successors claimed on several occasions that they had final authority over the Papal States, the Popes had always been able to reject their claims and, profiting from the Investiture Dispute, and the increased prestige it earned the church in Germany, had come to look upon themselves as sovereigns in their own right.

However, the emperor had one irrefutable argument to support his authority, and one that did not depend upon his disputed rights as King of Italy—he was the head of the Holy Roman Empire and as such wielded supreme authority over Rome. Even before handing him the imperial crown, his German electors acclaimed their sovereign 'King of the Romans', and the Pope himself conferred upon him the special title of Advocate and Protector of the Roman Church.

The question of sovereignty was a difficult issue, both in law and in practice, and was complicated further by the fact that the Pope and the Emperor disputed possession of Radicofani and Acquapendente, and there were more serious differences still concerning the Duchy of Romagna, the Duchy of Spoleto, the March of Ancona. Worst of all was the question of the Matildine inheritance. In 1115 the Countess Matilda had died without heirs, leaving vast estates, some of them fiefs of the Empire, some of the papacy, and some originally freehold which she had enfeoffed or granted to one or the other. The disputes arising from this complicated state of affairs had by no means been settled at the time of Barbarossa's election in 1152.

The peninsula also included the Kingdom of Sicily and the Republic of Venice, both of which shared a long tradition of Byzantine domination.

In 1152, the Kingdom of Sicily was governed by the Norman king, Roger II. Norman knights, descendants of Tancred de Hauteville, had first come to Southern Italy and Sicily to help the local nobles, officially still under Byzantine rule, to throw back the Saracens, who had invaded the country in 820–830. As the Normans pushed back or subjugated the invaders, they carved out principalities for themselves, and flouting the rights of what they called "those Greeks", swallowed up the small autonomous republics of Gaeta, Naples and Amalfi. By the end of the eleventh century, they had established three large principalities: the Duchy of Apulia and Calabria, the Principality of Capua, and the Duchy of Sicily. In 1127, Roger II, who ruled over the last two, also inherited the first. In 1130, he was crowned King of Sicily at Palermo, and in the same year Anacletus, the anti-pope, recognized Roger's title against a pledge of support for the Roman Church. Pope Innocent II added his ratification in 1139.

This did not, however, lead to permanent peace, for the popes never completely trusted the Normans, the less so as the latter, too, insisted on the right of nominating bishops of their own choice.

In law, Sicily was undoubtedly part of the ancient Byzantine Empire, and neither Charlemagne nor his successors, with the possible exception of Lewis II, had ever laid claim to the entire Italian peninsula. Hence, in about 1150, when the Byzantine Emperor Manuel Comnenus decided to assert his rights over Sicily, the German Emperor could scarcely oppose him in law. Still, as Advocate to the Holy See he felt in duty bound to protect the interests of the Roman Church, and to resist Manuel with might and main. But if anything, the Pope had more to fear from the German Emperor than from Manuel, for what was to make the former halt his victorious army half-way down the peninsula, especially now that the Byzantine hold over the south had become purely theoretical?

Venice was yet another bone of contention between Germany and Rome. In 812, Charlemagne had assigned this republic of islands and lagoons to Byzantium. Later, it achieved independence under its Doge. The papacy had never shown much interest in Venice—although Byzantine sovereignty over the republic was no more than a dead letter, the Pope never disputed it either in theory or in fact. As for the German emperors, their dreams of domination ought logically to have included Venice as well but, first, the emperors thought her too small to worry about and, secondly, Venice had close business links with Germany that made it more profitable to leave the republic alone.

In the Kingdom of Burgundy or Arles, unlike Sicily or Venice, the emperor's claims rested on straightforward rights of succession. This kingdom, known as Burgundy for short, or sometimes as the Kingdom of Arles and Vienne, lay between the Rhone—from lake Geneva to the sea, with a few enclaves in Vivarais—and the Alps. King Rudolf III (993–1032), having no descendants, agreed that, on his death, the kingdom should become part of the Empire. In 1032 the Emperor Conrad II was crowned King of Burgundy and in 1038 his coronation was ratified by a solemn assembly of bishops and priests at Solothurn.

The very size of the kingdom made it difficult for the emperor to exercise any real control over it, especially since he lived abroad and had virtually no administrative organization—except for an honorary arch-chancellor. Moreover, successive emperors took little interest in Burgundy, so little, in fact, that the nobility came to enjoy a considerable amount of independence. The Marquis of Provence and the Counts of Venaissin and Provence (descendants of the Counts of Barcelona), the Counts of Forcalquier and Nice, and further to the north, the Counts of Vienne, Maurienne and Savoy, were extremely powerful, as were the counts of Burgundy proper or the "Comté" as it was then called (the modern Franche-Comté). Arles in the Rhone valley and Marseilles on the coast, were beginning to achieve a measure of self-government, and so were well in advance of Besançon and Lyons in the interior.

Such then were the southern countries which together constituted one of the most interesting and attractive parts of the Holy Roman Empire. Their natural diversity was great, their geographic extent considerable, their economic and social structure extremely varied. In 1152, all of them—with their dynamic traditions, their many advantages and problems— came down to one on whom the German princes had seen fit to bestow the weighty crown of Germany: to Frederick Barbarossa.

CHAPTER FOUR

The Man and his Aims

ON 15 February 1152, Conrad III died at Bamberg, and on 4 March his nephew, Frederick, Duke of Swabia, was elected to succeed him. In the interval, the most powerful princes of Germany had been engaged in electoral bargaining.

Who were these men? First there were the Hohenstaufen, relatives of the late emperor, and headed by Barbarossa himself. They were descendants of Frederick of Beuren (died 1094) and owed their fortune to Frederick of Beuren's son, Frederick of Hohenstaufen, so-called after the castle he built not far from Beuren, in the Goppingen district east of Stuttgart and near Lorsch. For his loyalty to Henry IV during the princes' revolt, Frederick of Hohenstaufen was offered the hand of Agnes, the king's daughter, and granted the Duchy of Swabia. He died in 1105, leaving two sons. The younger became the Emperor Conrad III; the older, Frederick the One-Eyed, fought Lothar of Supplinburg for the crown in 1125. He died in 1147, and was succeeded by his son, Frederick Barbarossa. Barbarossa's cousin, the son of the late emperor, was a seven-year-old boy when Barbarossa himself was elected in 1152.

The Hohenstaufen were closely allied to the Babenbergs, originally from Bamberg. At the beginning of the twelfth century, Leopold, head of this family and holder of the Austrian March, had married Agnes, widow of Frederick of Hohenstaufen, thus becoming the stepfather of Conrad and Frederick the One-Eyed. Leopold of Babenberg and Agnes had three sons of their own, the oldest of whom, Leopold, was one of Conrad's most active supporters and, for his services, was allowed to add the Duchy of Bavaria to the Austrian March. He died in 1141, and his titles of Duke of Bavaria and Margrave of Austria passed to his younger brother Henry, nicknamed Jasomirgott after his favourite oath. The third brother, Otto, entered the church, and became the Bishop of Freising from whose chronicles we have been quoting. He was one of the most cultured men of his age, a born diplomat and a tireless worker for the Hohenstaufen cause. Henry Jasomirgott was a less dependable ally, particularly after his marriage to Gertrude, widow of Henry the Proud. The Hohenstaufen were also known as the Waiblingen (a name the Italians turned into Ghibelline) after one of their castles. They were bitterly opposed by the Welfs (Guelphs), a family to whom Henry IV had granted Bavaria in 1070. From 1125 onwards, the two rival clans were constantly at each other's throats, with one gaining the upper hand at one moment and the other at the next. In 1152, the Welfs were headed by Henry the Lion, ably supported by his uncle, Welf VI. Henry the Lion himself (born 1129 or 1130) was the son of Henry the Proud and Gertrude, daughter of Emperor Lothar III of Supplinburg, formerly Duke of Saxony. On Lothar's death in 1137, Henry the Proud inherited both the Duchy of Bavaria and the Duchy of Saxony. When he died in the prime of his life, in 1139, Conrad III took advantage of the revolt led by Henry the Lion and Welf VI, the younger brother of Henry the Proud, and confiscated the two duchies. In 1142, he agreed to give Saxony back to the Lion but handed over Bavaria to Leopold of Austria, who in turn passed it on to Henry Jasomirgott. The Welf faction remained powerful for all that; they owned vast estates not only in Saxony and in Bavaria, but also in Italy, so much so that, in 1151, Henry the Lion offered a formidable threat to Conrad's authority.

Nor were these two the only noble families of importance in Germany. Another leading house was that of Duke Berthold of Zähringen, who owed his title to a Swabian ancestor, and

Emperors from 962 to 1190

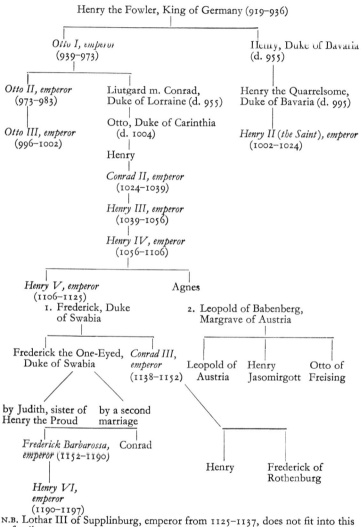

N.B. Lothar III of Supplinburg, emperor from 1125–1137, does not fit into this family tree.

43

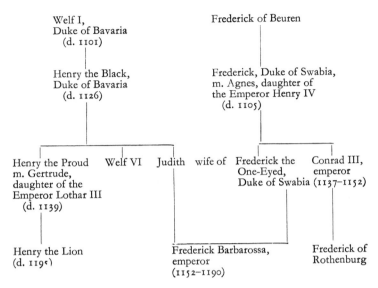

who also ruled over Breisgau, Zürich and Berne and had extensive possessions in the Kingdom of Burgundy, where he officiated as king's rector. The younger branch of his family held the March of Verona and the castle of Baden. Although Berthold's sister had married Henry the Lion, the family was not implacably opposed to the Hohenstaufen, but rather sought to wrest what concessions it could from both parties.

Other important nobles were Otto of Wittelsbach, Count Palatin of Bavaria, and Count Henry Ratzeburg, both allies of the Hohenstaufen. As for the other nobles, their attitude was far less clear-cut. Albert of Ballenstädt, Margrave of Brandenburg, gave considerable support to Conrad who had invested him with Saxony (previously confiscated from Henry the Lion) but understandably began to waver in 1142, when Conrad revoked the gift. We also know that Adolf II of Schauenberg, Count of Holstein, guarded his independence and stood aloof from both factions, but we lack reliable in-

formation about the stand of Vladislav II, Duke of Bohemia;
that of the Duke of Upper Lorraine, a descendant of Gerard
of Chatenois; that of the Duke of Carinthia; that of the Margraves of Misnia and Lusatia (members of the Wettin family);
that of Herman of Stahleck, Count Palatin of the Rhineland,
and that of many others.

As for the princes of the church, we know that most of
them were anxious to heal the rift between the two hostile
factions, though some tended to support the Welfs while
others, elevated during the reign of Conrad III, no doubt
championed the Hohenstaufen family. The second group included Arnold of Wied, Archbishop of Cologne; Hillin,
Archbishop of Trèves; Conrad, Bishop of Passau (a descendant
of Leopold of Babenberg) and, quite naturally, Otto of
Freising.

When all these men met in late February 1152 to elect
Conrad's successor, they reached a fairly quick understanding.
Three reasons helped them to sink their differences. To begin
with, they were all tired of a quarrel that seemed to have so
little point. Its origins went back to 1125, when the pontifical
legates had helped to elect Lothar instead of the Hohenstaufen
nominee and had undoubtedly had a hand in arranging the
marriage of Gertrude, the king's daughter, to Henry the
Proud. The ensuing revolt, confiscations and battles had torn
Germany in two, but for the rest had helped nobody and
decided no issues. Secondly, a number of electors realized that
Welf, with his ungovernable temper, might find it difficult to
impose his will on a nobility that bore him little love. Finally,
the majority of the electors would have found it embarrassing
to extricate themselves from a situation they themselves had
created in 1147 when, in Conrad's lifetime, they had agreed to
elect Henry, his son, to the throne. Since Henry had died
shortly afterwards, it seemed only logical to keep the crown in
the hands of the Hohenstaufen family, the more so as the
emperor, on his death bed, had handed the royal insignia to

his nephew, Frederick Barbarossa, thus clearly indicating his own preference. Barbarossa, moreover, was related to the Welfs—his father had married Judith, a sister of Henry the Proud and of Welf VI at a time when there was some hope of a reconciliation between the two families. Frederick, as cousin of Henry the Lion, was, according to Otto of Freising, "the cornerstone, that might, perhaps, bind together these two receding walls".

A move by Frederick Barbarossa himself had helped to smooth over any remaining difficulties—he declared himself willing to compensate his rival if he was elected. He made this promise in the absence of the pontifical legates, and the German electors, who had felt somewhat humiliated by Lothar's subservience to the Holy See, were only too anxious to settle things among themselves before a representative of the Pope arrived. And so they quickly agreed to elect Frederick Barbarossa King of Germany and Rome, with one voice. On 9 March, Frederick was crowned at Aix-la-Chapelle.

Born in 1125 or 1126, Frederick Barbarossa was 27 or 28 years old on the day of his election. He was a man of medium build, broad shouldered and muscular, with a rather long face and a fair, almost red, beard—hence his Italian nickname. He was extremely vigorous and spirited, an enthusiastic sportsman (excelling at riding, hunting and swimming) and always ready to throw himself into any new venture. He was a man besides who, despite his youth, had many political achievements to his credit.

We know next to nothing about his childhood and upbringing. Doubtless he had the best military education that could be given to a young German prince, and doubtless, also, he reacted to it with his usual enthusiasm. And though he must have received some sort of schooling, better perhaps than the smattering of learning that fell to the lot of most young nobles, he never mastered the Latin tongue. By contrast, he acquired a sound grounding in politics, and this not only by way of theoretical lessons from clerks of the Chapel Royal, including the Abbot of Corvey, and later the Abbot of Stablo, a man of wide culture, who possibly helped to round off the young prince's education: his whole life was spent in the thick of important events, and this was his practical apprenticeship.

His father, Frederick, Duke of Swabia, was anathematized by the Pope shortly after Barbarossa's birth for trying to raise up another king against Lothar III, in the person of his brother Conrad of Hohenstaufen. Soon afterwards, Frederick of Swabia was forced to the bitter conclusion that, though it is simple enough to instigate revolts, it is quite another matter to stop the nobility from changing sides once the glow of victory has faded. In the end, he, with all his retainers, had been forced to submit. These were Barbarossa's earliest memories, these the subjects he heard discussed in his family circles, these the basis of his reflections in later life.

Then, with the election of Conrad, his uncle, as King of the Romans, came ten years of apparent tranquillity during which he acquired political and administrative skills, first from his father, confined to his native Duchy of Swabia and anxious to increase the family fortunes, and later, when his father retired to a monastery in Alsace, and left him in charge of all the estates, from personal experience. It was then that the future emperor began to appreciate the disadvantages of the feudal system—civil wars resulting from private feuds were rapidly leading to a complete breakdown of order throughout Germany. Fighting by his uncle's side against Conrad of Zähringen in Bavaria, Barbarossa was able to see at close quarters how these petty rivalries undermined the authority of the crown, and prevented the king from governing the country. This was a lesson he never forgot.

On his father's death in 1147, Barbarossa became Duke of Swabia. Previously, two important events had occurred in his life: at some date unknown he had married a young German woman, Adelaide of Vohburg and, shortly before his father's death, he had taken up the cross to follow his Uncle Conrad and Louis VII, the King of France, to the Holy Land, there to resist Turkish attacks against the Christian community.

This crusade, badly planned, poorly organized, and obstructed by Manuel Comnenus, the Byzantine emperor, proved a complete fiasco. The German expedition which had set out before the Capetian host, ran into trouble first in the Balkans, where the population resented their harshness, next with the Greek authorities and finally even with the French contingent. Once in Asia Minor, they engaged the Turks and, in October 1147, suffered a shattering defeat at Dorylaeum. Conrad retired to Byzantium whence he set sail for Acre while the main body of the army, led by his half-brother Otto of Freising, was hacked to pieces near Laodicea. The remnants of the German and French hosts assembled in Syria a year later, laid siege to Damascus but, because of bitter jealousies, were forced to abandon the enterprise. Conrad, discouraged, returned to Germany in the autumn of 1148.

This ignominious failure provided young Frederick with further proof, if such was still needed, that only a king with great personal authority could hope to enforce discipline over his feudal retainers. The crusade, moreover, gave him his first opportunity to mix with nobles outside his own family circle and to make new friends. It was during these months that he met first Otto of Freising; Henry Jasomirgott; Henry, Bishop of Ratisbon; Vladislav, Duke of Bohemia; and the Margrave of Styria, whose acquaintance was to stand him in such good stead. Moreover, his courage and loyalty during the crusade earned him general esteem, the friendship of his uncle, Welf VI, and above all, the confidence of Conrad III.

For it seems that it was during these months that Conrad first thought of drawing the electors' attention to his valiant nephew and that Barbarossa's dream of empire first took shape. The next two years, which were marked by a new and violent rupture between Conrad and Henry the Lion, passed quickly, and then the dream had suddenly become reality—albeit it was darkened by the disunity of the German princes.

This deplorable situation summoned up all of Barbarossa's extraordinary powers of leadership. The new emperor held the noblest ideals of service, and was at all times ready to defend the cause of justice and right—as he saw it. This explains his two crusades, his love of fairness and his desire for unity. Moulded by his aristocratic education and accepting its ethics, Frederick was always loyal, more so, perhaps, than any other man of his age, though even he was, at times, forced, like all great statesmen, to resort to expediency and artifice. Again, though he was generous by nature, gave fully of himself, was a staunch friend and an indulgent enemy, as monarch he was sometimes forced to keep his friendships in bounds and to measure his indulgences.

His warm qualities were, moreover, balanced by a steely will. Courage always runs the risk of turning into brutality, strength may become violence; when loyalty is deceived or generosity abused, they can quickly turn into cruelty. If roused to anger, Frederick could be extremely harsh, although perhaps he felt that the cruel punishment he meted out to Milan and to some of his opponents was dictated by necessity. Nevertheless, here was an obvious flaw in his character, a failing that was common and perhaps even essential in any ruler of his day and age. Still, Frederick was far less afflicted by it than any of his peers.

For one thing, his military prowess and fervour were tempered by deep piety, by the firm conviction that the Christian faith imposes ineluctable moral obligations on all true believers. His private life was without blemish, and he never forgot his Christian duty to succour the weak. Frederick was deeply involved in the life of the church, took measures to stamp out heresy, helped the monasteries, and, as we saw, did not hesitate to take up the cross—indeed, he held this to be the most noble deed of all, and a duty superior to all temporal acts. True, his faith and Christian humility did not stop him from attacking the Holy See, but he always claimed that his opposition was purely political and, as such, fully justified.

He had, besides, the natural confidence of the born aristocrat —not because he was vain or despised common people but because, like all the nobles of his day, he believed that he had been set above the rest by the Almighty. Typical of his class, his family and his rank, he thought of himself as a noble among the nobility, a prince among princes, a king born for great achievements.

As a statesman, his most outstanding characteristic was the lofty conception of his duties and of his position. He was the king, he was the emperor, he was majesty itself. And so he ruled over his subjects with an iron hand, in strict accordance with the Royal Proclamation, with feudal custom and with Roman law, in which latter he became an expert. When it came to his theoretical and practical prerogatives, Frederick was at his most intransigent: his word was law, he *was* the Empire.

And having attained sovereignty over it, he was determined to make it great, to help it fulfil its heroic destiny. He was and remained a man of burning ambition—in youth, manhood, and even in old age. Nor was his ambition fixed on narrow objectives, and he never fell prey to mysticism or the lure of esoteric doctrines. He wanted to be the most perfect of knights, the greatest leader in battle, the best-loved monarch, the most renowned of emperors. These high ideals ceaselessly spurred him on to new ventures and never allowed him to feel discouraged in the face of even the most serious set-backs. He was a born optimist, self confident and contented but without a trace of false pride. Providence had chosen him and he would prove worthy of her trust.

His chief political asset, besides his natural gift for leadership, was his extremely alert practical intelligence. At times, like any king, he must have indulged in grandiose daydreams of world-shattering victories and accomplishments—after all, was he not the Emperor? But he never allowed these reveries to confuse his judgment; all his decisions, all his actions, were based upon common sense. His outstanding ability can be seen in his acute analysis of the situation and problems facing him in Germany on his accession, and in his long campaign to subdue Italy. In a crisis, he was always adroit and realistic, always ready to negotiate, not directly, for this was not his method, but through diplomats whom he invariably chose with great discernment.

He was a brilliant politician, fond of power and responsibility, a tireless leader, a man whose physical strength and enormous vitality were fed by a love of action. German affairs, the Italian question, ecclesiastical and religious disputes, West and East, ideas and practical problems, all were grist to his mill. Had he been stupid or clumsy, had his character been less noble and his ambitions less lofty, he would have been no more than an ineffectual dilettante, ever engaged on some new project. But, as we have said, he combined idealism with intelligence and considerable practical leadership, both in peace and war, both as governor and as head of a nation whose people revered his stern moral qualities.

Yet at times Frederick's very strength led him astray; his perseverance turned into sheer stubbornness and sometimes paved the way for defeat. It would take him a long time to abandon a course on which he had embarked, possibly because he found it difficult to go back on earlier decisions. This, perhaps, was his gravest fault, and one that, on occasion, caused this remarkable leader to lose his head.

The grand design Frederick revealed in 1152 was in keeping with his character. His programme, though not perhaps clear in all its details, was nevertheless one that encompassed every aspect of imperial policy.

It can be put in a few words. Faced with a Germany in which disorder and anarchy were rampant, Frederick was determined to re-establish the full glory of the crown which, since 1125 at least, had become tarnished. Shortly after his election he wrote letters to various notables, including Pope Eugenius III, informing them that he would work to re-establish and strengthen the honour of the kingdom and the empire—*honor regni, honor imperii*—and that, if he failed in this task, he would not only have failed in his duty to Germany and the empire, but would have forfeited his own honour.

Now, while some rulers might have concentrated on restoring the "honour" of Germany first, and others on repairing the prestige of the Empire, Frederick believed that the two went hand in hand: he would strengthen the German kingdom in order to strengthen the empire, eradicate anarchy in the part the better to repair the whole.

The empire Frederick had in mind does not seem to have been the universal kingdom embracing all Christendom. Doubtless some of his bishops and nobles had this vision, and who knows but that Frederick, too, may not have nurtured it, but he was far too much of a realist to be led astray by such idle hopes. The empire Frederick wished to restore was the Holy Roman Empire, comprising the three kingdoms of Germany, Italy and Burgundy.

Of these three, the last was relatively unimportant—Frederick knew that once Germany was pacified, Italy held the key to imperial glory. In making the conquest of the peninsula his long-term aim, he not only continued in the Ottonian tradition, but also satisfied his keenest personal ambition. His aims were not, as Johannes Haller has tried to show, commercial advantage or control of the trade routes from Bavaria and Austria to Venice—this theory could hold only if trade between Germany and the Adriatic was highly developed, when in fact it was not, or if Frederick was capable of being swayed by considerations that were entirely alien to his spirit.

Once his goal was fixed, Frederick took stock of his resources. The power of the German crown, unlike the French, was not, as we have said, backed by vast private resources. However, Frederick's personal wealth, inherited from his family, was by no means negligible. Apart from some land in Thuringia, his possessions were chiefly concentrated in the Duchy of Swabia, and particularly in the Rhineland: between Basle and Freiburg, round Worms and Spires, in the Lauter valley, and in Alsace. For all that, other princes and the Welfs, in particular, were very much richer. But Frederick held three other trumps and these he played with consummate skill.

Firstly, upon his election, he at once made full use of his basic right of office—the Royal Proclamation—to call upon his princes to desist from their petty feuds. At the same time he made it clear that he was not prepared to relinquish any of the traditional crown rights and that, while fully endorsing the Concordat of Worms as an attempt to clear up the confusion between temporal and spiritual authority, he intended to maintain crown control over all episcopal nominations. Secondly, by asserting that the power of the throne was based on the willing co-operation of the princes, and thus publicly recognizing their power and natural rights, he appealed to their sense of honour and so gained the willing co-operation he required.

His third trump was Germany's entrenched feudal system. With his tight grip on reality, Barbarossa must have realized, even before his accession to the throne, that this system was too much a part of German life, and indeed of his own outlook, to be simply set aside, but he did not intend to become its victim. Instead he would make full use of it, i.e. of the ties between lord and vassal, to bend the country to his will.

His was a dangerous and difficult programme. By giving free rein to feudalism, by being too generous or cordial towards the most powerful nobles, Frederick ran the risk of weakening his own authority, of jeopardizing the very objects he had set himself. However, whenever there was a clash of interests, Frederick invariably put the crown first and, if necessary, backed up his determination by reliance on the strong network of feudal alliances to the House of Hohenstaufen he had so assiduously built up.

His approach in Italy was not nearly so clear-cut, though he was equally sure of his final objectives.

In the first place he wished to be King of Italy, in fact as well as in name. Nobles and townsmen alike, great and small, must all accept his authority, and though he was prepared to grant them a measure of local freedom, they were not allowed to interfere with his general plan. Here, as in Germany, he wished to rule with the co-operation of the people. But whereas, at home, he made concessions to his princes because they were his peers and hence entitled to every consideration, in Italy he felt that what concessions he made were purely due to his generosity, and hence not subject to discussion or negotiation. Whenever the Italians opposed his authority or refused to co-operate with him, Frederick used force—brute German force—to bring them to heel.

As for the rest of the peninsula, though he did not wish to establish permanent and direct sovereignty over it, he nevertheless considered it part of his sphere of influence, and felt that he had the right to intervene as a last resort. Hence he accepted the existence of the Kingdom of Sicily but refused to let the Sicilian ruler meddle in the affairs of his neighbours, and expected him to bow to the emperor's authority. In short, the *honor imperii* did not call for conquest and annexation of Sicily, but only for its relegation to a subsidiary role. Some historians, it is true, deny this, and assert that in the first years of his reign, Frederick drew up plans to take the Kingdom of Palermo by force. The truth of the matter is difficult to discover, since whatever his plans, Frederick never took positive steps in that direction.

In any case, his foremost concern in Italy was to reach agreement with the Pope, ruler over vast territories in the peninsula and a man of considerable influence in Sicily. On this point the imperial programme was clear. The Holy See and the Empire both derived their authority from God, and so ought to work together in harmony. Frederick, for his part, would do his utmost to help the Roman Church in the performance of her religious duties, and as her Advocate and Protector, would assist her in fighting her enemies, both in the Papal States and abroad. But in exchange, the Pope would have to respect the emperor's prerogatives in Germany, and particularly his right to have a final say in the nomination and confirmation of bishops, all of whom owed fidelity to the crown. Moreover, the Holy See must respect the emperor's right to dictate general policy in the Kingdom of Italy, including St. Peter's Patrimony, and confine itself to questions of local and ecclesiastical administration. Last but not least, the Church must collaborate with him in Sicily and, in general, support the interests of the empire wherever they were threatened.

Thus the implementation of Frederick's vast imperial programme depended on the Pope's willing support, and Frederick, though he was clear on his other objectives, both at home and abroad, was quite uncertain as to what course of action he should follow if the Pope withheld his co-operation or refused to endorse the imperial project. As a Christian, he was, of course, in duty bound to submit to the spiritual authority of the church, but in matters of state he was equally determined to brook no interference from any one. No doubt he hoped that, if the Pope proved obdurate, the mere threat of force would quickly make him change his mind.

For the rest, the new monarch knew perfectly well where he intended to go—physically, intellectually, morally and politically, he was ready to play the part for which he felt he had been chosen. Moreover, he was wise enough to realize that co-operation would lead him more quickly to his goal than brute force.

In Germany, his great peace plan worked so well despite his later clash with Henry the Lion—simply because Frederick knew what was best for his country. In Italy, on the other hand, he never succeeded in enlisting the support of the princes, and was accordingly forced to use coercion time and again. Then, in 1174–7, after twenty years of bitter struggle, he seems to have realized the error of his ways, and elaborated a new strategy to reach his old objectives.

The chief weakness of his Italian policy, then, was his failure to feel the pulse of his southern neighbours, and nowhere was he more at a loss than in his dealings with the Holy See, an omission that was soon brought home to him and for which he had to pay very dearly.

CHAPTER FIVE

First Steps and Early Setbacks

HARDLY had he been crowned, when Frederick Barbarossa made it clear that the days of Lothar and Conrad were gone for ever, and that he would suffer no interference with the authority of the crown.

His first act after his coronation at Aix-la-Chapelle was to compose an address to Pope Eugenius III. In it, he respectfully informed the Pope of his election and offered him filial greetings. "We send you all our respect and love, and assure our Holy Mother, the Roman Church, and all her noble sons of our prompt and sure attention to justice and of our protection." Frederick also affirmed his desire to help the church by punishing all who disobeyed "the laws of the Fathers and the decrees of the Holy Councils".

Beyond that, his message contained several startling proposals. Frederick did not conceal the fact that, while prepared to defend *"the dignity of the Church"* he would also try to resurrect *"the grandeur of the empire in all its former glory"*. Very skilfully, he let it be understood that in order to achieve this twofold task he wished to work in close collaboration with the pontiff while maintaining his own freedom of action. On this point he most adroitly quoted the famous words of Pope Gelasius I (496–502): "The sovereign government of the world is based on the sacred authority of the pontiffs and the power of kings". Moreover, he in no way asked for confirmation of his election and, by signing his letter simply as "King of the Romans", he implied that, having been elected by the

German princes, he now expected the Pope to crown him emperor as a matter of course.

Eugenius III was no doubt mightily surprised to receive an epistle so very different in tone from those he had received on Lothar's and Conrad's accession to the German throne. At the same time he was sent a letter by Wibald, Abbot of Stablo, the late king's chief counsellor, who depicted the new sovereign as a prince of great valour "full of spirit, prompt in decision, successful in war, undeterred by obstacles, keen for glory, unable to bear injustice, affable, liberal, and a brilliant talker". This somewhat reassuring picture at least announced that the empire had passed into strong hands. And this is assuredly what the Pope must also have been told by the ambassadors Frederick sent with a plea for closer collaboration. One of these was Hillin, recently elected Archbishop of Trèves and who, having first sworn fidelity to the young king, now came to ask for the Pope's consecration—which seemed to augur well for the future.

In his reply to Barbarossa, the Pope stated, curtly but amicably, that he had duly noted Frederick's election and that he welcomed his plan to support the church.

In fact, the Pope had been asking for aid against the Communes ever since 1151, and Conrad, shortly before his death, had agreed to come to Rome's assistance. Moreover, Eugenius III was sufficiently experienced, and generous enough, to understand and perhaps even welcome the ambitions of the young monarch. Frederick, for his part, was unwilling to lead an expedition into Italy right away since, in his eyes, German affairs took precedence, but he was careful not to utter a blunt refusal. Pressed by the Archbishop of Cologne, he contended that the final decision must be left to his princes who, after due deliberation, advised their king to wait. Meanwhile, Frederick continued negotiations with the Pope whom he wanted to speed the arrangements for the imperial coronation in Rome and whom he had asked to annul the marriage to

Adelaide of Vohburg, Frederick's barren queen. Besides, having indirectly raised the Italian problem, he wanted to show that he was as anxious as the Pope to find a solution.

At the same time he indicated that he had not forgotten his third crown—that Burgundy, too, was part of the "glory of the empire". In April or May he renewed the Burgundian Rectorship of Berthold, Duke of Zähringen, granted him a domain and promised him help against William, Count of Mâcon, who was laying claim to Burgundy as successor to Count Rainald (died 1148). However, Frederick meant to retain personal control over the election of Burgundian bishops, and laid down what military contingents Berthold must contribute towards the Italian expedition.

In May of the same year, the Danish nobility asked Frederick to arbitrate between two rival contenders for the Danish crown and, at the Diet of Merseburg, he pronounced in favour of Svend, whom he reminded forcefully to acknowledge German sovereignty. However, all these activities were of minor importance—what was uppermost in Frederick's mind was the need to restore order in Germany and Italy.

It was almost certainly at this time that he promulgated his *Landfrieden* (Land Peace) as a means of checking anarchy at home and strengthening his own authority. Summoning his princes he made each of them swear in turn to observe the peace, once again skilfully associating the twin powers of the crown and of the aristocracy. As for the *Landfrieden* itself, the most impelling and original of its provisions governed the bearing of arms and trial by combat: the peasantry was to surrender all weapons, and only men with noble ancestors were permitted to fight duels. Some of the other stipulations deserve mention as well. Penalties were fixed for murder, assault and theft (in the case of murder the sentence was death, except for cases of legitimate self-defence or justified duels), and fines laid down for minor offences, including the selling of corn at a price above that fixed by the local Count.

The *Landfrieden* affected every stratum of society, but above all it meant that peasants and merchants could no longer resort to violence to settle their disputes. Moreover, Frederick let it be known that he was personally instructing his various counts as to the details of his new measures, thus proclaiming to all the world that justice was his exclusive province and that, despite the feudal system, the nobles, in matters of law at least, were no more than his agents. In the next few years, he strictly enforced the *Landfrieden* and even extended it to cover the unlawful levying of tolls.

At the same time he did his utmost to improve relations with the Welfs. As proof that he would not use his royal powers for his own enrichment, he gave up the Duchy of Swabia in favour of his cousin Frederick of Rothenburg, the late emperor's son. Possibly he had promised to do this to Conrad; at all events the gesture cost him little at the time, since, because of his cousin's youth, Frederick retained practical control of the Duchy. At the Diet of Ratisbon in June, he went further still, and granted Welf VI the Marquisate of Tuscany and the Duchies of Spoleto and Sardinia, together with all the estates of the Countess Matilda. He even encouraged Henry the Lion to challenge Henry Jasomirgott's claims to Bavaria, but added that it was up to an assembly of princes to decide the issue.

While enforcing the *Landfrieden* as a means of increasing the power of the crown, Frederick also hastened to assert his rights over the clergy. In approving the election of Hillin as Archbishop of Trèves even before the latter's consecration by the Holy See, Frederick showed right from the start of his reign that he intended to enforce the Concordat of Worms to the letter. In particular, he meant to make full use of his right to intervene in cases of dispute between the clerical electors and, if necessary, to veto any bishop-elect—as the Concordat had laid down.

This is precisely what he did during the election of the

Abbot of Prüm—when some of the assembled clergy raised the cry of simony, Frederick cut short their recriminations, and, declaring himself the sole arbitrator, ordered the candidate to be blessed. He took a similar stand during the election of a new archbishop of Magdeburg, a see that had been vacant ever since the death of Frederick of Wettin on 14 January 1152. When the electors could not decide between two of the candidates, Frederick sent both of them packing, called for a new examination, and then decided in favour of Wichmann who, as former Bishop of Seitz, did not have to be consecrated and was installed on 1 November.

The German clergy, anxious for law and order and not, on principle, opposed to royal authority, probably welcomed the intervention of a king who was more accessible than the Pope or his all-powerful legates; at any event, they did not protest. They even asked Eugenius III to send Wichmann the pallium, as a sign of his approbation. The pontiff refused, but, for the rest, did not intervene, since he, no less than the bishops, had come to realize that a new era had opened in Germany and that the young king was a force that he could ill afford to antagonize.

By the autumn of 1152, Frederick, finding that his most urgent problems had been dealt with and that he had made his strength felt, pressed on to further negotiations with the Roman Church.

His approach to the Pope was quite straightforward. He wanted his marriage annulled, he wanted to be anointed in Rome, and he wanted the Holy See to endorse his sovereignty over Italy. But he was careful to press his private claims separately, and, in fact, quickly succeeded in having his marriage set aside on grounds of close kinship. Moreover, the Pope did not order him to pay the least compensation to the unfortunate Adelaide of Vohburg. This out of the way, Frederick got down to the two other points, and since Eugenius III was temperamentally disposed to conciliation, and in any case needed German assistance to re-establish his authority in Rome and to ward off the threat of Roger II in Sicily, he was more than ready to fall in with the emperor's plans.

Talks were started in December 1152, and culminated in an official meeting in Constance. The Pope was represented by seven cardinals and the Cistercian Abbot of Chiaravella, while Frederick's cause was championed by the Bishops of Havelberg and Constance together with one German and two Italian counts. On 23 March 1153, they signed a solemn treaty which included the following clauses:

"1. The king (of the Romans) will cause one of the ministers of his realm to swear in his name, and will swear himself, putting his own hand in that of the Pope's legate, that he will neither declare a truce nor make peace with the (citizens of) Rome or with Roger of Sicily, without the free consent of the Roman Church and of Pope Eugenius or any of his successors. Moreover, the king will use the full power of his office to cause the Romans to submit to the Pope and to the Roman Church.

"2. The king, as Advocate and Defender of the Holy Roman Church will, to the best of his ability, maintain and defend the honour of the papacy (*honorem Papatus*), and all the regalia of Saint Peter which are in the possession of the Pope. And all those the Pope does not presently enjoy, the king will help to recover and to defend when they shall have been restored.

"3. The king will not cede to the Greeks any territory this side of the sea, and should the Greeks invade this country he will essay with all his might to drive them from it. He will execute and observe these clauses without deceit or retraction.

"4. By verbal pledge of his apostolic authority, the Pope together with the aforesaid cardinals promises, in the presence of the aforesaid legates of the king, to honour the king as the dearly beloved son of Saint Peter, to put no obstacles in his way when he shall have received the plenitude of his crown, to help him fulfil the obligations of his office, in maintaining, augmenting and increasing the honour of the kingdom (*honorem regni*).

"5. If any man whatsoever shall have the presumption or audacity to violate or sully the justice and honour of the kingdom, the Pope in his affection for the dignity of the crown will give canonical notice of his displeasure. And if such men after the apostolic warning shall continue in their refusal to pay due respect to the crown, the Pope will punish them with excommunication.

"6. The Pope will not cede any territories this side of the sea to the king of the Greeks. If the latter should have the audacity to invade this country, the Pope will essay with all the might of the blessed Peter to repulse him.

"7. All these clauses will be honoured by both parties without deceit or retraction, unless perchance they be altered by the free and mutual agreement of both parties."

This exceptionally important treaty, the precise interpretation of which was to give rise to many disputes between Pope and Emperor—no less than between modern historians—served to establish three major points. First, both parties agreed to co-operate in the joint defence of the papacy and the empire (a term that was not, in fact, used in the treaty since, at the time, Frederick was still no more than King of the Romans). Moreover, they granted distinct prerogatives to either signatory. And the fact that the "honour of the papacy" was coupled to the "honour of the empire" and that the Holy See was entitled to its own regalia (symbols of political power), showed that Frederick did not wish to restrict the Pope's authority to matters spiritual but was prepared to grant him full sovereignty over St. Peter's Patrimony. Second, the treaty represented a check to Byzantine aspirations in Italy, and third the king agreed to suppress the Roman rebellion and never to treat with either the Romans or the Sicilians separately.

Frederick had no doubt agreed to take military action

against the Roman Commune so as to hasten his coronation in Rome. As for Sicily, the Pope's obvious hostility to its rulers seemed to guarantee that Church and Sicily would never conspire against Germany, a guarantee that needed no special ratification, the more so as the Holy See had promised to work to increase the "honour of the empire", which at the very least must mean recognizing the empire's interests in the whole peninsula. Frederick, on the other hand, had to sign an explicit undertaking not to deal separately with the Sicilian crown.

At the time, and during the next few months, neither of the two signatories suspected that their respective interpretations were about to diverge; indeed, co-operation between Frederick and the Pope became ever closer. On the death of Eugenius III on 8 July 1153, his successor, Anastasius IV, in a gesture of goodwill, sent the pallium to Wichmann of Magdeburg, and in Germany Frederick did nothing of which the Holy See could possibly disapprove—he continued to work for peace and even forbade the bishops to dispose of church property. At the same time he prepared an Italian expedition. The Romans awaited it with trepidation, while the Pope nurtured hopes that it might result in the submission of William I of Sicily who had succeeded his father, Roger II, upon the latter's death on 26 February 1154.

Military operations in Italy, however, did not appeal to the German princes, who were more concerned with home affairs, and so forced Frederick to content himself with a relatively small expeditionary force. Before setting out, he wished to see the fate of the Duchy of Bavaria settled, and to show his goodwill towards Henry the Lion, he granted him, probably at the end of 1153, the Slav diocese of Oldenburg, across the Elbe. Later, in June 1154, he granted Henry the newly created sees of Ratzeburg and Mecklenburg. Finally, at the Diet of Goslar, also in 1154, when the princes at long last awarded Bavaria to the Lion, Frederick accepted their decision with pleasure, though in order to keep some hold over Henry and also not to antagonize Henry Jasomirgott, he did not invest him with Bavaria right away.

The summer was taken up with last-minute preparations, and then, in October, the royal expedition crossed the Brenner. It was a small enough party, more in the nature of a royal escort than an army bent on military conquest. Hardly had they crossed the Alps when difficulties arose. Near Verona, the royal party was attacked by armed bands, and though these were easily beaten off, henceforth the Germans were obliged to avoid the cities. In November, after a detour into Piedmont, Frederick set up his winter quarters in Roncaglia on the left bank of the river Po, below Piacenza.

It was here that he received his Italian subjects for the first time. On 5 December, he held a diet, attended by a large number of the Italian nobility, with whom he agreed on a new constitution, designed to reorganize the feudal system by limiting the freedom of minor vassals and increasing the powers of the leading nobles and so facilitating royal control over the country. By the new edict, no vassal could dispose of his fief without express permission from his overlord; the edict also laid down that any fief that was eschewed and not reinvested by normal hereditary succession within a year and a day, was to revert to the overlord.

These laws were in harmony with Frederick's policy of collaboration with the higher nobility. They made no mention of the position of the cities, some of whose representatives Frederick had received as well, and whose privileges he apparently respected. This at least is what emerges from a reference he made to the Communes when, on 22 December, he renewed his treaty with the Republic of Venice, delimiting her frontiers and recognizing that her territory, including Torcello, Murano and Grado, did not belong to the Kingdom of Italy.

Having done so, and without even trying to pose the problems he wished to solve, and seemingly ignoring the real forces at work in the country, Frederick advanced further into

Italy as confidently as if he were still at home. As his army progressed, the Italians were forced to take sides. While some, for instance Lodi and Pavia, welcomed Frederick as an ally against their rivals, others, like Milan, became increasingly hostile. The German army was not large enough to deal with them there and then and, wishing to reach Rome as quickly as possible, Frederick pretended to ignore their opposition, though his mind was already made up to deal with them later.

In Rome, too, he was greeted by darkening skies. Pope Anastasius IV had died on 3 December 1154, and while his successor, the English cardinal Nicholas Breakspear, who took the name of Hadrian IV, was not opposed to Frederick's imperial ambitions, he did not share Anastasius' confidence in the young king. Moreover, he believed firmly that the papacy must be free to exercise its ecclesiastical functions throughout the whole of Christendom, and that it must brook no interference from temporal rulers. He himself, before his accession to St. Peter's throne, had been on an extremely important mission to Scandinavia, in the course of which he had invested a new Archbishop at Trondheim, and, to the dismay of Germany, had attached the Swedish church in the See of Bremen–Hamburg to the See of Lund. Frederick, however, concealed what resentment he may have felt; his prime wish in 1155 was to see his coronation pass off without any trouble. Nor did Hadrian IV want to question any part of the Treaty of Constance, which he intended to turn to his own advantage. The most that can be said, therefore, is that both sides were reserved, that a tentative rapprochement had given place to mistrust.

This became crystal clear when Frederick asked the Pope for an official endorsement of the Treaty, and stressed the mutual benefits that would result from "an indissoluble bond of love between the crown and the ministry". In reply, if we may believe Cardinal Boso's account of these events, Hadrian called upon the king to swear to respect the life and property of the Pope and the cardinals, as if all at once the Holy See was in danger of attack from the Teutonic ruler. In fact, it was being threatened from quite other quarters.

The pontiff had by then lost all authority inside the Holy City and was being hard pressed in his very sanctuary. Locked inside the Vatican, within the precincts of the Leonine City, he refused to recognize the commune, and so increased the enmity of Arnold of Brescia. In the streets, disorder was rife, so much so that Cardinal Guido of Santa Pudenziana, returning from the Vatican one day, was assaulted and left for dead upon the ground. This outrage provoked an immediate reaction from Hadrian IV: he launched an interdict against the city. As Easter was close and the interdict prevented the crowds of pilgrims from entering the holy sanctuaries, thus threatening further violence, the senate called on the Pope, begging him to revoke his decision against the promise that Arnold and his followers would be banished from the city. Then Hadrian relented and proceeded solemnly to the Lateran where he presided at the Easter solemnities. Part, but only part, of the threat to the papacy had been averted.

In Sicily, Hadrian had refused to respond to the overtures of William I, who was quick to take umbrage. He declined to see the Papal legates, and then, at the end of May, attacked the papal estates, burned Ceprano and laid siege to Benevento. Hadrian could do nothing but excommunicate William and place his hopes in Frederick.

But the latter had come to realize that he lacked the military resources to subdue William, and that, after receiving the imperial crown, he would have to return to Germany, shelving his other Italian plans until a more opportune moment. Meanwhile, he was delighted to receive a deputation from Pavia, capital of his Italian kingdom, which, reviving an old tradition, offered him the iron crown of Italy. Unfortunately, this coronation involved him in a side issue—he was forced to uphold Pavia's claims against Tortona, and when the latter refused to accept his arbitration, he could only save his face by laying siege to the city, which did not surrender until April. On 17 April, Frederick was crowned at Pavia, and immediately left for Rome, travelling by way of Bologna, where he received jurists from the famous school of Roman law. When he reached the Holy City, Hadrian IV, in the wake of new disturbances, had just left for Viterbo, whither Frederick despatched a new embassy. Its mere arrival sent the Pope into a panic—he was trapped in the midst of the German army and above all he feared that Frederick might come to an understanding with the Romans. This fear was completely unfounded, and showed that Hadrian had no insight into Frederick's real motives.

Frederick now offered fresh proof of his goodwill, for, when Arnold of Brescia was captured and brought before him, he handed him over to representatives of the Holy See who put the rebel to death. Thus the life of a passionate idealist, dedicated to poverty and simple Christianity, came to a sad and untimely end.

Soon afterwards, two cardinal-legates called upon Frederick to make final arrangements for his coronation. In the name of his king, a German noble had to swear that no attempts would be made on the life of the Pope or members of the Curia; there was another round of manoeuvres and promises, and then finally, on 9 June, the Pope came to meet Frederick in his camp at Campo Grasso in the territory of Sutri.

Here a new shock awaited the pontiff, and one that helped to revive his worst fears: Frederick did not advance to hold his bridle and stirrup. When the Pope remonstrated that he had thus been denied an act of respect due to him as successor of the Apostles Peter and Paul, Frederick replied that he was not bound to this act of service. However, so insistent were the cardinals, that a new meeting was arranged, where Frederick did as he was asked in the name of an ancient custom.

Nor was that his only gesture of reconciliation. Thus, when the Roman senate sent ambassadors to persuade him that he ought to receive the crown from the Roman people themselves, as had the emperors of old, and not from the Pope, Frederick made them a strong and dignified reply: he held the empire by the right of conquest of his predecessors, Charlemagne and Otto; he had come to Italy not "to receive as a suppliant the transient favours of an unruly people, but as a prince resolved to claim, if necessary by force of arms, the inheritance of his forebears".

The Pope was now willing to proceed with the coronation, though Frederick's harsh rebuff to the city called for extraordinary precautions. The German army advanced during the night of 17–18 June and occupied the Leonine City. Next day the official ceremony was held in St. Peter's. Kneeling at the Pope's feet, Frederick swore "before God and the blessed Peter, to be, with divine help, at all times, to the best of my ability and intelligence, and in all good faith, the protector and defender of the Holy Roman Church and of the person of the Pope and of his successors". Then after a solemn procession, he heard the Litany and, prostrate before the confessional, was anointed between his shoulders and on his right arm. Next the mass was said and, after the Epistle had been read, Hadrian IV handed Frederick the sword and sceptre and finally the golden crown. Listening to the loud acclamations from the German knights on that day of 18 June 1155, Frederick knew that another great hurdle had been cleared: he was Emperor at last.

That self-same day, the Romans rushed down from the Capitol to assault the Leonine City. Bloody battles raged for the whole evening. In the end, the attackers were thrown back, but on the morning of 19 June the emperor and the Pope decided to withdraw to Tivoli, which they reached by way of Farfa and Poli. Tivoli was a dependency of the Holy See, and when the inhabitants offered Frederick the keys, he made a point of refusing and of enjoining the people to remain faithful to Hadrian IV.

Frederick now felt that there was little more he could do for the hard-pressed Pope, what with his slender resources and the plague decimating his ranks, exhausted by the heat of the Italian summer. He accordingly made for the north, razed Spoleto, which had paid him tribute in false money, and at Ancona, received envoys from the Byzantine emperor, Manuel Comnenus, and rejected their offer of a joint Sicilian campaign. In September, he crossed the Alps, having first put Milan to the ban of the empire, thus depriving the city of her regalia (the right to mint money and collect tolls). Now while this ban could not be enforced on the spot, Frederick had no intention of letting the matter rest there. When he eventually returned to Italy, he would deal with the northern cities from a position of strength; and not allow himself to be diverted by such side issues as the Pope's relations with the Romans—even if this meant deserting the Holy See.

Back in Germany, he set to work once more with great energy, banning the seizure by local lords of the personal property of deceased priests, and passing a host of other laws in the same vein. In October 1155, he invested Henry the Lion with the Duchy of Bavaria and, on 17 September 1156, in order to appease and compensate Henry Jasomirgott, he turned the latter's March of Austria into a Duchy. In addition, the new Duke was given some rather special privileges: Austria was granted in fee to him and his wife Theodora (the daughter of the Emperor Manuel Comnenus) jointly, and to their children whether male or female; if they should die without issue, they could bequeath the duchy to anyone they chose. Finally, the Duke was exempted from attendance at all diets held outside Bavaria and was only liable to render military service in Austria or her immediate neighbourhood. By this act, known as the *privilegium minus*, Frederick laid the foundations of modern Austria.

Another step he took to strengthen his authority was to enfeoff Conrad, his half-brother by his father's second marriage, with the Rhine Palatinate, which had reverted to the crown on the death of Hermann of Stahleck. As a result, Frederick greatly increased the influence of his family in the Rhineland, and particularly in the neighbourhood of Heidelberg, a city then rising into prominence.

Meanwhile Frederick did not lose sight of his original objectives—even when it came to choosing a new wife. In 1155, he asked the Emperor Manuel Comnenus for his daughter's hand but without success, possibly because Manuel wanted to make the marriage dependent on major concessions in Southern Italy. On his return from Italy, Frederick turned instead to Beatrix, the daughter of Rainald, the late Count of Burgundy, and an extremely good match since, after the death of her uncle, William, Count of Mâcon, who had seized the inheritance and even thrust the heiress into prison, she had come into her father's full estate. The man she married would thus be able to take a direct hand in Burgundian affairs, which Frederick dearly longed to do.

On 9 June 1156, the marriage was solemnized at a magnificent ceremony at Würzburg, and attended by a great concourse of princes. One of these, Duke Berthold of Zähringen, was bitterly disappointed. Like his father before him he had been *rector Burgundiae*, a post that was both influential and remunerative, and he knew that the marriage must put an end to all his privileges. In return, Frederick granted him the advocateship of the three sees of Geneva, Lausanne and Sion, a meagre recompense, and one that did not encourage Berthold's loyalty to the crown.

But by then, Frederick's major adversaries had been greatly reduced in strength. Peace reigned throughout the country, and the *Landfrieden* had considerably enhanced the power of the crown. It seemed to Frederick that it was high time to return to unfinished business in Italy.

From the end of 1155, his thoughts turned continually towards the peninsula, as he drew up plan after plan for a new expedition in the spring of 1158, this time with scrupulous attention to both military and diplomatic details. Frederick took advantage of the death, on 14 May 1156, of Arnold, Archbishop of Cologne and Arch-Chancellor of Italy, to bring new blood into the Italian administration. The most important and active of the newcomers was Rainald of Dassel, a young man who had gained much practical experience as provost of the cathedral churches of Hildesheim and Munster. Gifted with a lively intelligence, imaginative, energetic, courageous and pious, Rainald was a passionate supporter of the empire, and believed firmly that its authority should be extended over all Christendom. As Frederick's chancellor for the next eleven years, Rainald proved a most skilful negotiator and devoted servant. Unfortunately, sharing Frederick's great qualities as well as his defects, and being belligerent to boot, he was sometimes inclined to give intemperate advice.

At all events, with this lieutenant by his side, Frederick felt free to embark on his next great venture.

CHAPTER SIX

Breach of the Treaty of Constance and Frederick's Italian Expedition Summer 1156 — Summer 1159

A FEW days after Frederick's marriage, the situation in Italy was changed radically and quite unexpectedly—on 18 June 1156, Hadrian IV signed a treaty with William I, King of Sicily, at Benevento.

To explain the chain of events leading up to this treaty, we must go back to Frederick's return from Italy in the summer of 1155 when, as we saw, Sicily still represented a serious threat to the Holy See. Soon afterwards, however, the excommunicated King of Sicily was forced to raise the siege of Benevento, begun by him in May, so as to quell a barons' revolt in Apulia (encouraged by Manuel Comnenus) and the Sicilian threat to the papacy suddenly diminished, so much so, in fact, that the Pope was persuaded to call in William I as a possible ally against the Romans, who continued to prevent his return to the Holy City.

The Pope was further encouraged in this attitude by the fact that many of his cardinals had begun to question the wisdom of the alliance with Frederick, which they deemed not only deceptive but also quite pointless—deceptive because it was an alliance between two unequal partners, a weak church and an increasingly powerful empire, and pointless because Barbarossa had shown in 1154–55, that when it suited his book, he was prepared to overlook the interests of the church.

Moreover the alliance was dangerous, since Frederick's boundless ambition and the violence with which he threatened Milan and all those who dared to resist him, could only be prejudicial to the cause and rights of the Holy See. Hence these cardinals had come to feel that firmness towards Frederick was a far better policy than friendship, and that, before entering into any new agreements, it was necessary to re-define the respective position and objectives of both partners. One of the leading exponents of this view was Cardinal Roland Bandinelli of Siena, formerly professor of canon law at Bologna, and later Chancellor of the Roman Church under Eugenius III.

But in the autumn of 1155, while William I had still loomed threateningly on the horizon, a break with Frederick seemed out of the question. At Benevento, Hadrian IV had but recently received the homage of some of William's rebellious barons, and this at a time when William had fallen gravely ill. Early in 1156, he narrowly escaped assassination in a plot, and so shaky had his position become that, as soon as he was on his feet once more, he made up his mind to negotiate with the Holy See and to ask that the ban of excommunication be lifted. He accordingly sent ambassadors offering to pay homage to the pontiff, to swear fidelity, to make reparation for all the damage he had caused to the church, to support the papacy actively against the commune of Rome, and to grant the Pope considerable financial aid.

These attractive proposals threw the Pope and his cardinals into a great confusion. While some argued that any political settlement with William was an implicit violation of the Treaty of Constance (which did not explicitly exclude negotiation between the Roman Church and Sicily), others contended that peace with William would not only help to settle the Sicilian and Roman questions, but would also act as an effective check of Barbarossa's growing ambitions. There was yet another group of cardinals, who believed that what really mattered

74

was to reach agreement with William on the status of the church in the Norman kingdom rather than on more general political topics.

In the end, as Cardinal Boso has explained, the Pope and a majority of the Sacred College decided to reject William's proposals, who then resolved to have recourse to arms. This time, luck was on his side. Within a few weeks, he was able to bring the leaders of the rebellion to heel, recaptured Brindisi from the Byzantine forces, and once again laid siege to Benevento, with the pontiff and his cardinals within. Then William repeated his offer of negotiations and this time he could not be refused.

William now drove a hard bargain, forcing Hadrian to grant him major political concessions in exchange for ecclesiastical ones—hence the name of Concordat by which their agreement, signed on 18 June, became known.

The Holy See invested William I with the Kingdom of Sicily, the Duchy of Apulia, the principality of Capua and some minor territories. The king, for his part, took the oath of homage to the Pope, and agreed to pay a tribute of 1100 schifati. In Sicily itself, William was to keep his traditional authority over church appointments, but in Apulia and Calabria the Pope secured the right of appeal by clerics to Rome, the right of episcopal consecration, and the right of holding ecclesiastical councils.

This compromise was satisfactory to both parties—to William because it increased his realm and established his authority, to the Pope because it brought him control of churches that had previously been out of his grasp. In addition, William gave more concrete proof of his goodwill when, in November of that year, he helped the Pope to return to Rome.

When Barbarossa heard of the Concordat and of some of the steps the Pope had taken to re-assert his authority, he felt a keen sense of betrayal. He feared that the Concordat might endanger his entire Italian project, which hinged on papal support against William's kingdom. And Frederick was the more outraged in that he believed, with some justice, that the Concordat ran counter to the spirit if not to the letter, of the Treaty of Constance. Perhaps he forgot that in failing to come to the aid of the Pope in his hour of need, he himself had been the first to violate it. In any case, he was forced to revise his plans there and then: any idea of using Central Italy as a base against the northern cities was now out of the question.

This, in fact, was an intelligent assessment of the situation, but one that left Frederick in a quandary. Should he try to set up a few reliable pro-German military and diplomatic outposts, or should he win over the north by diplomatic overtures? And as for the Holy See, how far could he go towards severing diplomatic relations without jeopardizing his imperial ambitions? The answer to these problems was never satisfactorily propounded, and this was a major factor in Frederick's eventual downfall.

In any event, Frederick was forced to drop his original plan for a massive intervention in Lombardy and, at the Diet of Fulda, on 24 March 1157, he announced his decision to concentrate his attack on Milan. When first confiding this decision to his uncle, Otto, Bishop of Freising, Frederick had declared that God had entrusted him with "the government of the Holy City and the world (*urbis et orbis*)", thus for the first time laying claim to sovereignty over all Christendom and over Rome in particular—no doubt on the advice of Rainald of Dassel. In so doing, he not only challenged the power of the Pope but, against it, set up a magnificent dream of empire.

Before embarking on his new campaign, Frederick settled a number of domestic problems. To begin with he passed a royal prohibition against the levying of tolls along the Main between Bamberg and Mainz except for Neustadt, Aschaffenburg and Frankfort. In April 1157, he guaranteed the rights of the Jews in matters of law, residence, property, trade and commerce, and insisted that none of them must be forcibly converted to Christianity. He also opened negotiations with Vladislav, Duke of Bohemia, and in 1156, granted him the right to wear the royal insignia on certain festive occasions. All these measures were meant to strengthen the authority of the crown while Frederick was away in Italy, to fill the imperial coffers, and to gain new allies for the expedition.

Frederick also took more direct measures to enhance his prestige. Thus in 1157, when King Sven of Denmark was forced to submit to his rival Waldemar I, Frederick made certain that Waldemar did not escape from German tutelage. At the same time he established friendly relations with Géza II, King of Hungary, who promised to join the Italian expedition. Again, when Boleslav IV, who had seized control of Poland after ousting his brother Vladislav, refused to pay tribute to Frederick, the latter crossed the Elbe at the head of a small army and in the summer of 1157 captured Breslau and Posen, and forced Boleslav not only to render the required tribute and to pay large fines, but to participate in the Italian expedition and to bring his brother back from exile, which last promise Boleslav never kept.

At the same time, Frederick bestowed solemn privileges on the German churches, confirming their ancient rights, and putting church property under his personal protection. He also paid a visit to the Kingdom of Burgundy, there to take possession of his wife's estates, to receive the homage of the Burgundian nobility, and to improve the country's administration. At the end of February 1157, he arrived at Besançon, where he stayed for several months. Here, too, he confirmed the ancient privileges of religious institutions, placing the most important of them, including the church of Besançon, under his direct authority, banning the disposal of fiefs held from the empire, and asserting his rights by several other acts, the most famous of which was the golden bull he sent to the Archbishop of

Lyons which confirmed the latter's authority, and granted him various privileges, while solemnly proclaiming the emperor's sovereign rights over the city.

It was during his stay at Besançon that a serious incident further aggravated Frederick's relations with the Pope.

Since the autumn of 1156, Hadrian IV had scarcely communicated with the emperor, though he had never dared to adopt an openly hostile attitude to him—possibly because he was still in two minds as to which course of action he should pursue. At all events, the division within the Sacred College continued to tie his hands—a fact that for some reason has been overlooked by many modern historians.

The Concordat of Benevento had effectively united those who were wholeheartedly opposed to the empire and those who merely sought an agreement with Sicily. However, the majority of cardinals was still in favour of some measure of co-operation with Frederick and wished to restore the spirit of the Treaty of Constance. Hadrian, for his part, had increasingly begun to heed the call of the minority, headed by Roland, who asserted quite plainly that the interests of the Church demanded an alliance with Sicily and with the northern cities. They did not call for open war with Frederick but opposed the formal renewal of an alliance that, according to them, was bound to benefit Frederick at the church's expense. They proposed therefore to refrain from doing anything that might advance the imperial cause in Italy, and, wherever possible, to forestall the emperor's plans. The Pope, while agreeing with them in principle, refused to act without the unanimous support of the Sacred College, or at least of a majority of its members.

The Curia now evolved a twofold policy, intended on the one hand to bring home to the majority the benefits of an all-Italian alliance, and on the other hand to explain to the emperor, the world, and above all the German clergy, the reasons for this decision. If the emperor could only be made to see that the Church had no option in the matter, he might well be persuaded to change his attitude. Some of the cardinals, and even the Pope himself, it seems, concurred in this view, convinced as they were that Frederick's strength and determination had been grossly exaggerated, and that his behaviour in the peninsula in 1155 had shown that he sought personal exaltation and vainglory rather than concrete achievements.

Then an unpleasant incident gave the Holy See a chance of putting the emperor's resolve to the test. While returning home from a visit to the Pope, Eskil, the aged Archbishop of Lund was attacked by bandits on Burgundian soil and carried off into captivity. Hadrian IV protested at once to Frederick, on whose soil the outrage had taken place, and demanded immediate punishment of the perpetrators. When Frederick ignored the papal letter, no doubt so as to demonstrate his genuine displeasure with the Holy See, the Pope lodged a new, stronger, and more general protest, by which he hoped to force Frederick to show his hand—should Frederick merely react with recriminations or prevarications, the inference would be clear: he was not nearly as redoubtable as some of the cardinals feared.

It was a dangerous plan, for it threatened a violent break with the empire, but the Pope no doubt hoped that the unfavourable light the affair would shed on Frederick might arouse the opposition of the German clergy, and perhaps of the laity as well.

No other interpretation is, in fact, possible, though some historians have argued that Hadrian IV did not mean to provoke Frederick and merely failed to appreciate the full implications of his message to the king. This is to suppose the Pope naïve and clumsy to an incredible degree, and also to ignore the presence of the anti-imperialist group of cardinals in the Curia. Other historians, again, have argued that the papal message was meant, not merely to test Frederick's reaction, but to serve as a declaration of war, an hypothesis that would seem to be contradicted by the fact that the Pope retracted a few weeks later. The truth then must lie somewhere between these two theories: the Pope was trying to force the emperor to reveal his true intentions, and at the same time to rally his wavering cardinals, and the German bishops in particular, round the Holy See.

But let us return to the letter itself, which reached Frederick at Besançon in October 1157, and was handed to him by Cardinals Roland and Bernard. After recalling the outrageous attack on the Bishop of Lund and pointing out that the bandits had still not been brought to justice, the papal message continued with an exhortation to Frederick to show himself worthy of the kindness the Holy See had always shown him.

"You ought, most noble son," it continued, "to keep constantly before your mind's eye with how much joy and pleasure your Holy Mother, the sacred church, received you some years back; the cordial affection she has always borne you; the great dignity and honour she showed you when she so liberally *conferred* the imperial crown upon you; the manner in which she watched with benevolent attention over your elevation to the sublime honours, careful never to oppose your royal will in any way. Nor do we regret having in all ways satisfied your wishes, and had Your Excellence received still greater benefits (*beneficia*) at our hands—if this were possible— we should have been overjoyed at the great advantages and profits that might, thanks to you, have accrued to the church and to ourselves."

The reader might wonder why Frederick should have taken exception to so cordial a message, but in fact the terms *conferre* and *beneficia*, apart from their modern connotation, also had a specifically feudal one, denoting a grant of a fief by a lord to his vassal. In other words, the Pope was suggesting that Frederick was emperor by the grace of Rome and of Rome alone.

Rainald of Dassel was the first to read the Papal message, and when he was asked to translate it into German and unhesitatingly rendered *beneficium* as *fief*, there was a violent uproar among the assembled princes. In the ensuing turmoil, one of the Papal legates exclaimed: "From whom then does the emperor hold his empire if not from the Pope?" This brought the Germans to their feet, and Count Otto of Wittelsbach threatened the prelate with his sword. Frederick stopped him just in time, and ordered the two cardinals back to Italy, but only after their luggage had been searched.

One thing at least was now clear to the Pope: Frederick would neither recant nor allow himself to be intimidated. On the contrary, he had treated the legates with harshness, and in the days that followed, he directed a continuous stream of invective at the Roman Church. As a result, even the wavering cardinals came to see that agreement with the German emperor was no longer possible, and, indeed, after his shocking attitude in the Eskil affair, not even desirable. Thus the papal letter had achieved at least one of its objectives.

The Curia had, of course, hoped that the incident might also turn the German clergy against Frederick, but thanks to his indefatigable work for peace, thanks also to strong ties of kinship and friendship with several bishops, and above all to the able assistance of his Chancellor, Frederick had little to fear from that quarter.

He was the first to act. As soon as the Papal Legates had left, he addressed a circular to his entire kingdom in which he explained the nature of the papal manoeuvre and the indignation it had caused. He added that the legates had been dismissed for carrying blank letters with the seal of the Pope, empowering them to seize the treasures of the German churches. Moreover, by affirming that the imperial crown was a *beneficium* from the Holy See, the Pope had uttered a lie against a divine institution and a denial of St. Peter's doctrine. "Such then," he concluded bitterly, "was the message of paternal love, one that was meant to foster unity between the Church and the Empire." And he added an appeal to his princes to rise up against "the ignominy threatening us and the whole empire".

A few days later, Hadrian IV sent his version of the story to the German bishops. He recounted that his legates had gone to Besançon with a letter conferring upon Frederick "the glorious *beneficia* of the imperial crown". Though he was careful not to explain the dubious use of the term *beneficium*, he dwelled at length on the rest of the proceedings, and quite particularly on the threats offered to his legates, their expulsion from Besançon, and the consequent break of contact between Germany and the Holy See. The Pope begged all prelates to make the emperor see reason and to avoid a clash in which the German clergy would be the main losers. "This matter concerns not only us, but also you, and every church." The message ended with a denunciation of the aggression of some of Barbarossa's evil counsellors, and quite especially of Rainald of Dassel and Otto of Wittelsbach.

As soon as the emperor heard of this letter, he replied with a circular to the German clergy. In it, he once again set forth the view that the empire was his by the choice of princes and by virtue of the unction he had received, first at the hands of the Archbishop of Mainz and then by the Pope himself. The rest of the story, he wrote, was "long and painful". It had all begun with a painting in the Lateran (of Lothar kneeling before the pontiff) and had ended in the recent clash at Besançon. He, for his part, was not prepared to give way in a matter that involved questions of principles and justice.

The German prelates, anxious above all to see the empire live at peace with Rome, had been delighted by the signing of the Treaty of Constance, and fully shared Barbarossa's objections to the Concordat of Benevento. In any case, in a serious conflict, they could not possibly side with the Pope against their powerful and authoritarian king—even had they wanted to. And so, in a letter they wrote at the beginning of 1158, they informed the Pope that, to their mind, the legates had been expelled from Besançon because of the insult they had offered to one whose empire was his by the choice of the princes and by divine right. They accordingly advised the Pope to issue a new letter that would soothe the emperor's understandable anger, and to have the Lateran fresco destroyed.

This reply amounted to a resounding victory for Barbarossa —the Curia had clearly failed to appreciate how close and firm the association between the emperor and the German clergy really was. Hadrian IV was now forced to climb down, and in June 1158, he sent two other cardinals to Germany, with letters explaining that he had not used the term *beneficium* in its feudal sense, and that he had never had the least intention of claiming temporal sovereignty over the empire.

The Curia, though forced to swallow the Pope's retraction, remained extremely wary of Frederick, and as he was now determined to assert his authority over Italy, new complications were bound to arise.

On his next expedition to Italy, Frederick intended to make straight for the cities in the Po valley, and on no account to cross the Apennines. Immediately after his return from Besançon, he began to assemble a large and well-equipped army, made up of German contingents reinforced with troops from Bohemia, Hungary, and Poland. He took personal command of his entire host, drawn up under the respective banners of their princes. He also added a host of mercenaries and gave instructions that Italian reinforcements should await him across the Alps. Finally, he took steps to maintain discipline, to "organize" pillage and arson, and to appoint sutlers, the price of whose produce he took care to fix well in advance. In short, it was at the head of a highly disciplined and well-found army that he set out from Augsburg in June 1158.

Rainald of Dassel and Otto of Wittelsbach were sent on ahead to explain that the sole purpose of the expedition was the suppression of the Milanese rebellion, and Frederick's ambassadors were, in fact, able to enlist the support of several cities and of many Italian nobles. Piacenza signed a treaty in which she promised to provide military and financial aid (a hundred knights, a hundred archers and 600 silver marks) against Milan, with whom she was at war. Lodi, Como, Pavia and Cremona also joined the imperial camp. In these and other communes, many citizens took the following oath: "I swear fidelity to my Lord Frederick, Emperor of the Romans ... to help him protect the imperial crown, to preserve his honour in Italy . . . to restore his regalia ... and to obey his every command".

And so Frederick crossed the Brenner at the head of his army. This time he was not accompanied by his uncle Otto, the chronicler, who was ill and died a few weeks later. According to the pre-arranged plan, Frederick joined up with the promised Italian contingents and then made straight for Milan. The city resisted bravely for a month, but faced with the overwhelming might of the enemy and laid low by famine, she capitulated on 1 September. Besides imposing heavy fines and demanding 300 hostages, Frederick barred the city from coining money or levying dues and demanded an oath of fidelity from all the inhabitants, and the right to build a castle in the town centre (an extremely humiliating condition). Milan was moreover forced to promise not to interfere with the rebuilding of Como and Lodi. She would be allowed to elect consuls according to her own laws, but they were henceforth to be invested by the monarch. These terms were relatively lenient—Frederick wished to show that he had not come as an enemy but as a sovereign anxious to restore peace and order.

Above all, he hoped that by making an example of Milan, he might quickly bring all Upper Italy to heel. So confident was he, in fact, that he sent part of his army back home, though he took good care to keep Henry the Lion and other leading nobles by his side.

After spending some time in Lombardy, Frederick proceeded to Roncaglia, where he had convoked a diet of leading Italian bishops, barons, and townsmen. His intention was to cement his authority by solemn edicts, and to define his principles of government.

Four jurists from the celebrated Bolognese school were charged with compiling a list of regalia in accordance with Roman law and tradition, regalia which the Emperor, seeing himself as a new Justinian, was anxious to revive. They acquitted themselves well—their extremely long list included authority over public roads, navigable rivers and their tributaries, ports and landing places, the collection of tolls, the minting of money, the imposition of fines, the administration of vacant or confiscated fiefs, the contracting of marriages, the conscription of carriages, wagons or boats, the levying of exceptional taxes for royal expeditions, the authority to nominate magistrates and to build palaces in various cities, imperial control over mines, fisheries and salt pans, the confiscation of the goods of all people convicted of *lèse-majesté*, and a full or half-share in all treasure found on public or church property.

Frederick published this list on 11 November and decreed that although all these prerogatives were his by right, he would nevertheless cede them in perpetuity wherever documents could be produced establishing formal claims to them. For the rest, all regalia that had been usurped illegally must be restored to him, although he might, if he wished, forego some of them as a special concession. In fact, most bishops were able to produce written proof of privileges granted to them by various emperors since Otto I, and so were well content, the more so as Frederick also restored certain rights they had lost, legally or otherwise, to the communes. Hardest hit by the new edict were the cities, few of which could proffer official proofs of their privileges.

The new Imperial policy for Northern Italy was thus based upon the supreme authority of a single ruler, and the abrogation of most urban privileges, except in cities that had proved particularly loyal or useful. The clergy, on the contrary, was drawn into fruitful co-operation, Frederick believing that he had nothing to lose from granting them concessions because he counted on swaying of all episcopal elections. As for the lay nobility, a second edict, which applied to Germany as well, was issued in the same spirit as the first. It forbade the disposal or splitting up of fiefs, even in cases of succession, and quite particularly of fiefs that went with public offices (duchies, marches or counties), and called for increased military levies by the king's tenants. The entire programme was designed to increase the power of the greatest nobles who could be relied on to put pressure on their vassals, by threatening to revoke their fiefs.

A special edict extended imperial protection to "all those pursuing studies in one of the schools". This famous decree, which was applied, first of all, in Bologna, has been called the first university charter: by it, students were entitled to form autonomous communities of scholars or *studia*.

Finally, to ensure that his decisions would be carried out without fail, Frederick, in a further edict, ordered all male inhabitants in the Kingdom of Italy between the ages of eighteen and seventy years, to swear to maintain the peace and to take no part in any war-like enterprise or alliance. This was the crowning clause of his Roncaglia code: Frederick believed that if the Italians, of their own free will or of necessity, submitted to its rules, his imperial dream might be realized at long last. Moreover, he felt confident that all those who still harboured resentment would have been taught a salutary lesson by the capitulation of Milan. In the event, the emperor completely misjudged the Italian mood.

At the time, both the nobility and the bishops put a good face on his new edicts, the more so as what he demanded was customarily accorded to any emperor during his actual presence in Italy. Some went further and threw in their lot with Frederick, for example the powerful Count of Biandrate or the Marquis of Montferrat who, in 1159, was rewarded with important privileges in Asti.

The reaction of the cities was far less enthusiastic, indeed reticent. Some of them raised no serious objection to the edicts, not only because they felt that they had been an inevitable response to the defiance of Milan and her allies, but also because they hoped, by siding against Milan, to obtain major concessions from the emperor. This was the line taken by many of Milan's traditional enemies, among them Lodi, Pavia, Piacenza and Cremona. In Lodi, Otto of Morena, judge and consul, and his son Acerbo, ardent supporters of the empire, even wrote a celebrated paean of praise about "the great accomplishments in Lombardy by the very holy Emperor Frederick". In other cities, too, there were many who were anxious to support Frederick, hoping that he would respect the hard-earned rights of the communes. Others again, while agreeing that the emperor was fully entitled to exercise his imperial prerogatives whenever he was present in his Italian kingdom, nevertheless felt that he had no power to interfere with their *natural* liberties.

Between these two extremes—those who were for Frederick unreservedly and those who sided with the communes—the majority of Italians trembled.

The edicts of Roncaglia, coming as they did so soon after Milan was crushed, did not augur well for the future—they suggested that the emperor was determined to impose his will forcibly on even his most devoted supporters. And so, Italy at large clung to her worst fear, her age-old antipathy Frederick made a few alliances, and a handful of, mostly self-seeking, friends, but he received no solid backing for his plans of further expansion. Worse still, a few cities began to bridle at once. Thus Genoa retorted that she would only restore to Frederick what rights he could establish in law, and immediately strengthened her ramparts. In January 1159, Milan refused to allow the king's legates to invest her consuls.

Moreover, she launched a fresh attack on Lodi and Como, in clear breach of the surrender terms. Brescia came to her aid, as did the small fortified town of Crema. Since the king had sent part of his contingent back to Germany, he was in no position to fight a major battle, and had to content himself with laying siege to little Crema in July 1159. But so fiercely did the inhabitants resist him and so ingenious were they in constructing new engines, that Frederick was obliged to send for reinforcements to Germany. The siege continued for six months and was waged with unparalleled violence and cruelty, Frederick going "so far as to attach to his siege engines prisoners from Crema in the hope of preventing the beleaguered from firing their arrows and stones". Those within the city walls replied "by slaying on the ramparts all Italian and German prisoners".* Crema finally capitulated in January 1160, and while Frederick spared the lives of the defenders, he ordered their town razed to the ground. The bitterness of this campaign showed, perhaps better than anything else, how hostile much of Lombardy had grown to the German invader.

The Diet of Roncaglia also increased the fears of the Holy See, which at once adopted a more trenchant anti-German policy. Hadrian IV realized clearly that the occupation of Northern Italy was only the first step and that Frederick was aiming to seize all Tuscany, the Papal States and Rome. Frederick, for his part, did nothing to reassure the Pope by messages of peace or goodwill, and his counsellors encouraged him to persist in his intransigence.

In fact, it was during 1158 that many of those who had been counselling Frederick to come to terms with the Pope—his uncle, Otto of Freising; Wibald, Abbot of Stablo; and Archbishop Anselm of Ravenna—disappeared from his circle of advisers, leaving the field to his energetic and skilful chancellor,

* E. Jordan, *L'Allemagne et l'Italie aux douzième et treizième siècle*; (Paris 1939) p. 69.

Rainald of Dassel. Rainald was convinced that the empire was bound to triumph if only it proved courageous and strong enough in battle, and so impressed was Frederick with Rainald's wisdom and loyalty that, in January 1159, he appointed him Archbishop of Cologne.

There followed a series of intrigues, secret negotiations and unpleasant incidents. In pursuance of the Concordat of Benevento, the Pope established very close relations with William I of Sicily, who granted him enough financial assistance to strengthen the walls of the Holy City and to put the papal administration back on its feet—to the great dismay, not only of Frederick but also of the Romans. By way of reward, Hadrian IV interceded with the Byzantine emperor, Manuel Comnenus, who agreed to stop his attacks on Sicily, at least for a time. The Pope, moreover, brought home to Manuel that German expansionism posed a threat to Byzantium no less than to the Holy See, thus forestalling Frederick's attempts to win over the Greek sovereign. The Pope had previously been informed that German agents had been sent to Tuscany, the Papal States and Rome, where they were meant to organize active resistance, and that these agents were about to be joined and led by Count Otto of Wittelsbach.

The Curia, for its part, was busily engaged in secret negotiations with Milan and other Lombard cities, which were encouraged to sink their differences, and to unite against the common enemy. As a result, Bergamo and Brescia took their differences to the Pope, and when Frederick tried to interfere, Hadrian IV threatened him with an interdict. Shortly afterwards, the emperor made it known that he desired to appoint Guido, son of the Count of Biandrate, to the archbishopric of Ravenna. The Pope, referring curtly and ironically to Guido's alleged qualities, declared that the church could not possibly spare a man of such exceptional merit from Rome, and accordingly refused to confirm him.

For all that, the Pope did not bear the entire blame for these disputes. Frederick's negotiations with Manuel had given the Curia just cause for disquiet, as had the despatch of imperial agents to Tuscany and, *a fortiori*, the emperor's decision, exactly why we cannot tell, to place his name before the Pope's in messages to Rome, and, flouting all tradition, to address the pontiff as "thou" (*tu*) instead of the customary *vos*.

It was in this atmosphere of mutual recrimination and mistrust that official parleys between the two parties were started in April 1159 at the request of Hadrian IV. The ensuing discussions merely served to show to what extent the papal attitude had hardened, and that most of the cardinals now stood behind their leader. True, there was a pro-German minority who felt uneasy about the Pope's pro-Sicilian policy and who wished to show that an understanding with Germany was still possible, but the great majority now believed that Frederick was an implacable enemy to the Church and had to be treated as such.

In any case, the two cardinals who appeared before Frederick in early April, proposed a straightforward return to the Treaty of Constance. Now, though that treaty in no way barred the Holy See from negotiating with William of Sicily, Frederick contended that it did, and proposed that a committee of arbitration be set up, consisting of six cardinals representing the Pope's case, and six bishops of his own. On hearing this proposal, Hadrian IV remarked that such arbitration was quite pointless, since nothing good could come of apportioning blame for the present crisis. This was also the view of those cardinals who still had high hopes in reconciliation.

The Pope, with the support of the majority of the Sacred College, therefore decided that the negotiations must be solely concerned with Frederick's obligation, under the Treaty of Constance, "to maintain and defend the regalia of the Blessed Peter". Cardinals William of Pavia and Octavian of Monticello were now sent to make the Pope's position clear to Frederick, whom they met at Bologna in May, and whom they acquainted with the precise papal interpretation of the expression "regalia of the Blessed Peter". This included the Pope's sole right to nominate magistrates in, and to wield supreme authority over, Rome. Moreover, in the opinion of the Curia, the emperor had the right to claim the hospitality of Rome and the Papal States only when he was on his way to be crowned. The cardinals further submitted a list of territories the Holy See claimed for its own (Tivoli, the Matildine estates, Ferrara, part of the Exarchate of Ravenna, some parts of Tuscany, the Duchy of Spoleto, and Sardinia). Finally, arguing this time about canonical principles rather than regalia, they recalled that Italian bishops had never been obliged to swear homage, but only fidelity, to their monarch.

The first two claims dealt with highly topical matters: Otto of Wittelsbach was in Rome without the Pope's permission, and the monarch himself was at that moment encamped on church territory. Frederick accordingly rejected both demands out of hand, declaring that, as for the first, since he was called the Emperor of the Romans, the city of Rome certainly belonged to him. However, he agreed to absolve Italian bishops from paying homage to him, but only on condition that they ceded all their regalia. Finally he challenged the very basis of the Pope's territorial claims which he called "new, serious and unparalleled", but proposed that a joint commission should be held to look into some of them.

In fact, a deadlock had been reached. The Curia, almost certainly, was willing to temporize on the territorial question, which had no doubt simply been raised as a bargaining point. On the other hand, the cardinals were seriously afraid of Frederick's designs on Rome and thought it absolutely essential to obtain strong guarantees upon this matter. Yet it is difficult to see how Frederick could possibly have given way, seeing that sovereignty over the Papal States was an essential part of his Italian programme, as was ultimate authority over the Italian bishops. Frederick's reply therefore was a curt refusal to negotiate upon what, for the papacy, were the most important subjects.

But even while Frederick was still corresponding with Eberhard, Archbishop of Salzburg, about the latest turn of events, and while Cardinal Henry was declaring that he could no longer understand German policy, which now seemed aimed purely and simply at conquest, the Curia took direct action: in June, Hadrian IV left Rome for Anagni, where he was closer to his Sicilian protector. From there, Roland, the Cardinal-Chancellor and chief instigator of the anti-German policy, carried the banner of St. Peter to King William I, thus demonstrating to all the world that the Sicilian was now chief defender of St. Peter's Patrimony. At the same time, secret negotiations were started with Milan and other Lombard cities, including the besieged Crema. In August, finally, the Pope threatened to excommunicate the emperor within forty days if Frederick continued to perpetrate his "injustices".

At the time Frederick held all the winning cards. To begin with, he had military strength on his side, even if, for the moment, his forces were depleted. In Rome, Otto of Wittelsbach was stirring up the people, while other imperial agents were working in the northern Papal States. Furthermore, Frederick knew that he still had strong supporters inside the Sacred College, chief among them Octavian of Monticelli, an extremely influential Roman aristocrat, related to many princes, including the Babenbergs. True, Frederick's threatened excommunication was bound to arouse even greater Italian hostility, but Frederick felt he was strong enough to cope with any repercussions.

It was at this point that Hadrian IV died—on 1 September 1159.

CHAPTER SEVEN

Hopes and Disappointments 1159 - 1164

FROM 1159 to 1164, Frederick kept losing Italian support. More than ever, he sought to crush all opposition as he reached out for Tuscany and prepared for an attack upon Sicily.

Fortune seemed to smile upon him when, shortly after the death of Hadrian IV, on 7 September, the cardinals met at St. Peter's to elect a new pontiff. Frederick immediately put pressure on the Sacred College to nominate a pro-German prelate or at the very least one who favoured his plans. He had cause for optimism, since Otto of Wittelsbach had been distributing largesse among the Roman senators and people and, moreover, since he could rely on the full support of Cardinal Octavian.

In fact, the members of the Sacred College had agreed beforehand to elect the new Pope by unanimous vote, and this, in fact, meant a neutral candidate, a man of peace and reconciliation. However, the temper of the city, around St. Peter's and even within, where crowds of the faithful were milling about while they waited for the announcement with growing excitement, was not conducive to calm—indeed, it seems likely that quite a few of the electors went over to the German camp simply to avoid trouble and violence. Even so, the great majority of the electors, having come to appreciate how grave a threat Barbarossa's policies posed to the Roman Church, came down heavily against Frederick's nominee.

This much at least is apparent from the confused and contra dictory accounts of the voting that have come down to us. It seems that initially there were three candidates: Cardinals Roland, Bernard (two of the papal ambassadors to Besançon) and Octavian, and that, on a second count, the supporters of Bernard switched to Roland, who thus gained at least twenty out of the thirty-two votes cast. We also know that, a few days later, twenty-two cardinals, among them four cardinal-bishops, had ranged themselves publicly on Roland's side while Octavian could muster no more than five supporters.

However, when Roland's party tried to place the papal mantle on the shoulders of their candidate, Octavian made to snatch it and, failing to do so, seized a duplicate from his chaplain, and had the doors of St. Peter's opened to his armed partisans, who acclaimed him Pope Victor IV. At this, Roland and the other cardinals retired into the fortress annexed to St. Peter's, whence they proclaimed their determination to implement the will of the majority. A few days later, thanks largely to the influence of the strongly anti-German Pierleone family, they were able to escape to Campagna where, on the 20th, Roland was consecrated Pope and took the name of Alexander III. On 27 September, the two new Popes excommunicated each other.

The coup, planned by Otto of Wittelsbach, having failed, Frederick used all his powers to rally support for Victor IV among kings, nobles and bishops, and to isolate Alexander III who, having only Sicily to fall back on, seemed likely to prove as impotent as had the anti-pope Anacletus thirty years earlier.

Meanwhile, Frederick made a show of impartiality by ostensibly "investigating" the claims of the rival popes, and did not fall into the error of rashly recognizing Victor IV. At his camp before Crema, he convoked a council attended by twenty German and Italian bishops and the Abbots of Cîteaux and Clairvaux, who obligingly suggested that he act as arbitrator between the two rivals. Early in 1160, Frederick invited princes and bishops from all parts of the empire to a synod in

Pavia, where he proposed to examine the circumstances of the papal election and to decide who was the true head of the church. With consummate skill, he presented himself as a completely disinterested party, swayed purely by a sense of moral obligation, and let it be understood that in the present exceptional circumstances he alone had sufficient authority to effect a reconciliation. While Octavian readily agreed to be present, Roland refused, on the grounds that he was the true pontiff, having been elected according to canon law, and that he alone had the power to convoke a synod. He did, however, agree to send a cardinal as an observer.

The council was solemnly opened, not on 13 January as had been planned, but after the surrender of Crema, on 5 February 1160. It was attended by no more than fifty bishops, mainly from Germany, Burgundy and Italy with a sprinkling from France, England, and other parts of Europe. Notable absentees included Eberhard, Archbishop of Salzburg who, though pressed by Frederick several times, merely sent the Provost of Berchtesgaden as his representative; and the Archbishops of Trèves, Lyons, Arles and Besançon. The Archbishop of Mainz attended with some fourteen of his bishops; other prominent guests were the Archbishops of Cologne, Bremen and Magdeburg, the provincial bishops of Trèves and Aquila, and the bishops of Ravenna, Bergamo, Mantua, Faenza and Fermo.

Most of the defectors sent their apologies and promised not to recognize either of the two candidates until they had heard the emperor's envoys. Louis VII of France and Henry II of England made a similar reply. Their attitude was dictated by prudence: they wanted time to digest all the information and had no wish to be rushed into a decision.

The synod was opened by Frederick, who said that it was up to the bishops, and not to him, to judge the issue. There followed accounts by the Roman canons and various witnesses, all in favour of Octavian. They recalled that during the life of

Hadrian IV, Roland and his supporters had unceasingly worked to undermine the Treaty of Constance, that they had concluded an alliance with Milan and Sicily, and had fomented an uprising against the emperor. As a result, Octavian had gained the support of the more reasonable section (*sanior pars*) of the Sacred College, who looked upon Roland as a mere trouble-maker and plotter. After this bizarre argument, the council voted for Octavian (Victor IV) although, according to the Provost of Berchtesgaden, there was some hesitation among those present. Frederick thereupon conducted "his" Pope in solemn procession to the cathedral of Pavia, where Victor IV was crowned Pope once again. Roland (Alexander III) and his partisans were excommunicated, and Milan and the King of Sicily ordered to make "*canonical reparation*" to the new Pope.

The emperor had apparently gained his end: he now had a Pope devoted to his cause. However, Alexander III was by no means silenced; indeed, on learning of the verdict and of the letter the synod had addressed to the whole of Christendom, he replied with a shattering decree of his own: on 24 March he excommunicated Frederick Barbarossa. His bull was short and to the point: the emperor had been guilty of violence and fraud. He was "the chief persecutor of the Church of God", he had convoked a synod on his own authority, he had shattered the unity of the church, usurped rights that did not belong to him; he had torn Christ's seamless robe and confused the privileges of the church with the duties of the crown. For all these reasons, and especially "since he had embraced the schismatic Octavian and had had the presumption to champion him while in full possession of the facts", Frederick was cast out from the Church and his subjects absolved from their oath of fidelity to him—"since no Christian can be bound by an oath to one who has been excommunicated".

Had this—not entirely unexpected—ban been uttered by a less astute and gifted man it might well have come to nothing, but in Alexander III, Barbarossa had found his match; no mean jurist, indeed one of the greatest experts in canon law of his day, Alexander's reputation for learning was already high in the schools of Bologna. He had an extremely clear conception of his office, saw himself as the chief defender of the Roman Church, a champion of ecclesiastical liberty now menaced from without. The defence of the Church called for firmness of purpose and strong action, and not for the fervent declarations of bygone times. Alexander III was of a cold and domineering nature, a jealous guardian of the prerogatives of the Holy See, but he was also a skilful diplomat, always ready to give ground on inessentials if the major principles could be preserved. Above all, he was a politician who, thanks to his bourgeois background and early training in Siena, had a natural understanding of Italian affairs, and this clearly gave him the edge on Frederick.

Frederick's excommunication was immediately declared null and void by Victor IV. It did not, in any case, trouble the emperor in his own states, where his authority remained all-powerful, but it did persuade some of the uncommitted prelates—for instance the Archbishop of Salzburg and the suffragans of Gurk, Freising and Bixen, as well as some Italian and Burgundian prelates—not to rush into Frederick's open arms.

Moreover, the excommunication served to alienate Frederick from Christians abroad, few of whom rallied to Victor IV. Bohemia and Denmark joined him in the end, but Hungary, Aragon and Castille sided with Alexander, as did the Holy Land in 1161. Louis VII of France and Henry II of England wanted, for political reasons, to join the anti-German camp as well, but neither of them dared to do so immediately, notwithstanding the urgings of their clergy. In the summer of 1160, the Synods of Beauvais (on behalf of the French bishops) and Newmarket (on behalf of Henry's continental bishops) pronounced against the so-called German Pope.

And so the campaign Frederick had begun so enthusiastically on 7 September 1159, first hung fire, and, as enthusiasm waned, ground to a halt. But failure invariably spurred Frederick on to more vigorous action. On the advice of Rainald of Dassel, he now began to harp on his imperial authority, presenting himself as the true champion of the Christian West, one set above all other kings, who, as ruler of Rome, was responsible to none but to God himself. Being divinely appointed, his authority was far greater than that of the Pope, who was in duty bound to heed the emperor's advice. This was also the purport of a play staged in the Bavarian Abbey of Tegernsee. It was entitled *Ludus de Antichristo*, and its first act showed the Roman emperor receiving the homage of all kings; the second act showed the emperor's victory over anti-Christ who had taken the church out of the Temple of God. At about the same time, the Italian poet, Archipoeta, extolled the authority of "Caesar Frederick, prince of all earthly princes, raised up by God above all other kings". This kind of praise no doubt raised the emperor's hopes and strengthened his determination to impose his will on Italy.

To that end, Frederick now decided to bring Lombardy to her knees and then to drive further into the peninsula. First of all, he would crush Milan—as a saying then had it: "Take Milan and you have taken all". After that, he would establish himself in the Papal States and install Victor IV safely in Rome. Having thus restored the empire to the greatness it had enjoyed under Charlemagne and Otto the Great, he would go on to crush Sicily. All this introduced a new dimension into Frederick's great vision: with the help of "his" Pope, he would replace papal with imperial sovereignty over Sicily, and oust the ruling dynasty by enfeoffing all Southern Italy to the imperial crown. Thus the schism would yet prove a blessing in disguise: before the Treaty of Constance, Frederick's aim had merely been to stop Sicily meddling in Italian affairs and to eliminate her as a major power but not as an independent state; now, on the pretext of forcing the "false" pope to submit, Frederick had found a ready-made excuse to subject the entire south.

Meanwhile he was still encamped in Lombardy, waiting for the reinforcements promised him on 25 July 1160 at the Diet of Erfurt. Not all the nobles and bishops present there had been willing to supply and lead the military contingents Frederick had asked for; the Archbishop of Salzburg, for instance, had merely seen fit to offer financial support, which Frederick, whether from anger or spite, had refused to accept. In fact, the archbishop had no objection to Frederick's Italian policy as such but simply disapproved of the schism. In any case, Frederick could afford to dispense with his troops, since the other German nobles contributed a considerable number, to which the Bishops of Novara, Vercelli and Asti, the Margraves of Montferrat, Vasto and Busco, the Count of Biandrate, and various nobles from Lombardy, and particularly from Lodi, Como, Cremona, etc., added large contingents of knights, archers and engineers.

In the spring of 1161, as soon as the German reinforcements had arrived, Frederick launched a large-scale attack on Milan. In effect, hostilities had never really ceased, but, in the summer of 1160, had degenerated into a series of skirmishes and one large engagement—the relief of Salzano near Como which had been besieged by the Milanese. In May, Milan was invested, and offered peace on terms that included the destruction of all her walls and towers; the filling in of her moats; the delivery of 300 hostages; government by an imperially appointed *podestà*; surrender of all regalia; the payment of large fines; the construction of an imperial castle at the city's expense; the promise never again to enter into an alliance with any other power; the expulsion of 3,000 citizens; and the promise to receive Frederick and his army whenever he chose to present himself. Against such harsh terms, Milan held out valiantly for almost another year, but on 1 March 1162 she was forced to surrender unconditionally.

Then the city was given over to pillage and fire on an unprecedented scale. The violence was meant to serve both as a lesson to Milan herself, which had flouted Frederick's imperial majesty since 1159, and also as an example of strictness to the rest of Italy. On 6 March, the inhabitants, with their consuls, their flags, and their *carroccio*—the war chariot of the Italian communes—flying the sacred banner of St. Ambrose, went in procession to Lodi, where they prostrated themselves before the emperor and begged his pardon. The sovereign attached their banner but made no other reply. Next day, he ordered them to hand over their consuls and 400 knights, and to widen one of the gates of the city, through which he proposed to make his solemn entry on the 26th. After ostensibly taking the advice of his Italian allies, he gave his final orders: "Houses, churches, even the cathedral with its campanile, the ancient walls, dating from Roman times, all were destroyed; of the entire city, not a fiftieth part was left standing".* As for the hapless inhabitants, they were assigned four unfortified localities in which they might settle not far from the ruined city.

His strength displayed, his anger assuaged, his ambition satisfied, Frederick now proudly announced that his principal enemy in Northern Italy had ceased to exist. Milan's allies, Brescia among them, hastened to submit, lest the same fate befall them. Piacenza, which had deserted the imperial camp, was forced in May 1162, to fill in her moats and destroy her walls, surrender all the regalia and castles, pay an indemnity, accept the imposition of a *podestà*, renounce any independent political existence, and promise to help Frederick "maintain his crown and empire in Italy and in Lombardy". Other communes, who had been less hostile to Germany, received

* E. Jordan, *op. cit.*

better treatment. Ravenna was allowed to keep her consuls, but these had to be elected in the presence of, and invested by, an imperial representative, and had to present themselves in person to swear fidelity to the crown whenever the emperor happened to be in Italy. Moreover, all citizens had to declare on oath that they ceded all their regalia and the administration of justice to the crown. To Cremona, one of Frederick's most faithful allies, the regalia and justice were solemnly granted as a concession in exchange for an indemnity, but the consuls were to be elected and invested on the same conditions as those imposed on Ravenna (June 1162).

All these measures constituted a strict application of the principles of Roncaglia: imperial sovereignty was established and publicly proclaimed over all Northern Italy. At the same time, Frederick continued the work of militarization he had begun in 1158, and quite especially the occupation and surveillance of all passes and ports, the acquisition and construction of castles, the enfeoffment of all the fortified towns to friendly nobles, and so on. In this way he acquired a series of bases from which to mount further attacks, though, in general, it is true to say that the hatred and rancour his troops aroused wherever they appeared, weakened his hand considerably.

Aware that victory engenders further victories, Frederick made immediate preparations for an expedition against Sicily. For this he needed naval support, and to obtain it he started negotiations, one day after the fall of Milan, with Pisa and Genoa, the two chief maritime cities in the north.

Pisa was traditionally on the side of the empire and so an agreement was quickly reached. On 6 April, Frederick granted the city the right to elect her own consuls, to administer justice, and to decide her foreign policy without reference to imperial wishes. The city's own territory and all her possessions in the county were "granted" to the commune in fief, and Pisa was also given the right to trade in the area bounded by Civita Vecchia in the south and Porto-Venere in the north. In return,

Pisa agreed to stand by the crown, and to launch a naval expedition against Sicily as soon as the imperial army had reached Apulia. Pisa further agreed not to sign a separate peace with the enemy; after victory, she would be given the cities of Gaeta, Mazzaro and Tripoli as well as half of Palermo, Messina, Salerno and Naples. Finally, and this was an unexpected clause, the emperor undertook to help Pisa against Genoa, in case of dispute between the two merchant republics.

Genoa, for her part, had never been friendly to Germany, with the result that negotiations dragged on until 9 June 1162. When a treaty was finally signed, it was similar to that with Pisa. In particular, Genoa was granted the right to trade from Porto-Venere to Monaco. The appointment of consuls, on which no agreement could be reached, was not mentioned in the treaty, and Genoa, unlike Pisa, did not give a blanket undertaking to stand by the crown but merely agreed to participate in the Sicilian expedition against the promise of the city of Syracuse, a certain amount of property (streets, shops, etc.) in the various districts Frederick proposed to occupy, and the right to trade throughout the whole of Southern Italy.

These negotiations left no one in doubt as to Frederick's next step: only the impending invasion of Sicily could have caused him to grant privileges that ran directly counter to the policy he had laid down at Roncaglia; indeed, even to start negotiations with a city that was as traditionally pro-Alexandrine and anti-imperial as Genoa.

Nevertheless, a few weeks later, Frederick was unexpectedly forced to postpone his expedition.

All this time, he had kept close watch on the movements of Alexander III who, after returning to Rome for a time, had decided to seek the safety of France. At the end of 1161, Alexander had left Terracina, reaching Genoa at about the time of Milan's capitulation, and after a short stay, he had sailed to Maguelonne in Languedoc, where he arrived on 11 April 1162. His aim was twofold: he wanted to avoid falling into

Frederick's hands and he also intended to win the support of the kings of France and England. Frederick understood his motives only too well, and sought to forestall him: he must see Victor IV solemnly established in Rome, even if this meant delaying the Sicilian expedition for several months.

To gain a fuller understanding of the subsequent events, we must go back to the Synod of Pavia. At the time, Frederick had used considerable force and argument to drum up support for Victor IV. On 26 May 1161, he had summoned a new assembly of bishops to Cremona—a meeting he was forced to adjourn to Lodi in June for military reasons. There, Frederick issued a new proclamation confirming Victor IV as the true head of the church and, on his behalf, excommunicating all hostile prelates, the Archbishop of Milan and the Bishops of Piacenza, Brescia and Verona amongst them, and deposing the bishops of Bologna and Padua. He also acknowledged letters of support from the kings of Norway and Hungary, and made it known that the majority of the abbeys of the order of Cluny had decided in favour of Victor IV. The Cistercians took the opposite line.

Everything now hinged on Louis VII and Henry II. Frederick resolved to put pressure on the former, believing that the latter was bound to follow suit for fear of becoming completely isolated. The emperor accordingly started direct negotiations with a number of nobles in countries bordering on France, among them Count Raymond-Berengar IV of Barcelona and the latter's nephew, the Count of Provence, whom he married to his niece, and the Count of Forcalquier. Next he sent messengers to the Bishop of Viviers, to the divided leaders of the church in Lyons, to various nobles in Mâcon and Chalon, and, most important of all, to Henry the Liberal, Count of Champagne, whose county bordered on Burgundy and Germany. In addition, he established contact with several French bishops, among them Manasse of Orleans and Hugh of Champfleury, Bishop of Soissons, and a King's Counsellor.

In this way, he was able to establish a pro-German party within the French court at the very moment when Alexander III, having just disembarked at Maguelonne, was preparing to send legates to Louis VII and Henry II, and incidentally to commit a serious blunder. Unaware of the advanced state of Frederick's negotiations (the treaty with the House of Barcelona and Provence had only just been signed), and thinking that the support of Henry II would prove more useful than that of Louis VII, whose favours he took for granted, the more so as the king's brother Henry, Bishop of Beauvais, was shortly to be promoted Archbishop of Reims, Alexander told his legates to begin their negotiations with Henry Plantagenet. When Henry quickly persuaded them to grant his minor son a dispensation to marry the King of France's daughter, he made them fall foul of Louis VII who did not want this union to take place immediately, lest he have to hand over the Vexin as a dowry. Louis accordingly let it be known that he was still uncommitted, and that he must first hear the views of the Count of Champagne and other pro-German counsellors in his court.

The first talks between the Count and Barbarossa had apparently been held early in 1162 and were resumed during May, when the Count, at the suggestion of Louis VII, called on Frederick in Lombardy, and proposed a meeting on 29 August between Louis accompanied by Pope Alexander and Frederick accompanied by Victor, on the bridge of St. Jean de Losne, spanning the Saône between Dole and Dijon. At this meeting, the papal question would be finally settled. Frederick at once informed the German bishops, the Archbishop of Lyons and the German lay princes of this proposal. Then he set off across the Alps for Burgundy.

News of the proposed meeting quite naturally filled Alexander III with deep forebodings, and he begged his French supporters to dissuade Louis VII from attending. When Louis countered that he had already given his word, and could not possibly go back on it, Alexander, in spite of the king's insistence, refused to honour the meeting with his presence, and merely agreed to send five cardinals as observers.

Then Louis began to have second thoughts as well. At Dijon, he learnt that Henry of Champagne had taken it upon himself to promise that, should one of the pontiffs absent himself from the meeting, the other would automatically gain recognition. Moreover, at Chalon and Cluny, Louis met a host of nobles and priests who told him that, across the Saône, Frederick was loudly acclaiming Victor IV as the true head of the Roman Church. Worse still, the Germans, or more probably Rainald of Dassel, had started a rumour that Louis had already made up his mind to fall in behind Frederick's Pope, and that the rest was a mere formality.

Frederick, for his part, had learned in Burgundy that, far from being a staunch supporter of Victor's cause, the French king, under strong pressure from his clergy, was about to patch up his quarrel with Alexander, and that it was only because he must not appear to espouse Alexander's cause in advance, that Louis had not called off the meeting. Unfortunately, Alexander III, as we saw, refused to accompany him, and Louis was afraid that, in accordance with the promise of the Count of Champagne, he might be forced willy nilly to recognize Victor. This explains why, on 29 August, the two kings "missed" each other—each appeared on the banks of the Saône and solemnly noted the other's absence.

For purely formal reasons, however, the two monarchs felt it incumbent upon them to arrange for a second meeting, on 19 September. Louis VII was now in a most embarrassing position. To keep his word, he ought, at the very least, to face the emperor and explain that unless Frederick promised to keep an open mind, Alexander could not possibly attend, and that no impartial conclusions could be reached in his absence. But the pro-German party insisted that it was up to Louis to produce Alexander, and the French king knew that if he failed to oblige them, he ran the grave risk of having some of his men seized as hostages. Across the river, in the imperial camp, they were perfectly aware of his predicament. For this very reason Frederick and Rainald had decided, well before the meeting of 29 August, to summon a council at Dole in which a large number of princes and prelates were about to renew their allegiance to Victor IV. Their very presence was expected to make a considerable impression on Louis VII who, if Henry of Champagne exerted further pressure by threatening to transfer his allegiance to the emperor, might well be forced to submit.

Frederick's council met on 7 September, the third anniversary of the pontifical election, and was considerably more impressive than some historians have claimed. A good fifty bishops attended, and although most of them were Germans, the Kingdom of Burgundy was represented by quite a large contingent. In addition, all the great princes of the realm were present: Henry the Lion, Albert the Bear, and Otto of Wittelsbach. The King of Denmark attended in person and the King of Bohemia was represented as well.

Unfortunately, the meeting was not nearly as successful as Frederick had hoped. Thus when some of the German bishops put up a pretence of re-examining the rights and wrongs of the disputed papal election, Victor IV rebuked them for being insubordinate. Again, when some of them remarked that he ought first to gain the support of all Christendom before speaking to them in this way, Rainald of Dassel retorted that since Victor enjoyed the full support of the emperor, the opinion of "provincial" kings and nobles was of little consequence. When this was reported to Louis VII, he was deeply offended. Moreover, on learning that the whole pontifical question had been brushed aside at Dole, he began to have serious doubts about Frederick's integrity.

His doubts were increased further when he learned that Frederick was stirring up the nobles in and around Dole against the French crown. All the same, on 19 September, he thought it advisable to turn up for the second meeting, if only to explain that, since Frederick had not kept his part of the promise to examine the papal question impartially, he himself was no longer bound by their agreement. But Frederick had decided not to meet Louis in person; instead he had sent Rainald, no doubt with orders to persuade the French king to go on to Dole. Louis, having expressed his surprise at the emperor's discourtesy, demurred. Rainald lost his temper and declared that "the emperor had never promised to share with anyone, and certainly not with petty kings (*reguli*), his jurisdiction over the Roman Church". The Capetian waited to hear no more, and giving spurs to his horse, put an abrupt end to the conversation. A few days later, he solemnly recognized Alexander III, and received him in triumph both in Tours and in Paris. In March 1163, he summoned a solemn council at Tours, at which seventeen cardinals, 124 bishops and more than 400 abbots endorsed his decision.

All hopes of reconciliation had been dashed, the rift within Christianity had grown wider still. Frederick's plans had come to naught once again, the more so as Henry II of England had meanwhile declared his support for Alexander III.

As ever, this setback merely served to strengthen Frederick's resolution: since diplomacy had failed, he would once again have to take up the sword, install Victor IV in Rome and proceed to Sicily. He had not been struck a paralysing blow, and though he had gained nothing, he had lost nothing either. Above all, he was still in full control of Northern Italy.

Ignoring the intrigues of Berthold of Zähringen and the King of France, pretending not to notice how coolly a great many German bishops had treated Victor IV at the Synod of Trèves, and scorning the ban of excommunication pronounced against him and his followers at Tours, he firmly rejected all Alexander's offers of reconciliation.

The first such offer came only one day after the abortive meeting on the Saône, when Eberhard of Salzburg promised, in Alexander's name, to grant Frederick a free pardon and to accept him as "the most powerful of all princes". In the summer of 1163, four legates, two of them cardinals, came to Nuremberg. Frederick, forced to receive them, suggested that an arbitration council be set up to settle the papal dispute. Now this was simply a return to Pavia and Alexander would not hear of it. In the spring of 1164, two other cardinals called on the emperor at Susa, between Mont Cenis and Turin, but were not even received.

From Burgundy, Frederick had gone back to Germany, where he intended to put his own house in order, before returning to the Italian arena. To begin with, he had to settle accounts with Mainz, which, in 1160, had rebelled against her archbishop and put him to death. Using the tactics that had proved so effective in Italy, Frederick revoked all the city's privileges, had her ditches filled in and her walls breached. At the same time, in defiance of the Concordat of Worms, and ignoring the protests of Victor IV, he installed Conrad, the brother of Otto of Wittelsbach, as the new archbishop, after rejecting the two candidates nominated by the chapter: Rudolf of Zähringen, whom he rightly judged to be an opponent of the imperial policy, and Christian of Buch.

Moreover, he came to the aid of Henry the Lion, Duke of Saxony and Bavaria, who had so loyally supported him at Dole, and who was now quelling an uprising by his rebellious vassals.

In 1158-9, Henry had founded the town of Lübeck and, in 1160, had transferred the episcopal see of Oldenburg to that city. This had forced him to enter Holstein in order to ward off the Wends. All this, and his authoritarian manner, had aroused the opposition of some of the local nobles. At the same time, he was drawn into a series of sporadic engagements in Bavaria to protect his interests in the salt trade at Reichenhall and tolls from the trade routes into Italy. In 1158, he created the city of Munich at the point where these trade routes crossed, thus running foul of the Bishop of Freising, and unleashing the wars that, according to Archbishop Eberhard of Salzburg, ravaged the entire province in 1161. Here, as in Saxony, Barbarossa rallied to Henry's cause, anxious as ever to pacify Germany before returning to Italy. For the same reason he imposed a settlement on Poland, forcing Prince Boleslav IV to cede Silesia (the diocese of Breslau) to his two nephews, the rightful heirs. The diocese was divided into Upper and Lower Silesia, and though both remained Polish in theory, they were, in fact, treated as German principalities.

Despite these successes, Frederick nevertheless failed to impose his will on Germany in two important respects. To begin with, the number of bishops supporting Alexander III kept increasing steadily, and now included not only Eberhard of Salzburg but also Hillin of Trèves, and the bishops of Metz and Verdun. Archbishop Wichmann of Magdeburg, who owed his promotion to the king, remained undecided, but the new Archbishop of Mainz, Conrad of Wittelsbach, after wavering likewise, went over to Alexander in 1164. In Burgundy, defections were commoner still. At Lyons, the canons were divided, and Guichard de Pontigny, the prelate elected by Alexander's party, refused to step down in favour of the emperor's candidate.

Frederick also failed, despite blandishments and threats, to persuade his princes to participate personally in his new expedition or even to supply troops.

But the emperor was undeterred. In October 1163, he once again crossed the Alps with a small band of men, and set up camp in Upper Italy where he was joined by his old companions in arms, and tried to obtain reinforcements from friendly Italian nobles and cities.

His plan was simple: he would capture Rome and then, with

the help of Genoa and Pisa, make straight for Sicily. In the spring, he had sent Rainald of Dassel and Victor IV ahead to central Italy with instructions to prepare the way for the Pope's installation in the Holy City. Rainald had freely employed his considerable talents and boundless energy. Within a few months, working in Tuscany, the Duchy of Spoleto, the March of Ancona and Romagna, and relying almost entirely on his political skill and the prestige of the empire, he was able to set up a host of imperial strongholds, all of which proved far more redoubtable and durable than those of Lombardy.

Rainald's chief aim was to implement the principles adopted at Roncaglia, and to establish the emperor's authority over all Italy. The better to deal with any opposition, he went over the head of Welf VI, an uncle of Frederick and of Henry the Lion, who had been invested with Tuscany and the Duchy of Spoleto in 1152, and placed all his vassals and towns under direct crown control. Moreover, he ousted all bishops favourable to Alexander and had them replaced with more reliable men.

At the same time, he started negotiations with the communes. The most important cities, such as Lucca, were allowed to keep their consuls, on condition that they agreed to annual investment by the sovereign. These cities were, moreover, allowed to retain their regalia, except for the coining of money, and in exchange for these privileges, which were not granted in perpetuity, they agreed to pay an annual rent. They promised to swear fidelity to Frederick, and agreed to supply troops for the emperor's attack on Rome, Apulia and Calabria. The smaller towns were placed under direct imperial protection, on the pretext of guarding them against attack by the major cities. On 8 November 1163, Gubbio was thus granted "protection" and confirmed in her possessions against an annual rent of sixty livres and a further contribution of 100 livres towards the war on Sicily.

Finally, in the rural districts, imperial officers, either German or Italian, the latter chosen from the most stalwart imperialists, were appointed to keep watch over the nobility and the overland routes. New counts and *podestàs* were appointed everywhere, and, to a far greater extent than in Lombardy, Rainald succeeded in gaining control of strategic castles. He also built a new fortress at San Miniato, some twenty-five miles southwest of Florence, and turned it into his chief stronghold. His enormous building programme greatly impressed his contemporaries; Cardinal Boso explained that he brought the Emperor "impregnable citadels and other great fortresses, all of them garrisoned and defended by Germans. He also appointed Germans as princes and lords throughout Lombardy and Tuscany, so that no Italian could resist his will".

It was thanks to Rainald's spade work that, despite papal opposition and in the face of indifference by his own princes, Frederick was able to make such rapid progress when he entered the peninsula in the autumn of 1163. With the help of minor vassals, loyal servants and devoted ministers, he now had a real chance of imposing his will on the whole country.

But then Frederick's very determination and Rainald's ruthlessness came to his enemies' aid. In Northern Italy, they raised a loud clamour about German oppression, and even the most staunchly imperialist cities, such as Cremona and Pavia, began to protest against foreign tyranny. In Lodi, the anonymous chronicler who stepped into the shoes of Otto of Freising and Acerbo of Morena—both fervent admirers of Frederick—went over to Alexander's camp, and began to sing his praises. But it was Venice that, in the winter of 1163, became the chief centre of opposition. From the very start of the papal schism, the Republic had sided with Alexander, and this had been a source of considerable annoyance to Frederick, who was incensed further when Venice offered refuge to all the Italian bishops he had deposed. The republic was not a little anxious about the emperor's stranglehold over the Lombard cities, and feared his ambitions in Southern Italy and Sicily, whence he could dominate the Adriatic coast much more effectively than the feeble king of Sicily, and thus threaten her very lifeline. As a precaution, she therefore signed an agreement with William I and Manuel Comnenus, after negotiations encouraged by Alexander III, by which all three parties undertook to oppose any German attempt to spread further southward. Now, when Frederick had signed his treaty with Genoa, he had had high hopes that the Venetians would throw in their hand. In this he was badly mistaken: the republic might perhaps have submitted under the threat of a direct assault but she could not possibly tolerate an ostensibly peaceful alliance that not only strengthened her rival, but also threatened her most vital commercial interests. Venetian silver now began to pour into the coffers of the Northern communes, with the sole object of fostering rebellion. In March 1164, when Frederick told the Diet of Parma that he was about to march on Rome, and that he had turned Sardinia into a kingdom under Oristano, an adventurer without morality or talent, but a faithful servant of Genoa, Venice had had enough, and directly joined Verona, Vicenza and Padua in what became known as the League of Verona, and was overtly hostile to the emperor.

This was a serious set-back for Frederick and all the more dangerous because these cities guarded the Brenner and Tarvisio Passes—the two principal routes from Germany to Italy. He reacted promptly by declaring war on Vicenza and Padua, taking good care to make important concessions to neighbouring cities so as to dissuade them from joining the rebels. In particular, he granted Treviso, Ferrara and Mantua important privileges (regalia, fortifications, etc.) that went far beyond the spirit of Roncaglia. For all that, these cities failed to render him the assistance he so badly needed, and, worse still, what German contingents arrived in answer to an urgent appeal in April, proved pitifully small. As a result, Frederick's attack on Verona in June proved an abysmal failure.

He decided to return to Germany and shortly afterwards arrived at Ulm. In the meantime, on 26 April, Victor IV had died at Lucca, where Rainald of Dassel had at once persuaded the cardinals to elect as his successor Guy of Crema, who took the name of Paschal III. Frederick had not been consulted but hastened to send his approval, and in so doing committed another blunder—by failing to consult his bishops, he merely strengthened Alexander's hand.

By the summer of 1164, imperial policy was thus in serious difficulties right across the board. Opposition to the emperor's pope was day by day growing more vocal, nor was he yet in Rome. On the peninsula, the cities which had been subdued were in ferment, and Frederick was once again forced to postpone his Apulian expedition.

He could, however, take comfort in the fact that the past five years had not been entirely wasted. His excommunication by Alexander had proved no crippling handicap, for although some German prelates had refused to recognize Victor or Paschal, they none the less continued to accept Frederick as their emperor and to pay him homage as such. In Italy, Milan, his principal and most redoubtable adversary had been completely destroyed. A fair number of Lombard cities and most North Italian nobles supported the empire, and in Central Italy, too, his allies were very solidly entrenched. In fact, no emperor before him had held so much power over the peninsula. Moreover, at home, his star was in the ascendant and his reputation untarnished.

No wonder, then, that Frederick shrugged off his setbacks as so many minor irritations, and once again decided to strike back with redoubled energy.

CHAPTER EIGHT

A Time for Courage and Resolution
1164 - 1168

FREDERICK spent the summer of 1164 assembling an army
for a new expedition. Victor's death had in no way changed
his original plans; he was convinced that only an unfortunate
combination of circumstances had snatched success from his
grasp. This time, he would march straight on Rome and put
an end to the schism, foist his pope upon the Holy City, and
thus cow his opponents throughout Italy. Sicily would have to
wait for a while.

Frederick had obviously come to realize that his nominee
had little chance of gaining the confidence of Christianity at
large by peaceful means. While Victor IV had been alive, this
truth did not have to be faced, but his death and the election of
Paschal III had brought it to the surface with a vengeance.
True, Eberhard of Salzburg had died in June 1164, and was
replaced by Conrad, Bishop of Passau, who was related to
Frederick through the Austrian dukes, but even he was unwilling to range himself on Paschal's side, and Alexander's
party continued to grow in strength—in Germany no less
than in Italy. Frederick was forced to take strong counter-
measures and, as a first step, he took the chancellery from
Rainald of Dassel, who had been undiplomatic and clumsy, and
had displeased Frederick by nominating Paschal on his own
initiative. The chancellery was handed over to Christian of
Buch, Provost of Merseburg, whose election as Archbishop of
Mainz Frederick himself had prevented in 1161. Rainald, for
his part, continued as Arch-Chancellor of Italy and as Arch-

bishop of Cologne, in which capacity he was entrusted with many difficult missions.

Thus he was asked to conduct the extremely important negotiations with Henry II Plantagenet. Henry, though a supporter of Alexander, had at first been careful not to take sides in the papal dispute for fear of driving Louis VII into the arms of Germany. However, when he heard of the talks at St. Jean de Losne and saw his worst fears confirmed, he had decided to take prompt action and had declared publicly for Alexander. At the same time, his attempt to assert the authority of the crown over that of the English church had brought him into conflict with Thomas Becket, his own nominee for the archepiscopal see of Canterbury, and who now, in the name of church liberty, raised strong objections to the king's views as set forth in the Constitutions of Clarendon (January 1164). In October 1164, possibly fearing arrest, Thomas had fled to France, where Louis VII was quick to welcome him. Becket then called on Alexander III at Sens to explain his conduct, and while he did not receive the Pope's full blessing, he was nevertheless rewarded with a papal condemnation of several basic provisions in the Constitutions of Clarendon. Faced with this unfriendly action, Henry II resolved to put pressure on Alexander, and made it known that he might well decide to transfer his allegiance to Paschal III.

Frederick was quick to step into this unexpected breach: though he realized full well that the King of England was hampered by his clergy's fidelity to Alexander, he hoped that, by simply widening the gulf between Henry and the latter, he might weaken the Pope's international standing, and, moreover, strengthen his own position at home, perhaps win over a few waverers, eliminate a few adversaries and, in short, inject new life into the faltering cause of his papal candidate.

It was to that end that he had sent Rainald of Dassel to Henry, who, after some useful talks in Rouen during April

1165, and despite the opposition of the Norman clergy, promised to recognize Paschal III and to marry his eldest daughter to Henry the Lion. (When that marriage finally took place in 1168, it sealed the alliance between the Guelphs and the Plantagenets.) Last but not least, Rainald brought back to Germany an English ambassador who had instructions to disclose his sovereign's promise to a diet that was about to be held at Würzburg.

Frederick made elaborate preparations for this assembly, whose sole purpose it was to express vigorous support for Paschal III and to proclaim to all the world that Frederick's will was law. The diet was held on 23 May, and attended by most of the lay princes of Germany and some forty German bishops. Also present, although we cannot tell how he insinuated himself into the meeting, was a "spy" of Alexander III who gave his master a full account of the proceedings.

The chief objective of the emperor, as we said, was to intimidate his enemies. First of all, the Diet heard Henry's promise to support Paschal at some unspecified future date. Then Frederick himself swore an oath. This was an extremely unusual step since, in general, royal oaths were sworn by a deputy. But Frederick's intention on this occasion was not so much to solemnize his pact with Henry II, as to make a lively impression upon the German bishops. He swore never, under any pretext whatsoever, to recognize "Roland or any of his successors", and never to allow any of the clergy consecrated by Victor IV, Paschal III or their successors, to be deprived of their benefices and dignities. This amounted to a plain and unequivocal declaration that, as far as he was concerned, the schism could only end in the removal of Alexander III. Imperial policy on this subject had never before been stated in such forthright terms.

So as to leave no doubts about their intention, Frederick then asked all the princes and bishops present to swear a like

116

oath there and then, and in the circular he sent out on 1 and 2 June he claimed that everyone readily complied. However, if we are to believe Alexander's spy, this was a wild exaggeration.

According to this man, only five of the bishops swore without reservations. Others demanded that Rainald of Dassel, who had been elected, but not yet consecrated, Archbishop of Cologne, should be the first to take the oath. Yet others refused to swear the oath on the ground that they would have to refer back to their archbishops. The majority consented, but only with the proviso that they might retract if no unanimous decision was reached. Frederick cut them short—the only excuse he allowed was the absence of a particular archbishop. He then ordered all the elected bishops, Rainald first, to be consecrated, and promised to keep a very close watch on their behaviour. Finally, he called upon all the lay princes to swear an oath of obedience to Paschal III within six weeks, and laid down sanctions against any who should refuse. As a result, the Cistercians were expelled from Germany, and many of his most loyal subjects, men who, since 1159, had been wrestling with their consciences without swerving in their loyalty and patriotism, were placed in an agonizing dilemma, among them Gero, the famous Provost of Reichersberg and Bishop Ulrich of Halberstadt. Conrad of Wittelsbach, Archbishop of Mainz, was forced to seek the protection of Alexander III, and his See was handed over to Christian of Buch. Conrad of Austria, the new Archbishop of Salzburg, was summoned to appear before a diet at Nuremberg in February 1166, and when he failed to attend, was deprived of his regalia. Finally, Frederick solemnly communicated his views to various kings, and particularly charged the Count of Champagne to convey his decisions to Louis VII.

In all this he seems, superficially at least, to have ignored many of the doubts he must surely have felt. As usual, he was persuaded that strength and determination alone would ensure victory, the more so as he believed he could fully count on the political, if not the ecclesiastical, allegiance of the German nobility and church. This is precisely why, in an edict of 26 September 1165, ostensibly dealing with clerical estates, he extolled the magnificent legislative edifice he had inherited from his noble Roman and Carolingian predecessors—Justinian, Valentinian, Charlemagne and Louis the Pious—heirs to the greatness of ancient Rome. Moreover, he kept close watch over the episcopal elections in Ratisbon (Regensburg) in 1164, in Passau and Spires in 1164, in Passau and Würzburg (where Harold of Hochheim was elected) in 1165, and in Constance (where Otto of Habsburg was promoted) in 1166.

And it was in an atmosphere of exalted imperial power and munificence that, shortly after the Diet of Würzburg, he organized a grandiose festival in honour of Charlemagne. As the eminent professor and historian Robert Folz has astutely pointed out, this celebration satisfied a variety of needs: it helped to link Frederick's reign to that of his revered predecessor (and this at a time when Alexander III had just canonized Edward the Confessor); it served to humble the Capetian dynasty by flaunting the Carolingian's far nobler pedigree; it recalled that the founder of Frederick's empire had been a German prince; and, most of all, it proclaimed that Frederick was wearing the mantle of one who had united the West under a single sceptre, ruling supreme as Lord temporal and spiritual. This last idea, which had first been timidly voiced after Besançon and more loudly by Rainald of Dassel at St. Jean de Losne, was now expressed most vigorously at home and abroad—at the Diet of Würzburg and in Europe at large.

On Christmas Day 1165, when another solemn diet assembled at Aix-la-Chapelle, it was decided to "exalt" the relics of the holy emperor and to take them to a place where they could be more easily venerated by the people. This transfer was witnessed by a vast assembly of princes and prelates on 29 December, which is called St. David's day in Germany, David being the very embodiment of a pious and sacred king. Frederick presided over the entire proceedings, assisted by the Bishop of Liège, and by Rainald, now Archbishop of Cologne. At the end, Charlemagne was solemnly canonized and 28 January proclaimed a holiday in his honour. Doubtless Paschal III had been asked for his blessing, but that was all, for Frederick believed that this act fell entirely within his own province—it was precisely what Charlemagne himself might have done in his place.

Frederick himself has left us an account of the ceremony, in a document published on 8 January 1166 in Latin (German translation by Robert Folz). After recalling that since his coronation he had ceaselessly striven to follow the example of the great emperor, Frederick went on to say:

"He himself (Charlemagne) laboured with all his might to win the rewards of eternal life. His works and countless deeds bear witness to his constant desire to increase the glory of Christ's name and to propagate the holy religion. Many were the bishop's palaces founded by him, many the abbeys and churches he enriched with diverse benefits and gifts, manifesting the munificence of his alms on either side of the seas. He was tireless in his efforts to extend the Christian faith and convert the pagan peoples in Saxony, Friesland, Westphalia, Spain, no less than the Vandals, all of whom he converted to the Catholic Church by word and by sword. And although no blade pierced his soul, the diverse pains and tribulations he suffered; the dangerous battles he fought and his daily readiness to lay down his life for the conversion of the infidel, made him a true martyr. And so we now proclaim and venerate him upon this earth as our elected and most holy confessor, whom we believe, having lived a holy life, and having been confessed and deeply repented of his sins, to have gone before the Lord, and amongst his own confessors to have been crowned a sainted and true confessor in heaven . . .

"For these reasons, through our faith in the glorious deeds and merits of the most holy emperor, encouraged by the requests of our dear friend Henry, King of England, and with the agreement and authority of the Lord Paschal and on the advice of all the princes both spiritual and temporal, we decided on the elevation, exaltation and canonization of the Holy Emperor, at a solemn court this Christmas at Aix-la-Chapelle, where his most holy body had lain hidden from his enemies and was shown to us by the grace of divine revelation. We have elevated and exalted him on 29 December for the praise and glory of Christ, to strengthen the empire, and for the salvation of our dear wife, the Empress Beatrix, and our sons Frederick and Henry, amidst a great concourse of princes and in the presence of the clergy and the people, singing hymns and canticles with great devotion and respect."

Never since Frederick's accession to the throne in 1152 had emotions run so high, had the people been so close to their king and leader, had his authority at home been so firmly entrenched.

It was against this background that Frederick felt free to discipline his clergy, and to promulgate laws governing the disposal of their estates. At the same time he passed such far-reaching legislation as the decree of November 1165 by which the Rhine was tamed by the construction of an aqueduct, the shifting of a coffer dam, etc. For the rest, Frederick tried, as ever, to keep the peace among his princes, for instance by helping Henry the Lion to suppress his northern vassals, who had once again risen in rebellion against his harshness.

During all this time, Frederick had never forgotten his resolve to return to Italy and to strengthen his authority there. Indeed, this project had never seemed more important and necessary than it did in 1165, for Alexander III, upon the election of a favourable senate, had returned from France, to make his solemn entry into the Holy City on 23 November. In so doing, he had tied the solution of the papal schism closer than ever before to the struggle for Italy, the more so as he began at once to spread his net over the entire peninsula. In April 1166, he confirmed the energetic, saintly and cultured Galdin as Archbishop of Milan—a city that no longer existed—and charged him to rally the dispersed inhabitants behind the anti-imperialist banner. At the same time, he continued the secret negotiations with the Byzantine emperor he had begun in July 1163, giving the Basileus to understand that he was prepared to recognize his authority over the Italian peninsula and even hinting that he might recognize him as emperor of the entire West. In return, Manuel Comnenus promised the Pope considerable financial aid.

It was at this point—on 27 May 1166—that William of Sicily died. Since his son and successor, William II, was still a minor, Margaret of Navarre, the child's mother, was appointed regent, and although opposition increased under her weak regime, Sicily remained firmly wedded to her alliance with Alexander III, who took care to keep the rebels in check, and skilfully engineered a rapprochement between Palermo and Byzantium. Manuel Comnenus, who needed a foothold in Ancona, not only welcomed the Pope's intervention but even offered his daughter in marriage to William II.

All this demanded a rapid, energetic reply from Frederick, who immediately despatched Christian, Archbishop of Mainz, to Italy with instructions to consolidate the German position in Tuscany, and then to intervene forcibly in the Campagna. Christian installed Paschal III at Viterbo and let it be known that he would soon be escorting him to Rome. Across the Alps, Frederick was making haste to assemble the various contingents supplied by his princes. Though some of these, Henry the Lion among them, defected, Frederick took no steps against them, believing as he did that his army was strong enough as it was.

And, in effect, the force he was able to muster in Augsburg at the end of the summer was most impressive, and its orders quite simple: to make straight for Rome.

Then Frederick descended on Italy with the effortless swoop of the eagle. He crossed the Brenner, gave rebellious Verona a wide berth and, at the end of November, reached Lodi, where he was joined by allied contingents and held a solemn diet. During the next few weeks, when he was forced to winter in Lombardy, he carefully avoided being drawn into local disputes. True, he listened patiently to the mutual recriminations of Genoa and Pisa, who had once again gone to war, but he postponed arbitration between them, thus jeopardizing the naval support of both. He also heard complaints from other Lombard cities about excesses by imperial officials, but dryly challenged their veracity without considering the rancour his attitude aroused. As soon as the weather allowed, he set off once more, crossed the Romagna, and laid siege to Ancona, which Manuel Comnenus had secured with a small Byzantine garrison.

Meanwhile, Christian of Mainz, now joined by Rainald of Dassel, marched on Rome. Before entering the city, he decided to come to the aid of Tusculum, then at war with Rome and the Holy See, and on 29 May inflicted a terrible defeat on the Roman army. It was therefore with some justification that Paschal III, who was with the German host, wrote to beg Frederick to hasten to Rome, for it was "the time of reaping the harvest and gathering the grapes".

Frederick accordingly raised the siege of Ancona, and drew up before Rome on 24 July. He immediately occupied Monte Mario and next day attacked the castle of St. Angelo. When the German soldiers were thrown back, they turned on St. Peter's Church, and, unable to breach the walls, set fire to the nearby church of Santa Maria in Turi. In the face of this savage profanity, the papal defenders retreated and abandoned the entire right bank of the Tiber to Frederick's forces. Alexander III betook himself to the fortified castle of the Frangipani, close to the Coliseum and a short distance from the river. From there, with the help of the massive grants sent to him by the court of Palermo, he hoped to organize the defence, and inject new spirit into the Romans.

Unfortunately for the Pope, Frederick now made an extremely adroit move: through Conrad of Wittelsbach, the former Archbishop of Mainz, who had gone over to Alexander several months ago, the emperor proposed that both popes should abdicate and that a new council be summoned with instructions to nominate a new pontiff. He also promised to release all prisoners. When Alexander dryly refused, as no doubt Frederick had hoped he would, the emperor was able to put all the responsibility for further bloodshed in the Holy City upon the Pope. Frederick's agents accordingly spread the rumour that Alexander valued his tiara more than the freedom of his flock, with the result that the volatile Romans turned against their pontiff and forced him to flee disguised as a pilgrim. Fearing the Pisan fleet, which was cruising off Ostia, Alexander did not dare to board the galley the Sicilian court had had the foresight to send up the Tiber, but travelled overland to Benevento, where his cardinals later joined him.

In the meantime, Frederick was left in sole control of Rome and, on 30 July, had Paschal III solemnly enthroned in St. Peter's. On 1 August, Paschal returned the compliment when, repeating the 1155 ceremony, he once again placed the imperial crown on the heads of Frederick and Beatrix. A day earlier, Frederick had proclaimed that the prefect of Rome derived his authority from him and not from the Pope, and made all fifty members of the senate take an oath of fidelity to "the Lord Emperor Frederick, promising to help him to protect and preserve the imperial Roman crown and to maintain his judicial rights both in the city and outside, and never to participate by their counsel or their acts in any undertaking which might result in our Lord Emperor's shameful captivity, loss of limb, or other harm to his person; to suffer no senatorial investiture (*ordinatio*) except from him or his representative, and to observe all the aforementioned promises honestly and in good faith.

123

"The Lord Emperor confirms the senate for ever in its present status and will even exalt it, by investing it in person, receiving its submission, and by granting it a charter bearing a gold seal, and listing all its privileges, to wit, the imperial approbation of the senate and the emperor's protection of all the just possessions of the Roman people, all of which are derived from the empire."

Frederick thus took the reins of Roman power into his own hands and declared Rome his capital. His dream of a new Holy Empire had finally come true, and as he surveyed his Kingdom of Italy from the Roman heights, he felt free to shrug off his opponents in Lombardy and Sicily. He had reached his goal and now savoured his triumph to the full.

Then destiny struck him a cruel blow. During the evening of 2 August, an extremely violent storm broke over Rome, and as the rain poured down in torrents, the foul sewers began to overflow into the streets. The downpour continued for several days, and the foetid summer atmosphere did the rest: plague spread like wildfire among the German army, turning a brilliant political and military operation into a major disaster. Rainald of Dassel was one of its first victims and, fearing the loss of his entire army, Frederick gave orders for an immediate withdrawal to the healthier air of Upper Italy. The disease continued to decimate his ranks during the retreat, and two of his cousins, Frederick of Swabia and Welf VII, died on the way.

To add insult to injury, Frederick's enemies now declared with glee that this was God's judgment on one who had dared to lift his hand against St. Peter's successor and had profaned a holy sanctuary. And, indeed, many who had formerly revered him suddenly ceased to look upon him as their charismatic leader, one born to imperial majesty and greatness, the natural heir to Charlemagne's throne. He was only an ordinary mortal after all, an invader who must be fought and driven out. This was the view of Pontremoli, a tiny town between La Spezia and Parma, which barred Frederick's retreat and forced him to take to the mountains, whence he reached Pavia on 12 September.

Upon arriving in his "dearly beloved city", Frederick had time to take stock of his deplorable situation. Ever since the spring, Lombardy had been in a ferment of agitation. At least three forces had combined against him: Venice and the League of Verona; Archbishop Galdin; and Cremona and her many allies who had long chafed under the whips of the German administrators. Unexpectedly, rapidly, and almost spontaneously, a new coalition had been formed.

Frederick's Italian opponents fell into two main factions, linked only by their common desire to throw off the German yoke. There were those who found Frederick's administration excessively harsh, the military and fiscal decisions of his officials intolerable and their brutality execrable and who, finding themselves unable to make their voices heard—as, for instance, in Lodi, in November 1165—had come to the conclusion that the only alternative was force. But at heart they had not lost their profound respect for the emperor and did not question his rights in the peninsula; they were only concerned with the way in which these rights were being exercised. This was the attitude of Cremona, of Lodi, of Parma, and many other cities.

The second group was made up of those who had always opposed the Germans in general and the emperor in particular in the name of the natural liberty and autonomy of their communes. They, too, had no objections to the empire as such, but thought it should be a loose confederation of counties, duchies, bishoprics, cities, etc., each with clearly defined privileges and rights. This was the view of the dispersed Milanese, doubtless also of many Veronese, and of others, strengthened in their attitude by the Pope and Archbishop

Galdin, who hoped that, by fostering this kind of opposition, they might unite the entire nation behind them.

In the spring of 1167, Northern Italy was thus largely divided between those who supported the empire in principle, believing as they did that it served the best interests of their cities, but who wanted the monarch to act with more moderation, and the defenders of civic autonomy. The former became known as Ghibellines—so-called because they basically supported the House of Hohenstaufen, whose castle of Waiblingen the Italians rendered freely as *Gibelini*, and the latter as Guelphs, so-called after the Welfs, the Hohenstaufens' traditional enemies.

In the spring of 1167, the Ghibellines held the upper hand. Not only were they driven on by a sense of betrayal, when the emperor turned a deaf ear to their pleas, but they were also the stronger party because they had been far less harshly treated by the imperial agents than the Guelphs. In February, Cremona began to put out discreet feelers; in March, she signed a pact with Mantua, Brescia and Bergamo; on 7 April, she summoned representatives of several cities to Pontida where it was decided to rebuild Milan and make her a member of the alliance. Next, Cremona busied herself with smoothing out difficulties and encouraging other cities to join a league based upon one simple objective: to force Frederick to recognize all those rights and liberties that the communes had enjoyed under Conrad and his predecessors. Moreover, the league promised to guarantee the territorial integrity, the economic rights (tolls) and the military and institutional independence of each new member.

Frederick learned of these developments at Pavia on 12 September. At the same time he was told that several of the Lombard cities had expelled their *podestàs* and imperial officials, proclaiming their independence, shutting their gates on all Germans and sending for their expelled bishops. On 21 September, Frederick replied with a decree putting the rebellious cities to the ban of the empire, upon which the communes took to arms.

Unfortunately for him, Frederick no longer had an effective striking force of his own, and while he expected that many of his Italian allies—the Marquis of Montferrat, the Count of Biandrate, and the citizens of Pavia—would come to his aid, he also knew that they could not provide him with the number of men he so badly needed. He accordingly sought reinforcements from Germany, and to that end, wrote a letter to the Bishop of Freising, informing him of the rebellion, and of his intention to put down Milan, Piacenza, Cremona, Bergamo, Brescia, Parma, Mantua and the March of Verona. We do not know what the Bishop replied, but in any case no reinforcements were sent.

Moreover, time was on the side of Frederick's enemies, who were busily organizing their forces while Frederick himself remained cut off in Pavia. On 1 December 1167, the League of Verona entered into solemn union with the League of Cremona, and formed a new alliance which became known as the Lombard League. It was made up of sixteen cities, all of whom promised to fight for independence, not to make a separate peace, and to restore Italy to the happy state she had enjoyed under Henry V, Lothar III and Conrad III. This promise they sealed with an oath, and though the words we quote below were those spoken by the consuls of Mantua, the others spoke in much the same vein:

"I swear to assist Venice, Verona, Vicenza and Padua, Treviso, Ferrara and Brescia, Bergamo, Cremona, Milan, Lodi, Piacenza, Parma, Modena, Bologna and all men and countries, whoever they may be, who enter into league with the above-mentioned cities, and all others who, in agreement with us, swear this oath; and I also swear to oppose every person who shall try to harm us or make war upon us, and anyone who demands more than it has been our custom to grant from the time of King Henry until the coming of the

Emperor Frederick. And I shall not betray any of these afore
mentioned cities, or any who are with us in this League. And
should I learn of anyone plotting against us, or asking me to
join in such a plot, I swear to inform the general assembly or
the council with the utmost speed.

"Also I shall not make peace or sign any treaty or truce
without the joint consent and advice of the aforementioned
cities, and I shall help all those who have taken this oath
against any who may try to harm them. And I shall ensure that
all male citizens between the ages of fourteen and sixty who
live with me, swear this oath in the month following my own
oath, with the exception of clerics, paralytics, mutes and blind
people. And this oath shall be valid for twenty years commenc-
ing from next Easter.

"I swear to act as leader and guide, to defend the cities of
Venice, Verona, Vicenza, Padua, Treviso, Ferrara, Brescia,
Bergamo, Cremona, Milan, Lodi, Piacenza, Parma, Modena,
Bologna and every city and country that takes this oath in
alliance with the above-mentioned cities. I shall, in all good
faith, work for the interests and the common good of the
above-mentioned cities, and defend the principles of all those
who have taken this oath upon the orders of their rectors, or
at the command of their elected magistrates. And if perchance
I should be granted the opportunity to enrol yet another city,
nation or person into our League, I shall take full advantage
of it, in the common interest of the above-mentioned cities.
And I shall execute all this to the best of my ability and power."

On the day they took this oath, all members of the League
also agreed to send one consul each to a communal assembly
which was to have overall authority and would appoint two
"rectors" to wield power for one month at a time. Various
resources were to be pooled, and particularly all financial aid
from Venice, Sicily and Byzantium.

Faced with so resolute a response, Frederick thought it best
to return to Germany. As the passes on his direct route home

were unsafe, he decided to cross Savoy, but when he called a halt outside Susa the inhabitants closed the city gates upon his host, took up arms and forced Frederick to flee in disguise. He reached Burgundy in March 1168, after taking the road over Mont Cenis, only to find that most of the Burgundian nobles and bishops had declared for Alexander, and that, at Lyons, Guichard de Pontigny had, after a fierce struggle, seized the archepiscopal see from his rival. Frederick did not stay long but hastened back to his own people.

Italy now seemed lost to him for ever. Day by day, more and more of the peninsula fell to the insurgents. He still held Central Italy, but this was small consolation when Lombardy with its navigable waterways and great cities, with its command of the Alpine passes and the Apennine coastline, had slipped from his grasp. The work of ten years, the great Christian edifice he had been on the point of completing in the summer of 1167, was suddenly destroyed and Alexander's party in the ascendant. In England, Henry II Plantagenet, was embroiled in his quarrel with Thomas Becket, and, constrained by his clergy, did not give the least sign that he would fulfil the undertakings he had given at Rouen and Würzburg.

In these circumstances, which, if any, options were still open to Frederick?

CHAPTER NINE

A Time for Reflection 1168 - 1174

WHEN Frederick Barbarossa returned to Germany in the spring of 1168, a combination of factors helped to make his stay a very long one: lack of resources to mount a new Italian campaign; the realization of the serious nature of his setback; the need for new measures to strengthen his authority within Germany; and the desire, perhaps at first unconscious, to reflect, to rethink his entire policy.

And so he remained at home for six long years, during which he arrived at the conclusion that his aggressive policies in Italy would henceforth have to be tempered with a large measure of diplomacy and tact. Moreover, while at first he had looked upon diplomatic endeavour as a mere expedient, a means of gaining time, by 1174, on his return to the peninsula he had come to appreciate that it was extremely valuable in itself, and by 1177 he had reached the point of making negotiation the cornerstone of his foreign policy.

As a consequence, he gradually discarded the principles he had laid down at Roncaglia, and in 1177 threw them overboard completely. For this reason, the years of 1168 to 1177 may be called the middle period of his reign, when years of violent conflict made way for reflection and new experiment which, in turn, paved the way for the greater wisdom and renown Frederick was to enjoy in later life.

At home, however, he had no need to modify his tactics as of old, he continued to strengthen the authority of the crown and to collaborate with his princes. Moreover, he made sure that the cities and bishoprics under his direct authority fulfilled their financial and military obligations, and he saw to the military defences in his private domain, building or fortifying a host of castles in Swabia and Alsace. Thanks to his efforts, Beuren, Hohenstaufen, Waiblingen, Eppingen, Staufenberg, Schramberg, Schiltach, Selestat and Hagenau came to dominate the surrounding districts. Frederick also established his authority in the Lauter valley; in 1153, he had ordered the construction of a great new castle in Kaiserslautern to the west of Worms; in 1168, he added various annexes and then built or restored fortresses in Dahn and Trifels. In Franconia, he set up castles in Weinsberg, and in the Neckar valley. Near Frankfort, he built the great palace of Gelnhausen, and further afield, in Thuringia and Meissen, he likewise strengthened his defences. It is difficult to assign a precise date to all these constructions, but everything points to their completion before 1174. In any case, these years may be said to mark the peak of Frederick's power in Germany.

He also split up his private domain into districts, each with a governor in a castle-in-chief, surrounded by fortified and garrisoned towns (*burgs*). The governors were often granted estates in fief and helped Frederick to exercise his crown rights over various towns such as Goslar, Nuremberg and Bamberg. In this way he held control over vast tracts of territory in Alsace, between Saarbrücken and Mannheim, and across the Rhine, between the Main and Bavaria. Unfortunately, what documents have come down to us are rather imprecise on the subject, and German historians have not done much research on the subject.

To strengthen his authority further, Frederick tried to apply in Germany the feudal constitution he had promulgated at Roncaglia. In this way he hoped to put an end to the disposal of imperial fiefs, prevent their division on the death of the tenant, and, moreover, safeguard the wealth and power of his leading nobles. Frederick further demanded that his rights should be specifically recognized in every oath of fealty and homage, a provision that he later allowed to lapse, as did all his successors, who failed to grasp that it was an essential means of consolidating the power of the monarchy.

Having strengthened his political authority by his vast building programme, Frederick went on to tighten his grip upon the clergy. During all these years he kept a close watch on episcopal elections, and was quick to make himself heard wherever there was a dispute, often obtaining the promotion of men from his own court. In 1167, he intervened in the election at Ratisbon, and also tried to take advantage of a dispute in distant Cambrai; in 1169, he cut short discussions about the appointment of a new bishop in Bremen–Hamburg. Almost everywhere, he contrived to set up his own supporters: Hartwig of Lierheim in Augsburg (1167), Philip of Heinsberg (who replaced Rainald of Dassel) in Cologne (1167), Rapodo in Spires (1167), Raoul in Liège (1167), Ludwig of Tecklenburg in Munster (1169), Arnold in Trèves (1169), Egilolf in Eich-stadt (1171), Eberhard of Seeburg in Merseburg (1171), Frederick in Metz (1171), Reinhard of Abensberg in Würzburg (1171) and Conrad of Steinberg in Worms (1171). He tolerated supporters of Alexander in the Province of Salzburg on condition that they recognized the absolute authority of the crown. Similarly when Conrad of Austria died in 1168, and Adalbert of Bohemia, a champion of Alexander III, was elected to replace him, Frederick forced the new prelate to transfer all his regalia to the crown.

Frederick further increased his hold over the German clergy by limiting the powers of church advocates (1170), and by barring all but bishops invested with regalia from coining money. This last measure showed once again how concerned he was to keep all crown prerogatives under his direct control. It also bore witness to his interest in economic and financial questions, and to his determination to increase his country's wealth. To that end, he encouraged the clearing of forests, the foundation of new villages, and the emergence of a class of

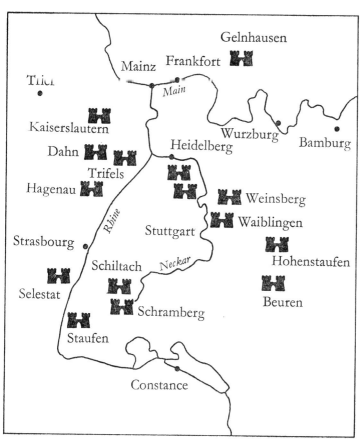

Frederick Barbarossa's Principal Castles

free peasants. In addition, he took active steps to promote trade by easing the travelling restrictions, and by establishing new markets. In 1173, he inaugurated four new annual fairs: two at Aix-la-Chapelle, to be held at the beginning of Lent and at Michaelmas (29 September), and two at Duisburg, one to be held on Laetare Sunday (the fourth Sunday in Lent) and the other on St. Bartholomew's Day (24 August). Each fair continued for fourteen days, during which time all traders were exempted from paying dues. Furthermore, currency minted in Duisburg, Cologne and Aix, three cities enjoying Frederick's special favours, was allowed to enter Flanders without any restriction, by a special arrangement with the Count.

In short, Frederick used his enforced years in Germany, which, as the historian K. Hampe has put it, were "poor in events but rich in durable results", to set his own house in order. He had always put his trust in the feudal system, but this system had turned against him, the more so as Frederick, unlike the King of France, could not boast wealthy or tightly clustered private estates of his own. As a result, he was forced to rule with a strong hand and unfailing vigilance over his vassals, and to proclaim insistently that they owed direct obedience to him rather than to their immediate overlords.

To that end, he also made certain that the German crown did not pass from the House of Hohenstaufen. Remembering his experience in 1167, when he had come close to losing his life, Frederick hastened to call a Diet at Bamberg on 24 June 1168 and, passing over his invalid heir presumptive, named his younger son, Henry, King of the Romans. On 15 August, when he had the boy duly crowned at Aix, he had taken an important step towards establishing an hereditary monarchy, incidentally, ensuring that, despite the extreme youth of the new king—he was only four years old—the crown now remained in Germany even while the emperor himself was abroad. To that end, all archbishops, bishops and other nobles were now asked to swear fealty and pay homage not only to Frederick, but also to his son.

At the same time, Frederick granted new privileges to his most powerful nobles, among them Albert the Bear, Margrave of Brandenburg (died 1170), and the Bishop of Würzburg. Henry the Lion, by far the wealthiest and most famous of Frederick's princes, continued to rule over Bavaria, the chief source of his wealth, with an iron hand, while pursuing a policy of territorial expansion in Saxony, and in what is today Schwerin and Mecklenburg, against the Slav inhabitants or Obotrites. There he carved out a vast domain and settled it with newcomers from the west, He also encouraged the expansion of Lübeck, Stettin and the recently founded Brunswick. Some of the lands he had conquered, colonized or converted to Christianity, for example the county of Schwerin, he granted in fief to German nobles; others he governed directly with the help of castellans, and yet others he restored to Slav chiefs who agreed to Saxon tutelage. (It was thus that Prince Pribislaw came into possession of Mecklenburg.) In short, by 1170, Henry the Lion had become a most powerful force in the land, and one, moreover, who, like so many German princes, was far too preoccupied with his own affairs to take any interest in Frederick's Italian schemes. This was yet another reason why the emperor made such haste to consolidate and increase his own possessions, for he knew that the burden of financing the next expedition would largely fall on his own shoulders.

He therefore allowed his princes to go their own way, and, as we saw, raised no protest when Henry the Lion absented himself from the imperial host in 1167. Frederick even came to the Lion's aid a year later when the latter clashed with Albert the Bear and the Count of Thuringia, and he also supported him against the King of Denmark who tried to occupy the Isle of Rügen, thus initiating a war that was to drag on until 1172. All Frederick had come to demand of his princes was that they should not actively interfere with his imperial projects.

Now it was precisely such interference that caused him to turn against the Lion, who, in 1170-1174, began to adopt a very high-handed attitude, and who, after his marriage to the daughter of Henry II Plantagenet in 1168, began to voice his opposition to Frederick's Italian policy in public. He became even more obstreperous when he learned that his uncle, Welf VI, who had lost his only son and heir during the plague of

1167, had agreed to sell all his rights and possessions in Central Italy, including the Matildine estates, to Frederick. As a result, Henry lost what personal stake he may have had in Italy and adopted a policy of "non-intervention" which, at times, bordered on rebellion—as Frederick found out by pure chance. And while Frederick thought it best to avoid an open break, he realized that he could not place the least reliance on the Lion.

Since the spring of 1167 and Frederick's escape, the German position in the peninsula had greatly deteriorated. The Lombard League had grown appreciably in strength, gaining the adherence of many new cities, chief among them Novara, Vercelli, Como and Asti. The League was better organized and more closely united than ever before, and the majority of its members was determined not to let internal disputes cause a major rift or weaken the common cause in any way. After numerous preliminary meetings, and lengthy discussions, a general assembly gathered at Lodi on 1 December 1168, the anniversary of the first oath of allegiance, and adopted a common charter. By it, reprisals within the league and the imposition of new taxes were outlawed, and all taxes introduced within the last thirty years repealed. The members further agreed not to give asylum to fugitives from allied cities and, under no circumstances, to appeal to the crown.

In short, the League was veering increasingly to the Guelph point of view, for their decisions amounted to a virtual rejection of the emperor's sovereignty; by taking taxation and justice into their own hands and, above all, by rejecting the crown as the supreme court of appeal, they revealed their determination to achieve full independence.

In fact, ever since the summer of 1167, the League had been continuously engaged in political no less than in military campaigns. They had made war on the Count of Biendrate, the Marquis of Montferrat, the Marquis of Busto, the Marquis of Vasto and a host of other Ghibelline lords. They had invaded the imperial manors and evicted the king's representatives. They had rebuilt the ruined city of Tortona, had expelled all bishops who supported Paschal III, and at Lodi, as the anonymous successor of Otto of Freising and Morena tells us, had replaced them with supporters of Alexander.

But their chief act of defiance was to construct a new city, intended to serve as a symbol of their unity. The entire League shared the expense, and other cities, such as Genoa, also contributed handsomely. The site was well chosen: south of the river Po at the junction of the Tanaro and the Bormida, in the confines of the Marquisate of Montferrat and close by the route from Asti to Genoa. The members all agreed that the new city would be a commune, governed by freely elected consuls, and placed under the protection of the Pope, in whose honour it would be named Alessandria. The humiliated Germans could do no better than pour scorn upon what they called this "city of straw". Their scorn gave way to fury at the end of 1168, when Alessandria was protected by powerful ramparts and inhabited by several thousand people, drawn chiefly from the neighbouring villages.

The year 1168 was thus a year of great progress for the Guelphs, no less than for Alexander III who, sensing the strength of the anti-German forces, did his utmost to help the League financially and otherwise, and, incidentally, used it as an excuse to withdraw from other diplomatic commitments and particularly from his links with Manuel Comnenus.

Since 1162–3, the two men had been in almost continual contact, initially with a view to forging a vast anti-Germanic alliance embracing Byzantium, Sicily and France. Later, when Louis VII showed little interest in this alliance, and when the death of William I left a power vacuum in Sicily, Alexander, who had meanwhile returned to Italy, was left with Manuel as the only one on whose active support he could count. At the time of Frederick's retreat, Manuel had taken advantage of this fact, sending a messenger, Jordan by name, ostensibly with instructions to "help and serve the Pope". Cardinal Boso has given us some details of just how the Byzantine emperor proposed to do this:

"He (Jordan) declared that Manuel wished to join the Greek Church to the Mother of All Churches, the Holy Roman Church, so that, for the good of all, they should once more be united as they had been in ancient times, and so that, under a single divine law, and with one head over them, the two clergies and the two peoples, that is the Latin and the Greek, might live together in perpetual harmony. Moreover, should a suitable occasion and an acceptable opportunity arise, it was only right and proper that the Holy See grant the Basileus the crown of the Roman Empire, which had always belonged by right, not to Frederick the German, but to Byzantium."

Though Manuel's extraordinary proposition promised the Holy See a vastly increased flock, Alexander III was enough of a realist to appreciate its shortcomings and pitfalls. To begin with, the actual absorption of the Greek into the Roman Church was to take place at some unspecified future date and Alexander knew full well that the Byzantine emperor was even more determined than his German rival to keep the whip hand over his bishops and clergy. Moreover, the political portent of Manuel's proposal was at variance with the principles of the Holy See which, ever since the ninth century, had held that the centre of the empire must remain in the West. Finally, Alexander III realized that the mass influx into the Church of the Greeks would shake the very foundations of Catholicism, and thus arouse great hostility among his own flock. Sicily would certainly put up a stiff resistance, since the new alliance was bound to constrict her freedom in the Mediterranean, and Venice could be expected to think and act in much the same way.

The Pope therefore informed Jordan that he had to consult his cardinals; at the same time, he let it appear that he felt rather pessimistic about their decision. Soon afterwards, however, no doubt so as to preserve Manuel's goodwill, he sent the Bishop of Ostia and the Cardinal of the Church of Santi Giovanni e Paolo to the eastern court. In 1168, Manuel dispatched further ambassadors to Benevento, with much the same proposals—including restitution of the imperial crown "as reason and justice demand". Alexander III then informed him that he could not consent to proposals that were contrary to "the statutes of the Holy Fathers", and might involve his people in a war, when his basic mission on earth was to preserve the peace. The Greek chronicler, John Kinammos, explained that the chief difference between Alexander and Manuel was the choice of a capital for the new empire; in fact, the real obstacles were of an entirely different order.

Now, in 1168, even while he was continuing his negotiations with Byzantium, the Pope also decided to form an alliance with the Lombard League and, indeed, to make this the very basis of his policy. Not that he was enamoured of the communes and their conception of liberty, but, as an Italian and a realist, he knew that far from constituting a threat to the Roman Church, the League was following the path he himself had outlined in 1156-8, when, as Cardinal-Chancellor he had begged the Pope to rally to the support of Sicily and Milan in an attempt to prevent the Germans from seizing all Italy, and imposing Paschal III on Rome. The cause of Italian liberty had become a condition *sine qua non* of the preservation of ecclesiastical liberty.

Frederick, for his part, was convinced that the alliance between the League and Alexander III, solid though it appeared to be, was not unshakeable, especially while he himself still had a foothold in the peninsula. Thus no cities in Central Italy had made common cause with the League, and while some, for instance Florence and Siena, had changed over to Alexander, they had done so on purely ecclesiastical grounds. Furthermore, in 1168, the emperor had consolidated his hold over these areas, where local fighting—quite unrelated to the struggle between the Guelphs and Ghibellines had once again broken out. He had strengthened the administration with new German blood, investing Bidulf, one of his most faithful servants, with the duchy of Spoleto, and granting Conrad of Lützelhard, his trusted counsellor and expert on Italian politics, with the March of Ancona and the Exarchate of Ravenna. It was also at about this time that Welf VI sold Frederick the Matildine estates and his other interests in Italy.

Nor was the emperor unduly worried by the apparent strength of his enemies. True, the Lombard League and Venice offered a serious challenge, but Sicily, under her regent, had ceased to pose any kind of real threat, and Alexander III, despite his strength and persistence, his growing prestige and the many new adherents to his cause, had been unable to oust Paschal III from Rome. Indeed, when Paschal died on 20 September, the emperor had good reason to felicitate himself upon the successor, John, Abbot of Struma, who took the name of Calixtus III. Moreover, in November, when the new Roman senate was elected, it proved as strongly pro-imperial as the old.

At the time, Frederick was unable to take advantage of the situation since, as we saw, he was still busy in Germany. Meanwhile, all he could hope to do in Italy was to open negotiations. But negotiations with whom?

He could not deal with all his adversaries at once, for in that way he would merely have thrown them more closely together, nor could he treat with the Lombard League, which to him was a band of insolent rebels. There only remained the Pope, with whom his differences were not of a kind to prevent an honourable treaty. Frederick accordingly decided to let it be known that he was anxious to bring the schism to an end and to restore Christian harmony.

It would seem that secret contacts between Frederick and Alexander were first made as early as the summer of 1167, but we cannot be sure whether they were, in fact, initiated by the emperor. At all events, we know that the Abbot of Cîteaux, the Prior of Grande Chartreuse, and possibly the Bishop of Pavia, served as intermediaries; that at the beginning of 1169, Frederick summoned the former and the Abbot of Clairvaux and asked them to sound out the Holy See. In March, the two abbots went to Benevento, where Alexander III evinced surprise that they brought no concrete proposals from the emperor. He now insisted that the whole Italian question must form part of any discussions and that representatives of the Lombard League must participate in them. In April, the two abbots returned to Bamberg and made their report. No further action was taken at the time, and though contact was not completely broken, there were no fresh developments during the next few months.

Early in 1170, however, the emperor sent Eberhard, Bishop of Bamberg, and a supporter of Alexander, on an official mission to the Pope. The ambassador declared that he was bearing genuine proposals, but asked the Pope to grant him an audience outside Sicilian territory, for reasons of imperial prestige. Alexander III agreed, and, with his cardinals, betook himself to Veroli, in church territory south of Rome. He was careful, however, to advise the Lombards and invited them to send representatives. He also promised them not to sign a separate truce, and not to waver in his resolution to make the settlement of the Italian question an integral part of any agreement.

Now Eberhard's instructions were to deal with no one but the pontiff, and when he explained this on his arrival at Veroli, Alexander agreed to see him alone, but warned him that he would inform his cardinals and the League of whatever was said. The Bishop then disclosed that Frederick was ready to cease all personal attacks on Alexander, and that furthermore he was prepared to recognize all bishops ordained by him, provided only that Alexander made peace and abandoned the Lombard League.

Alexander's reply, short and to the point, was given in the presence of all interested parties. He declared that he could not possibly agree to proposals that glossed over all the real problems, to wit the 1159 election, the situation in Rome, and the general situation in Italy. He noted wryly that, though he had been described as a false pope, he was suddenly seen to have acted within his rights when confirming new bishops, and poured scorn on the idea that the emperor, as a layman, could judge the validity of ecclesiastical ordinations. In short, he rejected the proposals *in toto*. Negotiations were at an end.

Was this, in fact, a victory for Frederick's enemies? Some historians appear to think so, others, on the contrary, hold that the emperor deliberately put forward proposals the Pope could not possibly accept. According to this view, he was anxious to put the blame for the continued hostilities on Alexander, while showing his own people that, faced with the strengthened alliance between the Holy See and the Lombards, he had no option but to fight on. As in most human affairs, the truth lies somewhere between these two extreme views.

In fact, if Frederick really sought to score points in this underhand way, he failed utterly in his purpose—no one in Italy blamed Alexander for the breakdown of the negotiations and even in Germany, there were suggestions that Frederick must change his attitude. On the other hand, Frederick gained one advantage, for his offer to the Pope had seriously upset the Lombard League, and triggered off a number of violent disturbances. Some of these were, no doubt, due to internal rivalry, but others clearly reflected the fear that the Pope might yet sign a treaty over the heads of the cities. Alexander III reacted strongly. In March 1170, he sent out a circular that was meant to still fears in Lombardy, the bull *Non est dubium*.

Alexander's bull was aimed at preserving the unity of the League. It stipulated that any act liable to weaken the alliance would call up ecclesiastical sanctions. The pontiff affirmed the strong bonds between the League and the Holy See and stressed that the cities were fighting for the freedom of both Italy and the Church:

"There is no doubt or uncertainty that, with the help of divine inspiration, you have concluded your treaties of concord and agreement so as to defend both your own peace and liberty, and that of God's church against the aforesaid emperor Frederick, and that you have banded together so as, with courage, to throw off the yoke of servitude. And we, who hold your peace as dear as our own, know how closely you cling to the church and that you will stand by it in good times as in bad (from which God preserve you)."

In the interest of their common desire to defend the church, the Pope then informed the Lombards of his negotiations with the Bishop of Bamberg, and of the new measures he had decided to promulgate:

"1. If any inhabitant or city in Lombardy should swear an alliance without the consent of the consuls of all the rest, we order and command our legates to place an interdict, regardless of any contradiction or appeal, upon any party to such alliance and to excommunicate all consuls who may have endorsed this alliance or who may have rendered aid and counsel in its formation.

"2. Any city seceding from the League will forfeit the right to its diocese, and all those who have persuaded it to secede will be deprived of their dignities of office.

"3. Besides, since the rectors whom you have jointly appointed labour not only for the promotion of concord and peace, but also for their strong and firm preservation, it is our will and command that any city or any of its citizens who commit an offence by disobeying an order of these rectors, shall be barred from divine office in the city where offence has occurred, and that the sharp blade of anathema shall be brought down upon the chief transgressor.

"4. And if the flame of dissension should be kindled between cities, and if, perchance, discord break out among them, the consuls of such cities having acted in defiance of an order by the common consuls, we shall order divine service to be suspended in these cities and excommunicate the chief culprits and responsible consuls until such time as an equitable settlement shall have been reached."

The Lombard communes, for their part, took a new oath, far more precise than the one they had sworn in 1167. In particular, they pledged themselves to make war on the emperor and all his allies:

"I swear by God's Holy Gospels to make neither peace nor sign a truce or other agreement with the Emperor Frederick, his sons, his wife, or any speaking in his name, nor to ratify, personally or through the mediation of a third party, any agreement concluded by others. I shall work in good faith and to the best of my ability to prevent the entry into Italy of any army, great or small, from Germany or any other imperial country beyond the mountains. And if such an army should enter, I shall ardently give battle to the emperor and all who are on his side, wherever they may be, until the aforementioned army shall be driven out of Italy.

"I shall also oppose the Marquis of Montferrat, the Count of Biandrate, and all who are on the emperor's side, and I shall banish all those who aid the emperor from the city, towns and all places over which I have authority and I shall destroy or order the destruction of all their property. Similarly, I shall not receive into my city any knights or infantry serving under them. I shall not allow the emperor or any of his party to provision troops in my city and I shall prevent any who may wish to do so . . .

"Finally I, as consul, will ensure that all men in my city between the ages of fifteen and sixty swear this oath in good faith. Any who refuse will be put to death and their property and belongings destroyed."

By their several new undertakings, the Pope and the leaders of the League not only strengthened their old bonds, but

144

demonstrated that Guelph principles had won the upper hand in Italy, much to the dismay of such cities as Cremona, who feared that if the emperor should yet reach agreement with Alexander III, the Ghibelline communes would be the first to suffer.

In short, the collapse of the negotiations at Veroli led both to a strengthening of the bonds between the League and the Holy See, which posed a grave threat to Frederick, and at the same time to differences of opinion within the League itself, a development that, in the long run, favoured the emperor's plans. Frederick revised his strategy accordingly. Whereas from 1167 to 1170 he had aimed to weaken and divide his opponents by direct negotiations, he now decided to apply different pressures.

During February 1171, he met Louis VII of France at Maxey-sur-Vaise (between Toul and Vaucouleurs) and apparently asked him to inform the Pope that he was willing to hold further talks. He also proposed, no doubt, as a result of his disappointment with Henry II Plantagenet, to settle all outstanding problems between the empire and France, thus founding that long-standing alliance between the Houses of Capet and Hohenstaufen that, 43 years later, culminated in the war between the Welf Emperor, Otto IV, and Philip Augustus, King of France, and the battle of Bouvines. At the same time, the emperor made approaches to Manuel Comnenus and offered his son in marriage to one of Manuel's daughters. Similarly, to gain the support of Sicily, he offered his daughter Sophia to William II (1173).

However, during all these diplomatic overtures, he never allowed his preparations for his next military campaign to slacken. To that end, he sent Christian of Mainz to Central Italy who, as a first step, intervened in the dispute between Pisa and Genoa and, on 23 May 1172, brought about an agreement which was endorsed by Florence and Lucca. Next he attacked several rebellious cities in Tuscany, and vainly laid siege to Ancona in 1173. It is possible that he also started secret negotiations with Cremona.

In the enemy camp, too, they were busy organizing under the watchful eye of Alexander III. It was he who, in 1171, prevented the Byzantine marriage of Frederick's son, and who had a hand in the marriage of one of Manuel's sons to a daughter of Louis VII. In 1173, he intervened once again, this time to break the engagement of William II and Sophia. Meanwhile the Lombards had been gathering their forces and were preparing for battle. By the autumn of 1173, when Frederick, having first brought his recalcitrant bishops into line (Adalbert of Salzburg was deposed in 1174), announced that he was ready to lead a new campaign, the northern cities were ready for him. This did not, however, prevent Alexander III from keeping up contacts with Germany through the mediation of Louis VII, possibly in an attempt to prevent war even at this late stage.

One year later, Frederick was back in the peninsula.

CHAPTER TEN

War and Diplomacy 1174 - 1177
The Peace of Venice

IN 1173, Frederick Barbarossa let it be known officially that he was about to humble the Lombard League. He realized that he could count on little military support from his German vassals; as we saw, they would submit to, and stand by, their sovereign only when it suited their self-interest. And so the emperor's army was made up chiefly of Brabant mercenaries, men renowned and feared for their cruelty. From the very start, Frederick seems to have had major problems in paying them, but hoped to reward them with loot and pillage.

In September 1174, he crossed the Alps for the fifth time, marched on Piedmont and set fire to Susa, which had treated him so perfidiously during his retreat in 1168. From there he made for the Lombard plain, while Christian of Mainz, having raised the siege of Ancona, advanced to meet him with a small band of men. A good strategist would now have attacked Milan or, even better, Verona and Cremona, but Frederick was determined to bring down Alessandria, whose very existence was an insult to his honour and a daily reminder of his humiliation.

Unfortunately for him, the "city of straw", to which he laid siege in October, put up a much fiercer resistance than he anticipated. Moreover, most members of the Lombard League, far from reacting with panic, rallied to the support of their threatened sister city. Only Asti withdrew from the alliance, no doubt because of the emperor's proximity, or possibly in the wake of repeated attacks by the Marquis of Montferrat. Como, too, began to waver, but such new additions to the League as Ravenna, Rimini and Bobbio reaffirmed their solidarity with the rest. In addition to these three and a few nobles—the Marquis of Malespina, the Count of Camino, the Count of Bertinoro and even the Count of Biandrate who had recently changed sides—the League now comprised Milan, Lodi, Bergamo, Ferrara, Brescia, Mantua, Verona, Vicenza, Padua, Treviso, Venice, Bologna, Modena, Reggio, Parma, Piacenza, Tortona, Alessandria, Vercelli, Novara and Cremona, although the latter, no doubt worried by the ascendancy of Milan and the general strengthening of the Guelph cause, continued to maintain close contacts with Christian of Mainz.

While the Germans were marking time before Alessandria, the Italians assembled their army at Piacenza, and then marched to the aid of the besieged, threatening to sandwich Frederick between them and the city walls. In the face of this danger, Frederick decided to raise the siege (13 April 1175) and to withdraw to his "faithful" Pavia. His retreat took him through Tortona, whose loyalty to the League had been shaken by fears that Alessandria might steal her trade, and Voghera, where he was overtaken by the enemy host. But since neither the Germans nor the Italians were keen to join battle—the Lombards because they feared the formidable Brabanters, and the Germans because Frederick knew that his army was too small to score a decisive victory—Frederick offered to meet representatives of the League and to negotiate an honourable settlement.

A truce was declared there and then, and an agenda quickly drawn up. Each side was to be represented by three ambassadors, and it was agreed that, if the talks should break down, the consuls and delegates of Cremona would be asked to arbitrate between them.

Frederick, anxious to demonstrate his goodwill, chose

148

Italians as two of his ambassadors—one from Turin and another from Pavia. The League was represented by the two acting rectors, Ezelino, consul and *podestà* of Treviso, and the little-known Anselm of Dovaria. Their third ambassador may have been Gerard Pesta of Milan, but we cannot be sure.

The negotiations took place at Montebello, after both armies had first been disbanded. This was an extraordinary concession on the emperor's part, though it was not made, as even some Italians believed, purely as a sign of reconciliation— he simply could not afford to pay his mercenaries. However, there is little doubt that he was genuinely anxious to reach a peaceful settlement, convinced as he was that agreement with the rebel cities would once more give him control of the country and thus force Alexander III to submit.

More than ever, he was determined not to give way on the pontifical question—indeed, the recent measures he had taken in Germany showed that he was resolved to implement the decisions of the Diet of Würzburg (1165) in every detail. And though he was ready to make concessions to the League, here, too, he insisted that the members must respect his sovereignty and privileges, among them the investiture of all consuls, and swear fidelity to the empire. Even so, this represented a radical shift from the principles he had set forth at Roncaglia, and a major concession to the League's growing strength and unity.

On 17 April, the League presented the Germans with what has gone down in history as the *Petitio societatis Lombardiae*. It made the following fundamental points:

1. *Recognition of the emperor's rights*. The League in no way challenged the emperor's authority and was prepared to grant him all the rights his predecessors had obtained "without intimidation or violence". More precisely, Frederick and his heirs would retain the right to requisition supplies, and to hold markets in Lombardy, whenever they were on their way to Rome for their imperial coronations. Moreover, the cities

would all swear an oath of loyalty to the emperor. The emperor, for his part, would renounce all his other regalia (except for special concessions), restore all the property he had confiscated during the war and not impose any financial sanctions.

2. *City rights.* All the other regalia were said to be vested in the cities by natural right and not as a concession from the emperor. (This was, in fact, a basic Guelph principle.) The cities would be allowed to keep their consuls, ramparts and fortified encampments, and indeed add to them. They would be allowed to follow their local customs, and the emperor must guarantee their safety.

3. *Rights of the League.* The communes would be granted the right to enter into alliance with one another, and to band together against the emperor, if he should break his promises.

4. *The settlement of disputes.* In case disputes arose about the precise interpretation of any part of the proposed treaty, the consuls of the city or cities concerned could be asked to swear a solemn oath affirming their respect for justice and tradition.

5. *Reconciliation between the emperor and Alexander III.* The League made this a prerequisite of peace.

6. *The problem of Alessandria.* Alessandria must be recognized as a free city enjoying all the rights of the other Lombard communes.

When Frederick heard these proposals, he rejected them out of hand; he objected quite particularly to the last two clauses, on the grounds that the first was not the League's business and the second humiliating to his imperial majesty. Furthermore, the absence of any reference to the investiture of consuls, and the exclusion of the crown from the settlement of all disputes, were utterly repugnant to him. The matter was accordingly referred to Cremona for arbitration; meanwhile it was agreed to set up a joint truce commission, to which

Frederick appointed Philip of Heinsberg, Archbishop of Cologne, and three others, while the League was represented by Gerard Pesta, Albert Ganbara of Brescia and a Veronese delegate.

Early in May, Cremona, having examined the imperial objections and counter-proposals item by item, proposed a compromise solution:

1. On the subject of the emperor's rights, the Lombard position was acceptable on the whole, except that German emperors must have the right of requisitioning supplies, etc. every time they were in Italy and not only en route to their coronation.

2. While the cities must be free to follow their ancient customs and enjoy the right to raise ramparts, their consuls must be invested by the Emperor, from whom they derived all their liberties and privileges. Moreover, the League must restore all imperial property seized during the war.

3. While entitled to associate freely with one another, the cities must also undertake to come to the Emperor's aid should one of their number break its undertaking to him.

4. As for the settlement of disputes, the Lombard proposals were quite unacceptable—differences concerning the interpretation of the treaty must be settled by a joint commission consisting of six members, three nominated by the emperor and three by the League.

5. On the subject of the pontifical problem, Cremona pronounced unequivocally against the League, and declared simply that no one should seek to quarrel with the party of Alexander.

6. As for Alessandria, she could not be recognized as a free city, but her inhabitants must be granted the right to rejoin their old villages without molestation.

Frederick was quick to accept these counter-proposals, so quick in fact that we may take it he had a hand in their drafting. The cities, for their part, while willing to make concessions on the composition of the arbitration commission, would not consent to the emperor's investiture of their consuls or to the establishment of a joint arbitration commission which, in fact, gave the emperor a casting vote, though this was not stated explicitly in the Cremona document.

After further discussions, Frederick made a number of new concessions and, according to one of the Lombard negotiators, even went so far as to agree to all the cities' other demands provided only that they renounced Alexander III in favour of Calixtus. And still the communes demurred, fearing, with good reason, that once Frederick had vanquished Alexander, he would redouble his attack upon the League.

Though the negotiations had thus reached deadlock, both sides nevertheless agreed to maintain the truce. Frederick used the opportunity to make direct contact with Alexander III, and did not bother to advise Calixtus that he was doing so. While the emperor did not actually suggest the signing of a separate peace—the oath he had solemnly sworn at Würzburg would have prevented this, as would the opposition of all those German bishops who had been ordained by the schismatic Pope and whom he could not desert without seriously injuring his own authority—he hoped to wrest major concessions from Alexander and, incidentally, to undermine the Pope's alliance with the League. He accordingly invited three prominent cardinals, among them Ubald, Cardinal-Bishop of Ostia, to call on him at Pavia. Alexander III put no obstacles in their way but advised them to stand firm. Moreover, he instructed two of the cardinals to pay a prior call on the rectors of the League, who gave them a full account of the negotiations, and, in particular, mentioned Frederick's insistence that they denounce the Pope. The cardinals immediately assured the rectors that Alexander would not sign a separate peace with Frederick, and, indeed, made this clear to Frederick when he received them at Pavia.

For all that, their first meeting with the emperor was

extremely cordial—Frederick listened politely while the cardinals exhorted him to recognize Alexander III, and explained that the Pope could not sign any peace treaty that excluded the Lombards. But even while he listened, he had made up his mind that the war must go on—his diplomatic efforts had clearly failed once again. He accordingly withdrew from further talks and left it to the Archbishops of Mainz and Cologne and his Protonotary, Wortwin, to carry on the discussions with representatives of the League. From a somewhat unclear document, it appears that these were now informed that since the emperor had the sole right to ordain and invest imperial bishops, he was clearly entitled to set aside all appointments the Holy See had made since the inception of the schism. This the Papal legates refused to swallow, the more so as they learned that Frederick intended to impose still harsher conditions on the Lombards and on Alessandria in particular. They accordingly took their leave, as did the League delegates.

At this, the League decided to return to war, while the Pope proclaimed Alessandria a bishopric. Meanwhile, Frederick, unable to hire a large body of mercenaries, was forced to rely on the small band Christian of Mainz had led into Apulia, on his way to Sicily. It was against this background that Frederick now vainly appealed for help to his German princes and vassals, and quite particularly to Henry the Lion who, in the end, agreed to meet his emperor in Chiavenna, on the shores of Lake Como. Here Frederick recalled the many services he had rendered the Lion—against the Margrave of Brandenburg, the Count of Holstein, the Count of Thuringia and others. But Henry had only just returned from the Kingdom of Jerusalem, where his help against the infidels had been rewarded with near-royal honours, and his success had clearly gone to his head. He now refused to come to Frederick's aid, declaring that his "crusade" had exhausted his resources, and that after so

153

long an absence from home, his presence was urgently needed in Saxony. He added that, in principle, he was not, in any case, bound to serve his emperor beyond the frontiers of Germany. Doubtless he also gave Frederick to understand that, since the latter had seen fit to keep him out of the limelight during the earlier Italian campaigns, and had moreover acquired what interests in Italy he might have inherited from his uncle, Welf VI, he was only too anxious to wash his hands of the whole Italian business. Perhaps he even added that he thought Frederick was making a mistake and that, in his view, the sooner the quarrel with Alexander III was patched up the better. But whatever reasons he gave, this refusal to serve spelled the end of an alliance forged in 1155, and one that had cost the emperor the friendship of the Margrave of Brandenburg and of many other princes.

The Lion's defection—through arrogance or sheer selfishness, we know not which—might well have had the most serious consequences for Frederick's cause in Italy, had not his allies in the peninsula, Como among them, rallied to his support. Hence it was mainly with Italian troops that Frederick prepared to overcome his Italian enemies. In the spring of 1176, he left Pavia for Bellinzona where he expected further reinforcements, before advancing on Milan from the north, while Christian of Mainz, at the head of the small veteran army from Apulia, would be pressing in from the south. When they learned of this threat, the Milanese, reinforced with militiamen from the allied cities, decided to strike first and to attack Frederick in his camp at Bellinzona. But Frederick was already on the march and, on 29 May, surprised the advancing host at Legnano, some eighteen miles north of Milan.

The ensuing battle was bloody and extremely confused. The German cavalry, as was their custom, launched a fierce charge and broke through the front ranks of the Lombards, who fled in confusion. But the German onset was halted by the Lombard infantry, who had formed up in a square round their *carroccio*, and soon afterwards cavalry reinforcements from Brescia came racing up at the gallop and, rallying their fleeing comrades, attacked the German rear. Sensing the danger and displaying great personal courage, Frederick immediately threw himself into the thick of the battle and was unhorsed. Rumour had it that he was dead, whereupon his men abandoned their arms, horses and even the emperor's personal standard, and escaped to Pavia. Here, Frederick himself later joined them.

He had fought and lost once again, but he was enough of a statesman to accept the inevitable, and to cut his suit according to his cloth. He therefore asked Cremona, which had drawn ever closer to him, to mediate between him and the League. During negotiations that dragged on throughout June and July, Frederick proposed a treaty based on the original Cremona proposals, but now adding full recognition of Alessandria. But once again, although his wish for a reconciliation with the communes was now beyond doubt, the League refused to countenance any agreement that did not include recognition of Alexander III.

It was this insistence of the Lombards that forced Frederick to try yet another line of attack. Ever since the negotiation with the papal legates in Pavia, he, no less than Archbishops Christian of Mainz and Philip of Cologne, had come to appreciate that Alexander was not altogether the champion of civil liberties the League took him to be, and that he was ready to make a number of concessions in this sphere. Thus while the Pope certainly wanted peace on as favourable terms as possible for the Lombards, he took little interest in their specific legal and political claims. So far, Frederick's intention had been to come to terms with the League in order to undermine the Pope; and to achieve this he had been prepared to meet the League half-way. But since the Communes had rigidly championed Alexander's cause throughout all the lengthy negotiations that had been going on ever since April 1175, Frederick was left with only one solution: he must arrive at a settlement with the Pope, who might well prove more amenable than his allies.

Contacts were resumed towards the end of the summer, and on 21 October 1176, Christian of Mainz, Archbishop Wichmann of Magdeburg and Conrad, the Bishop-elect of Worms, together with Protonotary Wortwin, arrived at the pontifical court in Anagni, south of Rome. The cardinals delegated by the Pope to receive them declared immediately that they could only hold discussions in the presence of the plenipotentiaries of the League, the King of Sicily and Emperor Manuel Comnenus. The imperial ambassadors raised no objections in principle but added that, since military operations against the rebel cities had been suspended by mutual agreement, there was no reason why preliminary private talks should not be held without prejudice. Alexander III agreed, merely remarking that he reserved the right to inform the Lombards and his other allies of the outcome.

Frederick and Alexander III had been implacable adversaries ever since the Diet of Besançon, and the bargaining that now ensued was extremely hard, the more so as it bore on such widely divergent topics as the ecclesiastical dispute and the secular status of Italy. Frederick offered to recognize Alexander III, but insisted on safeguards for his territorial interests in the peninsula, and on maintaining full authority over the German clergy, which meant papal recognition of all bishops who had supported Victor IV, Paschal III and Calixtus III. Upon this point the discussion was acrimonious.

Nevertheless, the legates moved some way towards Frederick's position when they acknowledged that some of the Lombard claims were excessive. A fortnight later, both parties drew up the preliminary agreement of what became known as the Peace of Anagni.

By it, Frederick and his family would recognize Alexander III as Pope, restore to the church (and loyal bishops in

Germany) what possessions they had lost through the schism, and allow the Holy See to appoint the prefect of Rome. In particular, Frederick would return "the property of the Countess Matilda which had been vested in the Roman Church under Lothar and Conrad", and release all vassals of the Church who had fallen into his hands. In return, Alexander III undertook to recognize Frederick as emperor and to revoke his excommunication. The problem of the German bishops was to be settled on individual merit, but Chancellor Christian would certainly remain Archbishop of Mainz and Philip of Heinsburg Archbishop of Cologne, while Conrad of Wittelsbach would be granted the first German archepiscopal see to fall vacant. The Archbishop of Salzburg, a supporter of Alexander, would have all his property restored, and Bishop Gero of Halberstadt would make way for his predecessor, who had been deposed by the monarch. Enquiries would be made into the validity of the elections of the Bishops of Brandenburg, Strasbourg and Basle. While the Pope alone would have responsibility over all the churches in Italy and Burgundy, he would restore to Garsendonius, one of the schismatic bishops, the see of Mantua, and transfer his rival to Vicenza. The antipope Calixtus III would be granted an abbey. Finally, Frederick would conclude a peace with the Lombard League and Sicily and, if his efforts in this direction failed, accept the verdict— to be given within three months—of an arbitration commission consisting of pontifical and imperial representatives.

Three points may be made concerning this settlement. Firstly it had the merit of dealing with all outstanding questions and of providing a solution for most of them. Secondly, it called for some very real concessions on Frederick's part. Not only would he have to recognize Alexander III without reservations (this was an absolute condition), but he would also have to give way on such important questions as his territorial rights in Italy, the Matildine Estates and the fate of the schismatic bishops. Possibly his ambassadors, faced with

Alexander's determination, gave more ground than he had intended, so much so that Frederick may well have been tempted to go back on what was, after all, no more than a draft agreement. The treaty also represented a number of concessions on Alexander's part, though these were made chiefly at the Lombards' expense, Alexander merely exacting a promise from the Germans that they would not resume military operations against the communes. No wonder, therefore, that the League, informed at long last of the outcome of the negotiations, was extremely incensed and that it lodged the strongest of protests. In reply, the Pope informed them that they had nothing to fear, since they had three months of peace in which they could put forward what counter-claims they decided to make.

Frederick was quick to see how successfully he had set the cat among the pigeons, and during the next few weeks he manoeuvred skilfully to sow suspicion and foster division in the other camp. Although Como rejoined the League, many other cities began to waver; Tortona, Rimini and Ravenna defected from the League, and Treviso would have followed suit had she not been prevented from doing so by her bishop. A treaty between Cremona and the emperor was drawn up and duly signed on 12 December 1176, the emperor undertaking to defend the city against all her enemies and not to leave Italy without ensuring her safety; moreover, he promised that, if she were attacked in his absence, or if peace with the League was not signed by 1 June 1177, he would send her 1,000 knights. He also gave her a free hand over the towns of Guastalla and Luzzarra and promised that Crema, her rival, would never again be allowed to fortify her walls. The remaining communes within the League now saw that further resistance was futile.

To meet this new situation, Frederick once more modified his Italian policy. Having been forced to abandon his Roncaglia programme, he would henceforth rely on bilateral agreements with one Italian city at a time and grant each special privileges in turn. In pursuance of this policy, he followed up his agreement with Cremona by signing separate treaties with Rimini, Ravenna, Tortona and Asti, and by strengthening his ties with Pavia, Genoa and Turin and even with those of his vassals who, like the Count of Biandrate, had proved disloyal. Moreover, he sent emissaries to towns he had formerly thought too unimportant, among them Alba, Ivrea, Ventimiglia, Savona, Albenga, Mondovi and—in Emilia and Romagna—Imola, Faenza, Forlimpopoli, Forli and Cesena.

Frederick embarked upon this new campaign with great energy, and so successful was he that, at the beginning of 1177, he felt confident enough to call for a re-examination of the entire Treaty of Anagni: on 25 January, he proposed to set up a council with instructions to adjudicate between Alexander III and Calixtus III and, simultaneously, a congress to settle the whole Italian problem.

His proposals were rejected out of hand. The Lombard League, that is to say the Guelph cities in it, realized only too clearly that their attendance of Frederick's council would antagonize Alexander III, who might then be tempted to sign a new treaty that would isolate them even further. Alternatively, Frederick might try to overthrow the Pope, whereupon they would be faced with a greatly strengthened emperor, a new and hostile Pope, and rival communes ready to profit from their predicament. They had therefore no choice in the matter: they must rally to the cause of Alexander III, even though he had ceased to stand by them.

In any case their refusal was of no practical importance, since Frederick's advisers had already persuaded him to retract. Ulrich, Patriarch of Aquileia, who was specially called to Ravenna, declared that peace with Alexander was essential; Christian of Mainz pointed out that the advantages accruing from agreement with the Holy See were so great as to merit some loss of imperial prestige. Christian made the further point that once Frederick was reconciled with the Roman Church and had signed some sort of vague agreement with the Lombards, the Papacy would drop all objections to his wider Italian plans.

Frederick appreciated the good sense of their advice and since, in any case, he lacked the resources not only for war but even for protracted negotiations with the cities, he finally decided to put his signature to the Anagni agreement.

Nevertheless, the end of the road was as hard as the beginning. The Pope was exceedingly suspicious of Frederick—quite understandably so in view of the latter's fresh proposals to the communes—while the emperor, afraid to lose face, kept challenging clauses to which he had already agreed in principle. Thus, when the imperial agents saw Cardinals Ubald and Rainier and the representatives of the League at Modena, they could not at first agree to a suitable meeting place for Pope and Emperor. The Germans suggested Ravenna, but the papal legates bluntly refused to go to what they considered a pro-imperial city. After much haggling, the Lombard suggestion—Bologna—was accepted by all parties.

Alexander immediately embarked on a Sicilian galley which, after a rough voyage, brought him to Venice on 23 March 1177. There he was met by Frederick's ambassadors who now declared that Frederick had decided against Bologna after all, on the grounds that Bologna was too anti-German (Christian had treated her with great harshness), and that he greatly preferred Pavia, Ravenna or Venice. The Pope stated that he would first have to consult the League, and accordingly arranged a special meeting at Ferrara, where he arrived at the end of April. During extremely stormy sessions with the Lombards, who reproached him for his actions at Anagni, Alexander succeeded in allaying some of their worst fears. Then seven imperial emissaries arrived, headed by Archbishop Christian of Mainz. The Pope appointed seven legates as well, the most important of whom was Cardinal Ubald, and the League nominated four bishops (including two from the pro-imperial Turin and Asti) and three laymen, led by Gerard Pesta. The Germans once again suggested that Alexander and Frederick should meet at Pavia, Ravenna or Venice, and in the end all three parties agreed on Venice. It was further decided to head the agenda with the restoration of peace in Lombardy, and then to proceed to the best means of effecting a reconciliation between Frederick, the Pope and the King of Sicily, "this forming, so to speak, but a single question".

The delegates then adjourned to Venice where discussions were resumed in mid-May. Alexander stayed within the city while Frederick established himself in Pomposa. He was now fully determined to reach a final agreement with the Pope, and to resume his campaign against the League. To that end, he instructed Christian of Mainz to present the following declaration to the Lombards:

"The Emperor begs and commands you to render him justice in the matter of the regalia and in what is rightly his but has been taken by you; to implement the sentence pronounced against you at Roncaglia, and to grant him the rights your predecessors were in the habit of according to Henry the Old (Henry IV)."

In fact, these three demands amounted simply to a reformulation of the Roncaglia principles, and there was only one reason for raising them now: as an excuse for re-opening hostilities against the communes who, as the emperor knew full well, would find his conditions intolerable. And, in fact, Gerard Pesta delivered an extremely forceful rebuttal—he began by declaring that the communes were, of course, "ready to render justice to the emperor as their lord", and then went on to refute the three imperial claims one by one. Peace, he demanded, should be concluded upon the basis of the Cremona draft, which, *inter alia*, had made the recognition of Alexander III a prerequisite of any agreement.

Gerard's reply was all the more skilful because Frederick himself had accepted the Cremona proposals in 1175, and also because by insisting on imperial recognition of Alexander III, he placed a moral obligation on the Pope to reciprocate. But Frederick was resolved to wreck the negotiations with the League and, as Romuald, Archbishop of Salerno, tells us, instructed his representatives to "raise objections to some clauses (of the Cremona proposals) and to put specious interpretations upon them, whilst rejecting others". Deadlock was reached, and, no doubt following a procedure agreed upon at Ferrara, the matter was put before the Pope, who, knowing that the emperor was, in any case, prepared to recognize his claim to the papal throne, suggested that the settlement of other outstanding problems be put off until later. All he asked of Frederick was to sign a fifteen years' truce with the King of Sicily and a ten years' truce with the communes.

In this, Archbishop Romuald, representing William II, readily concurred, knowing as he did that Sicily was in no danger while Frederick continued to be hampered by Lombard opposition. As for the League, deserted by all her allies, she had no option but to bow to the Pope's decision. Now this was the last thing Frederick wanted, and he therefore declared that the truce was quite unacceptable to him. At the same time, in secret discussions with the two prelates, he let it be known that he might be brought round if he were made usufructuary of the Matildine estates for fifteen years. To this, Alexander III offered no objection but insisted that, at the end of this period, it must be up to the emperor and not the Roman Church, to produce written proof of ownership. Frederick then clinched the bargain by agreeing to a six years' truce with the communes.

Even so, the negotiations were far from concluded; indeed they again came perilously close to failure. Thus when the Pope, anxious to expedite matters, invited Frederick to move his headquarters from Pomposa to Chioggia, which was closer to Venice, the leaders of the Venetian popular party, anxious to gain concessions from their Doge, suggested that Frederick, with their help, take the city by force, after which he could force the Pope to sign any agreement he pleased. Frederick fell in with their plan, not so much because he still hoped to depose Alexander III, as to avoid the humiliating ceremonies which must accompany the rescission of his excommunication. The *populani* then put pressure on their unhappy Doge to admit the emperor into the city and, in the dark of night, rushed in upon the Pope.

But Alexander was not the man to lose his head. Ignoring the panic all round him, he firmly refused to deal with the *populani*, sent a message to Frederick at Chioggia and another to the Sicilian legates, who at once made ready their galleys, threatening to leave Venice and to ask their king to wreak vengeance upon the Doge. The *populani* immediately weakened and the insurrection was over. In any case, it had been frowned upon by Frederick's own counsellors, not least by Christian of Mainz.

Negotiations were now resumed, and on 21 July Frederick signed the truce with Sicily and the League. The text was careful to spare the susceptibilities of the Lombards; it laid down that the emperor and his son would observe the truce, as would all the German princes present, all the Italian nobles, all Frederick's allies, and the consuls of Cremona and Pavia. It stipulated further that, during the entire truce, the monarch would not demand an oath of fidelity from members of the League, nor pronounce any sentence, or take legal action against them. The separate treaty with Sicily referred to William II as King—proof that Frederick had come to recognize Norman authority over the southern half of the peninsula. Thus the war between the emperor and Sicily, Venice, Treviso, Padua, Verona, Vicenza, Brescia, Ferrara, Mantua, Bergamo, Lodi, Milan, Como, Novara, Vercelli, Alessandria, Cassino and

Belmonte, Piacenza, Bobbio, Parma, Reggio, Modena and Bologna, was over at long last.

On the same day, peace was officially signed between the Pope and Frederick, and when it was ratified at Venice a few days later, it became known as the Peace of Venice.

This text differed from the Anagni version in two respects. Firstly it laid down that, in addition to the emperor, the empress and their son Henry would swear in person to honour the peace, and, secondly, the difficult question of the Matildine estates was conveniently glossed over—the treaty simply stated that Frederick would restore to the pontiff all possessions that had formerly belonged to the Roman Church "except for what claims the empire could legally establish". Next day, two German counts swore to the peace on behalf of the emperor, and only then was Frederick himself allowed to enter Venice.

On 24 July, the Venetian galleys brought Frederick to San Niccoló del Lido where three cardinals absolved him from excommunication, while the imperialist prelates abjured the schism. Frederick was then greeted by the Doge, who escorted him to St. Mark's. Here the emperor prostrated himself before the pontiff, who, in tears, raised and embraced him and, leading him into the church, gave him his benediction. The next day, Alexander said mass in St. Mark's and when he left the church, Frederick obligingly held the stirrup and made ready to lead his horse.

But though he had been forced to humble himself before the Pope, Frederick was able to keep his head high. He never at any time appeared in the garb of the penitent and never demeaned himself by uttering recantations in public. His chief concern was to safeguard the cause of the empire, and this Alexander III had fully understood. Thus on 1 August, when Frederick took his oath to observe the treaty, he confessed his fault in the following proud words: "Let it be known to the entire world that although we are clothed in the dignity and glory of the Roman Empire, this dignity does not keep us from human error; imperial majesty does not preserve us from ignorance".

It was, then, through ignorance that he had sinned; he had been ill-informed, and if anyone was to blame, it was his counsellors.

On the same day, Sicily and Lombardy also swore to the truce, and on 14 August, Frederick sent a cordial message to William II stating that twelve German princes were about to do likewise. On the 17th, he renewed the treaty of 1155 with the Doge of Venice, restoring to the Venetians all the privileges they had been granted by the emperors Otto, Henry and Lothar, and also undertaking to preserve the peace between the republic and all the cities of the League that owed him direct allegiance. On 17 September, in an extremely respectful message to Alexander III, he confirmed his adherence to the Treaty of Venice, and once again had it sworn to by a dozen princes of the empire. Finally, he detailed Christian of Mainz to escort the pontiff to Rome. Alexander III left Venice on 16 October.

At this date, peace reigned throughout the land. Notwithstanding the obstacles and his own misgivings, Frederick had followed the path of negotiations through to the end. For a long time he had been undecided whether to choose Alexander or the League as his partner, but in the end, with great shrewdness and thanks to the wise counsel of his experienced advisers, he had decided in favour of the former. No doubt, he had been forced to cede some ground, to humble himself a little, go back on what he had proclaimed at Roncaglia and Würzburg. But in the last analysis, he had been the gainer. His authority and prestige in Germany remained intact, the more so as he had been able to safeguard the rights of the schismatic bishops. He was no longer at war with the Roman Church, and the Lombard League was on the defensive. A great many Guelphs had been rapped over the knuckles, and a fair number of cities had come to see that collaboration with the empire was the best policy. And above all, he himself had at last seen the advantages of co-operation.

After years of effort and frustration, a new hand had been dealt to Frederick, and he was quick to play it to good advantage.

CHAPTER ELEVEN

The New Policy 1177 - 1184

THE Treaty of Venice was the crowning achievement of Frederick's reign; it had the great merit, among others, of bringing peace to Italy, even if it was not a lasting one. In this sense, it marked more than the end of a period—it opened a new age, rich in promise. For having reigned during twenty-five years, Frederick not only changed his domestic approach, but, in 1182–3, put into practice an Italian policy that was far more realistic and dynamic than the old. All those who had described the Treaty of Venice as a defeat for Barbarossa, were taught better by the vastly increased prestige that accrued to him during the next few months. True, Frederick had had to pay a large price for his peace with Alexander III, but his imperial majesty was now recognized by all Christendom. To consolidate his position further, he decided to stay on in Italy for a while and to show himself to his subjects as a benevolent and understanding monarch. This he did during a glittering royal tour that brought him into contact with all sections of the population and took him to many cities.

The better to demonstrate his allegiance to the Pope, he ordered Christian of Mainz to escort Alexander III into Rome, which they reached on 12 March 1178—the Pope having first promised to respect the rights of the commune, and the senators having agreed to pay homage to their pontiff. On 29 August, Calixtus III was made to tender his submission, but, for the rest, he was treated with extreme leniency. This enabled Frederick to allay all fears at home and also to silence all opposition in Central Italy.

In the meantime, the emperor continued to pay state visits to all his loyal cities and to extend friendship to all the rest. He also made a tour of the March, stopping over at Ancona and Osimo, where he published an edict on the administration of justice on 4 December 1177. Then he proceeded to the Duchy of Spoleto, and on to Tuscany. Finally, by way of Pisa and Genoa, where he was received with acclaim, he reached Lombardy and Piedmont. On 7 July 1178, he signed a treaty with Asti, and showed his benevolence by recalling the castellan of a nearby imperial castle, and by promising not to replace him with any but citizens of Asti. He took the opportunity of his stay in Piedmont to reorganize his estates and to fortify those cities that assured him control of the most important passes (Turin, Ivrea, Annona, Asti, and others).

From Turin he crossed the Alps at Geneva, and descended into Burgundy. There, in his official capital of Arles, he received all the lords of Provence and Languedoc in great majesty, and on 30 July 1178, was ceremoniously crowned king. This was the first time an emperor had visited this region, and his presence clearly reflected the wish, after the somewhat humiliating Treaty of Venice, once again to exalt the empire. Frederick remained in Burgundy during the entire summer, and paid state visits to Lyons and Besançon. Then he made for home, and when he reached Spires on 31 October, he immediately attended to what business he had left unfinished in 1174.

This brought him into direct conflict with Henry the Lion, whose clumsy actions had caused resentment among his vassals, and who, moreover, had raised personal objections to certain clauses in the Treaty of Venice. In particular, he was opposed to the restoration of Ulrich to the bishopric of Halberstadt. Ulrich's schismatic successor, Gero, had proved extremely accommodating to Henry, and had granted him many ecclesiastical estates which Ulrich was now claiming back. When Henry refused to comply, Ulrich enlisted the support of many nobles, including Philip of Heinsberg, Archbishop of Cologne, who had a personal grudge against the Welf.

Frederick took the opportunity to show publicly that his friendship for his cousin had been strained too far. At the Diet of Spires, on 11 November, he not only refrained from censuring the protesting nobles, as he would surely have done in the past, but let it appear that he, too, deemed the actions of the Duke of Saxony quite deplorable. The gulf between the Houses of Hohenstaufen and Welf was now as wide as ever it had been.

Historians have wondered at Frederick's "real" motives and, as always, more concerned with originality than common sense, they have put forward many different explanations. However, in the light of Frederick's character and his general conduct since 1152, the true explanation is not nearly as extravagant as some have suggested. Since Frederick's German policy had always been based upon collaboration with the princes, and since the Lion was far and away one of the most powerful of these, Frederick had buried the ancient quarrel between the two dynasties, and had offered Henry his hand in sincere friendship. For twenty years he had loyally pursued this policy. There is no reason to believe, with some historians, that he was all the while biding his time to settle accounts— had he wanted to, he could easily have done so in 1164, or again in 1170. No, his friendship was meant to cement the *Landfrieden*, and all Frederick expected in return was that Henry would prove equally loyal. At Chiavenna, however, when Frederick had asked for reinforcements, he had been refused, and then the doubts he had felt since 1171 gave way to annoyance.

Both his own authority and the honour of the empire had been flaunted. Henry's arguments—his Palestinian campaign, his loss of all Welf VI's estates and rights, and his consequent disinterest in the Italian expedition, the fact that he was under no obligation to support foreign campaigns—all counted for little. Worse still, Henry had come to act the petty despot in Saxony, which he tried to turn into a state within a state, one that was a law unto itself. In 1172, he had led an independent crusade to the Holy Land, where the King of Jerusalem had received him with royal honours, all of which was a slight to Frederick. Moreover, by his continued collaboration with a prince who ceaselessly aroused the opposition of his peers, Frederick put an intolerable strain on the loyalty of his other nobles. In short, imperial prestige, the power and cohesion of the kingdom, political considerations and even public morality, all demanded a break.

But Frederick was anxious that justice should be seen to be done, and that he should not be suspected of misrepresentation or injustice. And so he had the complaint against Henry investigated with due regard for feudal custom and German principles of government.

As far as we can tell from the largely illegible documents, there were two separate trials, the first of which was held at Worms on 13 January 1179, before Henry's tribal (Saxon) peers judging according to the *Landrecht* or customary law, with Frederick presiding as impartial arbiter. Foolishly, Henry refused to attend the hearing, and he did likewise when the trial was adjourned until 24 June to Magdeburg. New charges were immediately levelled against him by Dietrich of Landsberg, a Saxon noble, who testified that the Lusatians had invaded his territory at Henry's instigation, whereupon the assembly put Henry to the ban of the empire.

When Henry refused to bow to this verdict, the offended parties appealed to the sovereign, who now ordered a second trial, according to the *Lehnrecht* or feudal law, in which the judges were Henry's peers without differentiation of tribe. Here Frederick himself appeared as chief plaintiff and charged Henry with treason—at Kaina and Zeitz in August 1179 and at Würzburg in January 1180. Since Henry again absented himself, all his fiefs were declared forfeit.

Frederick had thus skilfully eliminated his rival in strict accordance with feudal law and with the full approval of his princes. He now ordered Henry's estates to be partitioned, and at a solemn diet in Gelnhausen (April 1180) conferred the title of Duke of Saxony upon the Ascanian prince, Bernard of Anhalt, the younger son of Albert the Bear, thus helping to settle an old account. However, in order to prevent the House of Ascania, which also controlled Brandenburg, from becoming too powerful, he severed Westphalia (with Cologne and Paderborn) from the rest of Saxony and granted it, with ducal powers, to Archbishop Philip of Cologne. Moreover, he granted the Duchy of Bavaria to the faithful Otto of Wittelsbach (whose descendants were to reign in Munich until 1918), having first detached the March of Styria and raised it into a royal duchy, under Otto's younger brother. As a result of all these changes, Germany now counted ten duchies: the six Frederick had inherited in 1152 (Saxony, Bavaria, Carinthia, Swabia, Bohemia [now a kingdom] and Upper Lorraine) together with Austria, Styria, Westphalia and Brabant (formed out of Lower Lorraine).

Henry had meanwhile taken up arms, forcing Frederick to take the field against him in Saxony. Most of Henry's vassals quickly deserted his camp, and to make things worse for Henry, he failed to secure aid from Henry II of England, his father-in-law, or from Waldemar of Denmark. Frederick had little difficulty in capturing the city of Brunswick and then laid siege to Lübeck, which put up a valiant resistance until July 1180 when, seeing that all was lost, the Lion took refuge in the fortress of Stade in Northern Saxony, and ordered Lübeck to surrender. Then he sued for the emperor's pardon.

But the time for clemency and friendship had long since passed. Moreover, even had he wanted to, Frederick could not have undone the verdict of Würzburg—he had already received the homage of Bernard of Anhalt, Philip of Heinsberg and Otto of Wittelsbach. However, when Henry threw himself at his sovereign's feet during the Diet of Erfurt in November 1181, Frederick made a generous gesture: he granted him the cities of Brunswick and Lüneburg, but banished him from Germany for three years. In July 1182, the humiliated duke left for England, where he was well-received by his father-in-law. In 1184, he returned for a short stay, with Frederick's permission, and in the summer of 1185, he came back to Germany for good.

Henry's defeat had thrown Northern Germany into disarray. Bernard of Anhalt, for all his good intentions, was unable to impose his will on some of his more powerful vassals, particularly the Count of Holstein; nor was he the equal of Knut, the new King of Denmark, who refused to pay homage to Frederick and extended his hold over the Pomeranian coast. However, Frederick counted all this a small price to pay for the closer control that he had gained over Saxony.

At the same time, he also tried to increase his authority in the east and south-east, strengthening his links with Poland, with Hungary (which had grown increasingly independent since the accession of King Bela III in 1172), and with Bohemia. Here he had refused to sanction the abdication in 1173 of Vladislav in favour of his son Frederick, and had handed the duchy to Sobieslav I. In 1177, however, Sobieslav had proved refractory, whereupon young Frederick was raised to the dukedom with the emperor's approval and duly enfeoffed. Moreover, in 1182, the emperor helped Frederick to defeat Conrad, who was then fobbed off with Moravia, now turned into a separate duchy. In 1187, the Bishop of Prague was made a prince of the empire and as such became directly answerable to the crown.

In short, the defeat of Henry the Lion had helped the emperor to consolidate and extend his power throughout the kingdom, and it had other repercussions as well. In particular, it hastened that slow evolution in German society which had begun in the early twelfth century, and which has been the subject of a brilliant analysis by Heinrich Mitteis, the great German historian: the growing strength of the *Reichsfürsten*, or princes of the empire, a new social class that had first come to the fore when Frederick created the Duchy of Austria and granted Bavaria to Henry the Lion. It was these princes who forced Frederick—or rather persuaded him, for he largely concurred in their view—to reinvest without delay all fiefs that had reverted to the crown, a procedure typical of German feudalism and known as *Leihezwang*.

After 1180, these men were set further apart from the rest when the royal chancellery restricted the title of prince to a relatively small number of men—roughly a hundred. All of them—dukes, margraves, landgraves and princes of the church —ruled over vast territories, ranked above counts, swore homage to no one but the king, and held their fiefs solely and directly from him. It was this class that would subsequently be entitled to elect new kings, and their distinction was all the greater since, during the period under review, the German nobility began to form a rigid hierarchy, the *Heerschild*.

This development, which was accelerated further after Henry's expulsion, helped to produce the social divisions that Eicke of Repgau has described in his *Sachsenspiegel*, a work famous in the history of law and of German institutions. On the surface, the *Heerschild* helped to strengthen the authority of the crown by closer union between the sovereign and his princes, since it led to the disappearance of the old duchies with their purely ethnic, and later territorial, loyalties. However, it is questionable whether this strengthening of "Germanic cohesion" was not, in fact, achieved at the expense of the central authority, that is, the crown.

To begin with, the obligatory reinvestiture of repossessed or eschewed fiefs no less than the electoral system, prevented the accumulation of large royal estates, which, in the course of the centuries, might have come to extend over most of Germany. Even if, like the Capetian in France, the Hohenstaufen dynasty had been able to appropriate a large number of major fiefs by marriage or inheritance (and here it should be noted that Philip Augustus first accumulated estates by confiscation and conquest) it had no assurance that it could keep the crown as well—indeed the more prosperous the House, the more chary the electors would have been of casting their vote for it. Moreover, the princes of the Empire stood between the emperor and the vast majority of his subjects— as the result of the hierarchical structure of German society, they had direct and exclusive control over all the king's vassals in their territory. In this way they were able to extend their powers in counties previously under crown control, and over crown ministers dispersed throughout Germany and holding their offices in fief. At the same time, the royal tribunal became increasingly feudal in character and greatly diminished the scope of the royal chancellery. Thus while the emperor's prestige stood high, and while he enjoyed a number of special prerogatives and, of course, his place at the very tip of the pyramid, that pyramid was, in fact, the feudal system, with all the limitations it imposed.

Hence it is tempting to see the trial of Henry the Lion, which hastened all these social changes, as an error on Frederick's part. However, this is no more than historical hindsight—if we try to enter into the mentality of the age, we shall find that Frederick was neither rash nor foolish.

Firstly, he acted in accordance with his own principles of government—to keep the peace between his nobles. Furthermore, by relying increasingly on their support, and quite particularly by forging the closest possible links with his princes of the church, he hoped to repair what damage the crown had suffered in the wake of the Investiture Dispute. Finally, he was a man of his time—despite all the qualities that raised him head and shoulders above the great majority of his contemporaries, he was blind to the impossibility of reconciling the *honor regni* with the feudalization of public offices and the growing power of his *Reichsfürsten*. Frederick's entire life, his feelings, his attitude to events and to men, were suffused with feudal ideals as, indeed, they were bound to be. Thus while he strove to increase his own authority, he never once tried to step out of the feudal frame (though, as we saw, in 1168 he toyed with the idea of making the crown hereditary). He considered the homage of his princes the mortar that bound the state together, the more so as the reinvestment of fiefs enabled him to reward the best and most loyal servants among them. In short, he was content to be a feudal ruler, a supreme arbiter among his people and a respected leader of men.

For all that, he did not entirely neglect the interests of his House. In 1179, he bought the extensive allods of Count Welf VI in Swabia and acquired the counties of Salzbach and Pfullendorf which he made over to his son. He declared Lübeck a free city under the crown, and gave Franconia, where he owned large estates, a new constitution in February 1179. He also acquired new territory in Saxony, Thuringia and Lusatia as far as the banks of the Oder. In 1184, he strengthened his northern strongholds further by legislating on the construction of new castles.

More than ever, he tightened his hold over the clergy, reminding them that no elected bishop could dispose of episcopal property before he was invested by the crown, and defining the rights of bishops in confessional matters. He used his royal prerogatives over vacant sees to seize all movable goods, but above all, he kept his eye upon promotions and elections. When an ecclesiastical court at Salzburg found Archbishop Adalbert, a supporter of Alexander, who had never been invested with his regalia and who had been deposed in 1174 by decision of the crown, guilty of simony (9 August 1177), Frederick at once had him replaced with Conrad of Wittelsbach. In the same year, he also appointed loyal men to the episcopal sees of Bamberg and Ratisbon, while, as we saw, Ulrich was given back the See of Halberstadt. In 1178, new appointments were made to the Sees of Brixen, Paderborn and Spires; in 1179, at Bremen–Hamburg; in 1180 at Brandenburg; in 1182 at Constance and Eichstätt, and in 1183, Conrad of Wittelsbach was given back his original archdiocese of Mainz, while the See of Salzburg went to another Adalbert. These various promotions made it possible for Frederick to reward those bishops who had stood by him throughout the schism.

There were several unresolved differences between Frederick and the Pope, and these formed the subject of more or less secret and almost continuous negotiations during the two years of grace following the Treaty of Venice, when the church was also busily preparing for the third Oecumenical Lateran Council (February–March 1179).

The greatest point of dispute, besides the standing of the former schismatics, was the future of the Matildine estates, which the emperor thought so important that, after 1180, Italy once more became his chief concern.

Throughout these years, Frederick had maintained the most cordial diplomatic relations with Sicily. In Central Italy, his vigilant agents had prevented the cities from achieving any real measure of autonomy, while, in the Papal States, Christian of Mainz was busy defending Alexander III, who had been forced to withdraw from Rome in June 1179, and was now being harassed by squireens in the Sabina and surrounding districts, led by Conrad of Montferrat. During one of these operations, Christian was ambushed and taken prisoner by the rebels, who even had the audacity to nominate a successor to the anti-pope Calixtus III and assigned to one of their number the title Innocent III. This "pontiff", however, did not choose to accept the honour; instead he approached Alexander, who permitted him to enter a monastery. Meanwhile, the rebels continued unchecked, and when Alexander III died at Cività-Castellana on 30 August 1181, he was a sadly disillusioned man. His subjects had spared him nothing: the Romans even insulted his mortal remains as these were carried through the city.

Alexander was succeeded by Lucius III who, as Ubald, Cardinal-Bishop of Ostia, had headed the papal delegation to Anagni and Venice. An able man of venerable age, and even temperament, Lucius III was inclined to compromise and immediately agreed to discuss the Matildine estates with Frederick. He also promised to consider the future of the schismatic clerics in Italy, whose position had never been regularized, and whom the Lateran Council had condemned *en masse*.

Formal negotiations were begun in May 1182, through the mediation of Archbishop Conrad of Wittelsbach. Previously the Pope, who had returned to Rome in November 1181, had been expelled by the unruly citizens, who soon afterwards declared war on Tusculum and defeated her. Upon hearing of this, Christian of Mainz hurried from the Duchy of Spoleto, where he had settled as soon as his captors had released him, and repulsed the Romans. When he died of a malignant fever soon afterwards, on 25 August 1183, Lucius III, now isolated, appealed for help to Frederick, who suggested a meeting at Mantua, Brescia or Verona. Verona proving the most acceptable to him, the Pope set out for that city in the spring of 1184, and arrived on 22 July.

Frederick had meanwhile been able to restore order in Lombardy. In this he had been greatly helped by the fact that the Holy See, bogged down in Rome and Tusculum, had been unable to intervene in the north. In so great a quandary was the Holy See, in fact, and so anxious were the Lombard cities to secure their liberties in a friendly way, that Frederick felt encouraged to resurrect his old dream of empire, and to foist it upon the church, if necessary by armed might. Hence he was only too pleased to renew the truce with the League on its expiry in the summer of 1183.

However, as the Lombards realized full well, there could be

no real conciliation with Frederick until the problem of Alessandria had been solved. On 4 February 1182, Frederick himself had made this quite clear in the text of his peace treaty with Tortona (which had left the League before 1177). In it, he promised to protect the city and to revoke a number of privileges he had granted to other communes (for instance Serravalle) at Tortona's expense. In return, he had demanded that the power of the castellans be restricted and that Tortona should refuse entry to all inhabitants of Alessandria.

Now, the Lombards found it exceedingly difficult to accept the destruction of a city that had become a symbol of their union—and this was clearly what Frederick intended. Luckily, both parties were so anxious to reach agreement that they hit upon a compromise at Piacenza: early in March, the inhabitants of Alessandria were made to file out and, after the imperial army had wreaked symbolic destruction upon the city, were led back by one of Frederick's agents, who declared that, on this very spot, he was establishing a new city, to be called Caesaria. On 14 March the city was officially recognized and given a new constitution.

This difficulty out of the way, the remaining problems were quickly resolved and a peace concluded. Frederick's delegation to Piacenza was led by the Bishop of Asti; the Lombards were represented by various consuls and other city officials, among whom Gerard Pesta was conspicuously absent. Apart from Venice, Como and Alessandria, all the cities that had signed the truce of 1177 were represented, that is Treviso, Padua, Vicenza, Verona, Brescia, Ferrara, Mantua, Bergamo, Lodi, Milan, Novara, Vercelli, Piacenza, Bobbio, Parma, Reggio, Modena, Bologna; and in addition Imola and Faenza. General agreement was reached on 30 April, and sworn to by the plenipotentiaries of both sides, except for the delegates from Ferrara, Imola and Faenza. The peace was to be confirmed before 1 September by an imperial edict and by a ceremonial oath. This was also to be taken by the three cities which had not been a party to the preliminaries at Piacenza and, in addition, by Feltre and Belluno. In the event, it was on 25 June that Frederick personally ratified the peace at the Diet of Constance, in the presence of his nobles, the city delegates and the papal legates.

The high sovereignty of the empire was implicit in the stipulation that the cities were to be invested by the emperor with certain regalia. As for the rest, they would be examined by special commissions, composed of the local bishop and other citizens of good repute.

"As to the regalia which we have not granted you, our will is as follows. Let the bishop, and some men from the town, or from the bishopric, who are of good repute and considered fit for this duty, not bearing any grievance against the city or our majesty, swear to enquire in good faith and without deceit into everything that especially belongs to our excellency."

If this enquiry should lead to difficulties, it was further laid down that the sovereign might cede his regalia against an indemnity of 2,000 livres, or less in special cases.

The sovereign was, moreover, to invest all consuls except in cities whose bishops had been granted the special privilege of doing so in the emperor's name. In the absence of this concession, the consuls would receive their investiture every fifth year from the emperor in person, and in the interval, from his representative in Lombardy. Before being confirmed in their office they must swear fealty to the crown, and all men between the ages of fifteen and seventy years of age must do likewise. Finally, the consuls were given the right to administer the law in all cases where conviction would lead to a maximum fine of 25 livres; all other cases were to go before the imperial court in Germany or Italy, which would also act as a court of appeal.

These provisions not only satisfied Frederick's honour but also safeguarded his interests. In addition, he was granted various requisitioning rights whenever he was in Italy, though he promised not to stay too long in any particular place. The cities further promised to protect all his property and prerogatives in Lombardy, and to bring any refractory communes to book.

For all that, it would be idle to pretend that this treaty worked exclusively to Frederick's advantage. In effect, the Lombard cities won a number of major concessions: the right to consular rule, the right to build fortifications, and last but not least the right to maintain their old alliances.

"Cities are entitled to fortify themselves and to erect fortifications on their boundaries."

But above all, the question of the regalia was dealt with so tactfully that both parties were highly satisfied. Article I of the treaty is therefore worth quoting in full:

"We, Frederick, and our son Henry, King of the Romans, concede *in perpetuity* to you, the cities, districts and people of this League, all the customary regalian rights you hold both within and without the cities, so that, in every city, you may freely follow what customs you have observed *since time immemorial* in respect of requisitioning rights, forest and pasture, bridges, waterways and mills, and also in respect of armies, fortification and criminal and financial jurisdiction both within and without your city walls, and in respect of everything that is needful to you."

Thus, while making it explicit that all regalia were granted by the emperor as a concession, and were not vested in the cities as their natural right, the treaty also conceded implicitly that these rights—and their list was left vague and imprecise—had always been enjoyed by the communes ("since time immemorial") and were therefore given "in perpetuity". This was tantamount to declaring that the powers of the omnipotent emperor were circumscribed by custom. By agreeing to this compromise, Frederick showed that he had finally come to terms with political reality in Italy, that he had at last recognized the towns as an integral part of the social framework.

Does this mean, as quite a few historians have claimed, that Frederick had suffered a serious reverse, that he had been forced to set his sights lower? Far from it; neither he nor the League had won or lost; they had simply arrived at a mutually satisfactory compromise. For Frederick, the new treaty had many advantages over the Cremona proposals, and the Guelphs were pleased by its moderation. The new treaty was thus eminently suited to preserve the peace in Northern Italy, as, indeed, it was intended to be by both parties.

In addition, Frederick was given considerable scope for manoeuvre in that he could concede or withhold certain regalia at will; in that he could invest consuls or withhold recognition from them; in that he could requisition supplies, etc. In this way he could, if he wished, favour one city at another's expense, and yet be assured that all alike would "preserve and maintain the peace".

And having restored the peace, first in Germany and now in Italy, Frederick felt the hour had come when he could lay hold of the Matildine estates and St. Peter's Patrimony, two great prizes that had eluded him for far too long.

But he did not hurry. At Constance, he merely informed the Papal legates that he was anxious to settle all outstanding questions. Then he proceeded to Germany where, in May 1184, he presided over the Diet of Mainz, the most triumphant and splendid of his entire career. Here a multitude of princes and foreign envoys witnessed the knighting of his two elder sons, Frederick and Henry. This was, perhaps, Barbarossa's finest hour.

CHAPTER TWELVE

Success 1184 - 1188

A t the Diet of Mainz, when Frederick Barbarossa knighted his son, Henry VI—whom he had proclaimed King of Germany and King of the Romans in 1168—and proposed a meeting with Pope Lucius III, he was about to realize his old dream of an hereditary monarchy. At the same time he was determined to assume full control of Italy, as was his right according to the Treaty of Constance. Now, Frederick knew that both ambitions called for speedy negotiations with the Holy See—the Pope alone could bestow the imperial crown, and mastery of Central Italy was dependent on the settlement of all outstanding territorial disputes between the church and the empire.

The Pope himself was only too anxious to meet Frederick half-way, for he hoped, with the emperor's help, to return to Rome. He accordingly sped to Verona (see p. 184), where he was forced to cool his heels for many long weeks, while Frederick attended to more urgent business elsewhere.

Imperial agents had gone out with orders to secure the Alpine passes and the routes leading down to the Po valley, thus implementing the decisions Frederick had taken at Piedmont in 1178. They now regularized the collection of tolls, fortified the imperial castles, established small garrisons and invested new seigneuries and domains, *inter alia* granting Obizzo d'Este the Lion's former estates in Milan and Liguria (19 October 1184). At the same time, Frederick began secret negotiations with Milan, his former enemy, but now the most powerful and dynamic of all the Lombard communes and, moreover, a city with a commanding position over the major Alpine routes.

In Southern Italy, too, he was forced to think anew. As early as 1173, he had made overtures to the court of Palermo, which, as he knew, was uneasy about Manuel Comnenus' plans in the Central Mediterranean. The approach had proved unsuccessful because of Sicilian attachment to Alexander III. Even so, their fear of Byzantium had persuaded the Norman rulers to approve the Treaty of Venice and, after 1177, relations between Germany and Sicily had been cordial.

Quite possibly, Frederick used the discussions at Constance to establish even closer links with Palermo, although we cannot be sure. In any case, there was general agreement between the two parties, both of whom feared the ambitions of Byzantium; moreover, Frederick was perfectly prepared to recognize the Norman dynasty—indeed, in accordance with custom, he sealed the alliance by offering his son, Henry VI, King of the Romans, in marriage to Constance, the aunt of young William of Sicily and the daughter of Roger II. When their engagement was officially announced at Augsburg on 29 October, Frederick had taken a major step towards consolidating his hold over Southern Italy. However, this marriage did not ensure Henry's succession to the Sicilian throne, though, in the event, it did lead to that result. Hence many historians have seen fit, in retrospect, to congratulate Frederick on his foresight when, in fact, he knew that young William II had only been married for three years and might still produce an heir of his own. What Henry's engagement unquestionably did achieve was the diplomatic isolation of the Pope. In that case, why did Lucius do nothing about it or, at the very least, refuse to bless the union?

The most plausible answer is that Frederick, with his customary skill, had successfully played on the Pope's fears of Byzantium. At the time, Lucius was most apprehensive about developments in the Holy Land where, two years after the death of Manuel Comnenus in 1180, there had been a massacre of Roman Catholics. Moreover, the Pope, no less than the princes of the church in Jerusalem, held Manuel and his successor responsible for Islam's recent successes. Frederick now presented himself as a defender of the Holy Shrines, one who was ready to make good the failure of the Greeks in Jerusalem and, with the Pope's help, to oppose their designs upon Palermo.

Lucius had all summer to ponder about Frederick's sincerity, while he was kept waiting in Verona. Conciliatory by nature, but far-sighted, he was no doubt fully aware of the dangers of a close alliance, yet he also knew that he could not afford the luxury of open conflict with Germany. Thus, when negotiations were started on Frederick's arrival at Verona in October 1184, they might easily have proved successful had two new factors not cast a shadow over the proceedings.

One of these concerned the archepiscopal See of Trèves. Archbishop Arnold had died on 25 May 1183, and when the electors were unable to agree on his successor—the majority choosing Rudolf of Wied, the provost, and the minority Folmar, the archdeacon—they decided to refer the dispute to the emperor, who ordered a new election, decided for Rudolf (who again gained the support of the majority) and forthwith invested him with his regalia. In doing so, Frederick had acted fully within the terms of the Concordat of Worms and, being certain of the outcome, had even refrained from applying a law, recently ratified by the German princes, which gave him the right to fill all disputed sees without calling for a new election.

Unfortunately, Folmar appealed to the Pope who, basing himself on a decision confirmed by the Lateran Council, argued that it was up to the Holy See, and not the Emperor, to arbitrate in all such matters. Perhaps an amicable settlement might yet have been reached, had Conrad of Wittelsbach, who was still smarting under the blow the Treaty of Venice had dealt him, and some other resentful ecclesiastics, not seen fit to put the worst possible interpretation on Frederick's action. They now whispered in the Pope's ear that Frederick was trying to usurp full authority over the German church.

The other factor that made the Pope suspicious was the rumour, spread particularly by the Italian clergy, that Frederick, now reconciled to the Lombards, had no intention of expelling any of the former schismatics, nor of restoring any church property. These men found some ready listeners in the Curia, where many cardinals took the view that there could be no final settlement with the empire until all church lands in Central Italy had been restored—if this were not done, the Holy See would find itself in the impossible situation from which Alexander III had suffered so badly in his struggle with the crown.

And so the negotiations at Verona ended in deadlock. Frederick had previously sent a message to the Pope, proposing that the empire should be left in possession of all Italian church domains—without specifying what exactly he meant by this— against an annual payment to the Pope of one-tenth, and to the College of Cardinals of one-ninth of all imperial revenues in the peninsula, or alternatively that the church retain all possessions not under dispute and that a commission should be set up to enquire into and adjudicate as to the rest. On his arrival in Verona, Frederick repeated this proposal in person, asked the pontiff to crown Henry VI emperor, called for honourable and equitable treatment of all schismatic ecclesiastics, and, finally, demanded that Rudolf be confirmed as Archbishop of Trèves. He made no mention of any help he might render in restoring the Pope to Rome.

Lucius dryly, and with unexpected firmness, refused to crown Henry VI, claiming that common sense argued against the contemporaneous existence of two emperors. As for the schismatic ecclesiastics, he agreed at first to examine each claim on its merits, provided it were presented to him in writing; but then, invoking a recent decision of the Lateran Council, declared that the issue could only be settled by a commission, which he proposed to convene at Lyons. As for the archbishopric of Trèves, he called for a new election, all the while attempting to bring the discussion back to the territorial dispute.

Despite these differences, the meeting at Verona proved of great historic importance, for Frederick and Lucius agreed to prepare a new Crusade (first prayed for by Alexander III in 1179) and to outlaw the Catharist (Albigensian) heresy which, for the past twenty months and more, had been causing church and empire a great deal of trouble, particularly in Vaud and Languedoc. The imperial edict on this subject has not come down to us, but it was almost certainly similar in substance to the Pope's *Ab abolendum*—Frederick was second to none when it came to championing Christian truth and upholding the church as chief arbiter in all matters spiritual. In the temporal sphere, by contrast, he refused to brook any rivals, and considered it a matter of honour to uphold his privileges and prerogatives intact.

Thus when the Pope refused to grant him what he had asked, and the Curia began to intrigue against him, Frederick thought it was high time to quit Verona, which he did in early November. On the 14th day of that month, the Empress Beatrix died, and after going into retreat for a few days, Frederick once again manned the helm. On his orders, Henry VI took severe measures against Folmar's supporters in Trèves, Coblenz and Cologne, while Frederick himself prepared to deal with the Italian problem. As a first step he hastened to bring his negotiations with Milan to a successful conclusion and, to that end, published a violent indictment of Cremona, his former ally against Milan. He now blamed Cremona for the destruction of Crema, recalled that it was at her instigation and with her help that Milan had been razed in 1162, and charged her with having fomented the revolt of 1167, with detaching Lodi and

Parma from the German cause, and with the usurpation of imperial property and rights. The hapless city was forced to sue for pardon, which Frederick granted against payment of an enormous indemnity. Milan now declared herself satisfied, and on 11 February, in a declaration signed at Reggio, undertook to support the emperor against his enemies and to protect his interests in Lombardy, the March, in Romagna and "especially in the lands of the Countess Matilda", which Frederick had long coveted but had been careful not to declare publicly as his own. Milan was invested with most of the customary regalia against an annual payment of 300 livres, received the promise of Frederick's neutrality in any dispute with Pavia, and was granted permission to rebuild Crema. It was a resounding victory for the Ghibellines.

In Tuscany and Central Italy, where he stayed during the second half of 1185, Frederick employed quite different tactics. Here he took every possible opportunity to intervene in disputes between the communes and the aristocracy, siding systematically with the latter and forcing the cities—Florence, Siena and Lucca—to restore his sovereign rights. For this very purpose he installed a host of imperial agents, particularly in parts of the Matildine estates which these cities had seized and which Frederick now recovered one by one.

Within a short time, he thus entrenched himself in the centre, while in the north, his new alliance with powerful Milan forced most other Lombard cities to throw in their lot with the empire—except for Cremona, he had no need to ill-treat them or even to subject them to threats. Tuscany, Romagna and the March remained, as ever, his staunchest supporters. Relations with the court of Palermo had been cemented by marriage, and the Holy See was now completely isolated. This was the state of affairs when Lucius III died on 25 November 1185.

That very day, the cardinals, wishing to show their disapproval of Frederick's policy, elected by a resounding majority one of

Frederick's fiercest opponents: Humbert Crivelli, Archbishop of Milan. His family had suffered terrible hardship when the city was destroyed in 1162, and he had been made archbishop by the Guelph faction among the clergy for the sole purpose of driving a wedge between the commune and the empire. The new Pope, who took the name of Urban III, decided to keep personal charge of the important diocese of Milan, and through it to influence the church throughout Lombardy. Nor did he hide his resolve to resist and, indeed, attack Frederick with all the means at his disposal. For this reason, hardly had he been set on St. Peter's throne, when, against the will of the majority of the electors, he declared Folmar the true archbishop of Trèves.

The strength of character and obstinacy of the new Pope put fresh life into the entire Curia, but at the same time lost it the goodwill of most of the German clergy. Urban III was accused by them of being too impetuous and imperious, of entering into adventures that, ultimately, were not in the best interest of the church, of refusing to recognize even those of the emperor's prerogatives which had never been disputed, and of pursuing a policy which, if continued, was bound to lead to open warfare. This, at any rate, seems to have been the line taken by Conrad of Wittelsbach, who now rallied to the emperor's cause.

When Frederick learnt of the Pope's support for Folmar, he decided to act without delay, believing as he did that time and justice were both on his side. He made straight for Lombardy and, on 27 January 1186, at Milan, solemnized the marriage of Henry VI to Constance of Sicily, amidst the great rejoicing of the inhabitants and the leaders of the commune, who were flattered by this great honour. Since he could not ask the Archbishop of Milan, i.e. the Pope, to officiate, he prevailed upon the Patriarch of Acquileia to stand in, and at the same time to crown his son King of Italy. This was a direct challenge to Urban III, who had neither been informed nor consulted.

Urban then urged Cremona to lead a revolt against Frederick, and made similar approaches to all German bishops who had protested against Frederick's high-handed abrogation of their privileges and seizure of their property. His appeal was favourably received, not only by Folmar, but also by Philip of Heinsberg, Archbishop of Cologne, whose head had apparently been turned by the concession to him of the Duchy of Westphalia in 1180, and who had strong ambitions of his own in Northern Germany. On 17 May 1186, the Pope, in a gesture amounting to a virtual declaration of war, with his own hands consecrated Folmar Archbishop of Trèves. Since Rudolf of Wied, invested by the emperor, was still in office, this act not only contravened the Concordat of Worms, but ran counter to established German usage. Worse still, Urban III saw fit to nominate Folmar and Philip of Heinsberg his legates to Germany.

Frederick was stung to the quick, and his response recalled his early violence, and served as a reminder that the emperor, despite his 60 years, had retained all the vigour of his youth. Verona was cut off and all routes of access to the city closed, so that the Pope became a virtual prisoner, unable to communicate with the rest of the world—the imperial agents having issued a warning that any messenger who was caught would be mutilated or put to death. At the same time, Henry VI was given instructions to invade the Papal States at the head of a small body of men, and by June, he was in control of the entire north of St. Peter's Patrimony, had obtained the allegiance of Perugia against a grant of certain privileges, had captured Viterbo and Narni, and, acting as sovereign, had invested a Roman noble with Sutri. His ministers meanwhile clamped down on any Tuscan cities showing the least signs of opposition, and ordered Siena to restore to the emperor "the property and rights formerly in the possession of the Countess

Matilda". As estate after estate fell into Hohenstaufen hands, Frederick's position grew stronger and stronger.

As for rebellious Cremona, Frederick began with threats of military reprisals, but quickly let it be known that he was anxious for a reconciliation, and accordingly proposed a pardon on honourable terms. On 8 June, the city agreed not to wage war on Milan, Piacenza and Crema, to restore Luzzara and Guastella to the emperor, and to pay a heavy indemnity. By the 29th, the matter was settled, and on 6 August, Cremona was granted a royal pardon by Henry VI, who had meanwhile moved on to lay siege to Orvieto.

Before this happened, Urban III had addressed a letter (18 June) to the German bishops complaining of the emperor's invasion of St. Peter's Patrimony, of Frederick's unjust charge that the Holy See had incited Cremona to rebellion, of his having dispossessed the churches of Ivrea and Turin, and his wronging the clergy and cities of Tuscany. All of this, the Pope alleged, amounted to a refusal to follow God's law, by which "the full power of the twin blades (of State and Church) was to be wielded against malice or injustice, and for the good of all Christian people".

When Frederick learned of this letter and of the conduct of some of the Papal agents, he decided that, with Italy pacified and Cremona safely out of the way, he could safely return to Germany and deal with Folmar and Philip of Heinsberg in person. At the end of November 1186, he summoned his leading nobles and ecclesiastics to a diet in Gelnhausen, and had little difficulty in persuading them, even before the assembly began, that his action in Italy had been entirely legitimate, and that it was not he but the Pope who, by consecrating Folmar, had offended against both justice and tradition.

The bishops, convinced that the Pope had broken the Treaty of Venice, and was now provoking discord in Germany, unhesitatingly took the emperor's side. Wichmann, Archbishop of Magdeburg, on whose support Urban had counted, led the clergy in condemnation of the Holy See, and persuaded them to make their position clear in a strongly worded reply. It accused the Pope of "malice towards the emperor", of intriguing with Milan and Cremona, and of violating an ancient tradition when he had consecrated a German bishop of Trèves "before he had received the regalia from the imperial sceptre". The Pope was asked to bethink himself before it was too late, and to work for peace between the empire and the Church. He was reminded that the bishops were obliged "to preserve and maintain the rights and honour of the Empire by the oath they had sworn to the Emperor and his Illustrious Son, the August King of the Romans". As in 1159, the German clergy once again demonstrated that they had not the slightest intention of deserting their sovereign, who, moreover, had since grown considerably in stature and authority.

There was only one cloud in the sky: Philip of Heinsberg, Archbishop of Cologne, had not come to Gelnhausen, and had not concealed his continued support for Urban III. The Pope himself, replying to the German bishops on 19 February 1187, glossed over the entire German problem and the case of Folmar in particular, and simply insisted that, by refusing to restore church property in Italy, Frederick had offended against "peace and concord between the Church and the Empire". In other words, the Pope refused to retract.

Frederick was deeply incensed, but felt that he must deal first of all with the Archbishop of Cologne, who presented a challenge to his imperial authority far nearer home. Philip had sought to increase his estates in the Lower Rhineland at the expense of the crown; he had encouraged the growth of Cologne at the expense of the royal cities, and he had also interfered elsewhere, especially in Lower Lorraine. Worst of all, he was working in league with Frederick's enemies Folmar, the Duke of Brabant, Louis III, the Landgrave of Thuringia, and Count Adolf of Holstein, who resented Frederick's support of

Bernard of Anhalt; Philip had even made approaches to Henry the Lion, returned from exile in 1185, and to the King of Denmark, who disputed German sovereignty over the Pomeranian coast. At Easter 1187, Philip was brazen enough to preside in Cologne over a large meeting of his allies, who attended with armed supporters.

On 29 November 1186, Frederick had promulgated new peace enactments at the Diet of Nuremberg, and then, at the head of a small army, had crossed into Lorraine, intent on quelling any opposition that might arise over the succession to the County of Namur, which had fallen vacant. In February, Folmar, installed in Metz, had summoned a synod in Mouzon, where he excommunicated the bishops of Toul and Verdun for refusing to recognize him as Bishop of Trèves. On Frederick's approach, he fled to Reims to seek the protection of Count Henry of Champagne. The emperor immediately lodged a protest with Philip Augustus, King of France, who promised to keep an eye on the Count, whereupon Frederick turned eastward towards the diocese of Cologne.

Upon hearing this, Philip of Heinsberg cut the bridge over the Moselle which the royal army had to cross, and prepared to defend his city. In August, Frederick summoned his princes to Worms, accused the archbishop of *lèse-majesté*, and ordered him to appear before a diet to be held in Strasbourg at Christmas. This caused a wholesale defection from Philip's camp, his allies recalling the trial and downfall of Henry the Lion. Frederick, triumphant, now informed the Pope that he was anxious to arrange a new meeting, and that he was sending an ambassador to Verona. The Pope, however, was unwilling to receive the envoy and immediately left for Venice, where he intended to excommunicate Frederick, thus making their breach final and public. But death overtook him on the way—he died at Ferrara on 24 October 1187.

There was then a moderate party in the Sacred College which, although it had approved of Urban's initial stand and his determination to resist Frederick in Italy, had never been happy about his dealings with Folmar and Philip of Heinsberg. They now thought that a settlement ought to be reached, the more so as they were anxious to speed a new Crusade on its way, and accordingly obtained the (unanimous) election of the aged Albert of Morra, a former professor of law at Bologna. Albert had been made a cardinal by Hadrian IV, and Chancellor of the Roman Church by Alexander III, whose friend and confidant he had been in 1175–81.

The new pontiff took the name of Gregory VIII and, immediately after his election, informed Frederick that it was not the business of the Pope or his cardinals "to take up arms and give battle, but to serve God by prayers and good works".* As a further earnest of his intention he wrote a letter in similar vein to Henry VI, whom he addressed as "elected emperor of the Romans". At the same time, he quashed Folmar's sentence against the Bishops of Toul and Verdun.

Then, on 17 December, Gregory died suddenly at Pisa, on his way to a meeting with Frederick in Rome. Luckily for the emperor, the cardinals now chose Paul Scolari, Bishop of Palestrina, who took the name of Clement III, immediately launched a solemn appeal for a crusade, and asked Henry VI to escort him into Rome. Peace had come at last.

All that time, Frederick had never wavered in his resolve to restore peace and order to Germany. In December 1187 (some historians believe it may have been in July) he met Philip Augustus on the banks of the Meuse, between Ivois and Mouzon. Here the two kings renewed their bonds of friendship, and sealed their old alliance against the Welfs and Plantagenets. Philip undertook to evict Folmar from Reims, while Frederick promised Namur to Philip's father-in-law, Baldwin, Count of Hainault, thus overriding the claims of Henry of Champagne. Next year this promise was ratified at the diet of Erfurt, where Frederick not only confirmed Baldwin in the

---

* C. E. Perrin, *L'Allemagne, L'Italie et la Papauté de 1125 à 1250* (n.d.), p. 73.

succession, but raised Namur into a margravate, thus exalting Baldwin to the rank of an imperial prince.

In February 1188, Clement III reached Rome with a strong escort, commanded by Henry VI in person, and at once proved his determination to come to terms with the emperor. Agreement in principle was reached at the beginning of spring, and an official treaty drafted a few months later.

Meanwhile, Philip of Heinsberg had made his submission at the Diet of Mainz, the emperor granting him a free pardon. This act of generosity was not dictated by reasons of political expediency—Frederick had no need of that now—but was meant to serve as a public token of Christian forgiveness, for, at this "Diet of Christ", as it became known, Frederick left the throne vacant for the Saviour—he himself had already taken the cross, but had waited for complete victory before making his decision known.

And, indeed, by the end of March 1188, thanks to his firmness and diplomacy, Frederick had defeated his enemies on every front. At home, all resistance had come to an end, and in Italy there was now no city or noble who could have challenged the emperor's might. Henry VI was king of Germany and Italy, and the new Pope was a loyal ally—in short, Frederick had reached most of the goals he had set himself on his coronation in 1152.

CHAPTER THIRTEEN

The Tragic Apotheosis 1188 - 1190

FREDERICK BARBAROSSA'S announcement of his decision at the Diet of Christ revived old hopes throughout the West. For many years, the Holy See had been putting strong pressure on Capetian France and Plantagenet England, to come to the aid of Jerusalem, and, after the Treaty of Venice, Alexander III had hinted that Frederick might lead a new Crusade—a vague invitation that Lucius III had repeated officially. Finally, at Verona, when the Patriarch of Jerusalem and the masters of both the military orders issued a similar appeal, Frederick had promised to heed it.

But, deeply stirred though he was by the prospect of this glorious enterprise, he was prudent enough to defer his departure until the Holy See had shown its good faith.

When he eventually took up the cross, the situation in the Holy Land was very grave indeed. After the fiasco of the expedition led by Conrad III and Louis VII in 1148, the Latin States in the East (the Kingdom of Jerusalem, the Principality of Antioch and the County of Tripoli) were thrown into a state of turmoil, which their energetic king, Amaury (died 1174) could do little to stem. Rivalry between the various clans, the civil rulers and the heads of the religious and military orders, threatened to paralyse law and order, and there was an even greater threat from without. Unable to rely upon Byzantium for support, the Franks, as they were known, were left to bear the brunt of the onslaught by Islam, grown much bolder under Turkish rule. To the east, the Sultan Nūr-ed-Dīn was master of Mosul, Aleppo, Hamah, Homs and Damascus,

holding all the western provinces of the caliphate of Bagdad
In Egypt, to the south, the Vizier Sālah-ed-Dīn Yusaf ibn
Ayub, known as Saladin, had, in 1171, refused to appoint a
successor to the Fatimite Caliph of Cairo, recently deceased,
and attaching his country to the Abassid Caliphate, had brought
it effectively under Turkish rule. It was at this point that
Amaury had asked Henry the Lion to lead a crusade, which had
greatly encouraged the Franks but had done little to stem the
tide of Islam—indeed, upon the death of Nūr-ed-Dīn in 1174,
Saladin laid claim to his former master's lands. The Franks now
found themselves completely encircled and, to make things
worse, Amaury died, leaving his strife-torn kingdom to his
son, Baldwin IV, a mere boy, and a leper to boot.

For some years Saladin was kept busy fighting opposition
in Nūr-ed-Dīn's former possessions, seizing the County of
Edessa (to the north-east of Syria); western Antioch as far as
the Orontes, including the powerful fortresses of Archas,
whence he threatened Tripoli; and Baniyas, which overlooked
the Jordan and Tyre. For some time to come he was content
with minor raids upon the Franks—in 1179 on Tyre; in 1182
on Nazareth and Tiberias; and in 1183–4 on northern
Samaria and south-eastern Galilee. But in the spring of 1187,
taking advantage of the dissension caused by the death of
Baldwin IV in 1185 and of his nephew Baldwin V one year
later, and also of the folly of the Grand Master of the Templars,
he committed his forces to a full-scale attack upon Palestine.

The decisive battle was fought on the Hattin plain north-
west of Tiberias, and led to the virtual destruction of the
Kingdom of Jerusalem—all the Frankish chiefs were taken
prisoner. On 10 July, Acre capitulated, and Nazareth, Caesarea,
Nablus, Sidon, and Beirut followed suit soon afterwards. In
September, Turkish troops, advancing from the south, took
Ascalon, Ramlah, Gaza and Hebron. By the 17th, Saladin was
before the gates of Jerusalem, which fell to him on 2 October.
During the next few weeks, he concentrated his attack upon

Germany in about 1190

1. Duchy of Saxony
2. Duchy of Swabia
3. Duchy of Bavaria
4. Duchy of Upper Lorraine
5. Duchy of Austria
6. Duchy of Styria
7. Duchy of Carinthia
8. Kingdom of Bohemia
9. Duchy of Moravia

10. Duchy of Westphalia
11. Lower Lorraine and Duchy of Brabant
12. March of Brandenburg
13. March of Lusatia
14. March of Misnia
15. County of Holstein
16. Landgraviate of Thuringia
17. Franconia (several counties)

the County of Tripoli and the Principality of Antioch, and by the time Frederick took up the cross in the spring of 1188, only the cities of Tyre, Tripoli and Antioch still held out against the Islamic onslaught.

News of the fall of Jerusalem stunned the entire West. The Pope immediately put fresh pressure on Philip Augustus and Henry II Plantagenet to patch up their quarrel and to lead a joint crusade, but his efforts were cut short by the death of the English king on 6 July 1189. Hence he more than welcomed Frederick's earlier decision to come to the rescue of Jerusalem.

Frederick was swayed by the same deep religious conviction that had led him to accompany his uncle Conrad to the Holy Land in 1147; his aim now and then was to liberate the holy places in which Christ had lived and died. And so he took up the cross unflinchingly, as one ordained by God to serve the faith and to bring to successful conclusion a glorious task that would add to the lustre of church and empire alike. This is precisely what Arnold of Lübeck, the chronicler, meant when he wrote of the Crusaders: "Their leader and guide Prince Frederick, Emperor of the Romans, threw his powerful army into battle against the enemies of Christ's Cross not only for the greater honour of the Empire, but also for the glory of God". And this is what L. Alphandéry, one of the most intelligent and sensitive historians of the Crusades had to say: "By the grace of God, the might of the empire assumed a religious aura in its struggle with the Infidel. After the apocalyptic appeals of the people; after all the sovereigns and would-be leaders had been defeated, there came at last the imperial Messiah, in an atmosphere of exaltation slightly tinged with German hallucinations."

His unworldly aura notwithstanding, Frederick did not relax his grip on his more mundane concerns: even while he was calling upon his knights to join the Crusade and pardoning various princes who had offended against him—among them the Archbishop of Cologne, the Bishop of Utrecht, and the

Count of Guelders—he kept pressing Clement III to seal their friendship with a clear-cut document.

The pontiff, however, had his hands full with other matters. Back in Rome, his first task was to reach agreement with the commune, with whom he concluded a treaty on 21 May 1188. By it he promised to respect all communal institutions and to pay the salaries of all senators and city officials. At the same time he affirmed his sovereignty over the city, and reclaimed all his regalia. And then he, too, became engrossed in preparations for the Crusade, stepping up his efforts of mediation between France and England and between Pisa and Genoa, whose fleet he badly needed. All this quite naturally took precedence over the settlement Frederick sought, which, incidentally, explained why the emperor, too, kept dragging his feet over his departure.

At all events, on 8 February 1189, matters were speeded up when, following a proposal by Frederick, the dispute concerning the archbishopric of Trèves was settled: Clement III deposed Folmar, while the emperor persuaded Rudolf of Wied to stand down. Then the electors nominated John, the imperial chancellor, who was immediately invested by Frederick, to the satisfaction of all. This settlement paved the way for the more crucial negotiations at which Frederick was represented, first by Henry VI and his counsellors, and later by the Bishops of Würzburg and Bamberg and the Abbot of Herfeld, and the Pope by the Cardinals Jordan and Peter. Their deliberations culminated in the Treaty of Strasbourg, signed on 3 April, by Henry VI who had returned from Italy to run the German kingdom during his father's absence, and whom the Pope now agreed to crown emperor, in Frederick's lifetime. In return, Frederick recognized the Pope's sovereignty over the Papal State with a reservation of imperial rights (*salvo iure imperii tam de proprietate quam de possessione*), and evacuated Orvieto, Orta, Narni, Tusculum, Terracina, Tivoli and other cities and estates he had seized. Moreover, he annulled the oath of fealty all these cities, together with Viterbo, the Romagna and the Compagna, had sworn to him. Nothing at all was said in the treaty about the disputed territories in Central Italy (including the Matildine estates) which the empire continued to hold, in fact if not by right.

Clearly, therefore, Frederick had struck the best possible bargain, taking full advantage of the fact that, in the interests of the Crusade, Clement III was unable to resist his claims. Satisfied at last, he sent a message of felicitation to the Church on 10 April, and Henry VI did likewise a week later.

Even during his negotiations with the Holy See, Frederick was busily settling affairs at home; in particular, he made sure that Henry the Lion would not exploit his absence to work up some new intrigue. Henry had been greatly encouraged by the recent rebellion of the Archbishop of Cologne and, worse still, was on cordial terms with the new Archbishop of Bremen, who had a private grudge against Bernard of Anhalt, the chief beneficiary of the Lion's trial and fall in 1180. To cope with this new threat, Frederick, at a diet in Goslar, in August 1188, offered Henry the choice between three proposals: he must either declare himself content with a partial restitution of his confiscated lands, or he must accompany the crusaders at the emperor's expense; or, finally, he must leave Germany for a further three years. The Lion could not accept the first of these proposals, which would have meant renouncing most of his former possessions and jeopardizing his heritage, nor could he accept the second, which meant placing himself under Frederick's command—and so, in April 1189, he left once more on the familiar road to England.

At the Diet of Goslar, the monarch "with the agreement of his princes" also adopted a constitution that guaranteed the church's ancient right of asylum and defined the prerogatives of church advocates in the matter of ecclesiastical property. Shortly afterwards, in December, he repeated his decree that no bishop must grant in fee any of the offices delegated him by the crown, thus setting his face firmly against feudal abuses.

Finally, he tried to ensure sound government during his absence in a document that may be called his last will and testament. Henry VI, King of the Romans, of Germany and of Italy, was entrusted with the administration of the empire, while his elder brother, Frederick, who had become Duke of Swabia on the death of Frederick IV (the son of Conrad III and a cousin of Barbarossa) was invited to join the crusade. The Hohenstaufen estates in Swabia (ancestral possessions and the former property of Welf VI) and Alsace and, to a lesser extent, in Franconia, Western Bavaria, Lorraine and, after 1180, in Thuringia, Saxony and Lusatia, were to be divided between Frederick's four older sons—the fifth, destined for the church, was made Provost of the Cathedral of Aix-la-Chapelle. Henry VI received the largest portion, Frederick of Swabia was granted all fiefs in his duchy together with the county of Pfullendorf, and, on the death of Welf VI, all the allods Welf had sold to Barbarossa. The third son inherited Beatrix's dowry, i.e. the County of Burgundy; while the fourth, Conrad, was given the County of Rothenburg and a special domain in Franconia for his fiancée, Berengaria of Castille, the daughter of King Alphonso VIII.

When all this had been settled during the summer of 1188, Frederick turned his entire attention to the crusade—hence it was Henry VI who concluded the negotiations with the Holy See and signed the Treaty of Strasbourg.

Frederick decided to take the hazardous overland route to Syria—he lacked a fleet of his own, nor had he the resources to pay for the services of Genoa, which had, in any case, been bespoken by France and England. It was also by no means certain that the ports of the Holy Land would not have fallen to Saladin by the time the crusaders arrived. Moreover, with the experience he had gained in 1147-8, he hoped to avoid the worst pitfalls of the long march.

He took care to foster cordial diplomatic relations with all the countries he would cross, sending extremely courteous messages to the King of Hungary, the Chieftain of Serbia, the Byzantine emperor Isaac Angelus, and the Sultan of the Islamic principality of Iconium, who was hostile to Saladin. He also took stern measures to ensure discipline within his ranks, lest there was a repetition of the disorders that had so badly hampered the Second Crusade. Only men capable of equipping themselves at their own expense and of supporting themselves for two years were allowed to take the cross, with the result that Frederick's host consisted chiefly of knights from the upper and middle ranks of the nobility. Finally, he gave warning to all sutlers that their dealings would be closely controlled.

Then he summoned his crusaders to Ratisbon. He intended to make straight for the Byzantine empire, Isaac Angelus having agreed to aid and provision the expedition, on condition that no military action was taken or tolerated against any Greek territories. From Byzantium, the crusaders drawn up in battle order so as to guard against surprise attacks by the enemy, would make for the tiny Christian kingdom of Armenia, at the very gates of Syria. Finally they would invade all the lands occupied by Saladin, and take them by storm.

In answer to Frederick's call, some twenty thousand men converged on Ratisbon in May 1189. (Several twelfth-century chroniclers, overwhelmed by such vast numbers, and moreover in no way disinclined to magnify the might of the host, have wrongly put the figure at 100,000.) It was certainly the greatest army Frederick had ever commanded, and one that was made up of seasoned warriors, loyal to their great leader and the sixty-odd princes and nobles who proposed to accompany him.

On 11 May, battalion after battalion, each made up of 500 men, moved out of Ratisbon in great military splendour. The first stage of the journey passed without untoward incident —King Bela of Hungary kept his promise and, indeed, proved so helpful to the Germans that Frederick proposed to offer his son Frederick in marriage to Bela's daughter. In Serbia, too, Frederick was received in friendship—the chieftain even offered to place his principality under imperial rule. However, as soon as the crusaders had passed beyond Niš (Naissus) and were about to descend into the Morava valley, they were attacked by bands of Serbs and Bulgars who blocked their way and forced Frederick to take a roundabout route. But though supplies grew scarce and sickness struck down a number of his knights, the host managed to reach Byzantium at the beginning of August, and the success of the expedition seemed assured.

But once in Byzantium, the crusaders were faced with new, and far more serious dangers—Isaac Angelus had never had the least intention of honouring his promise to Frederick. To begin with he remembered the outrageous behaviour of the German soldiery in 1147, and he was also afraid that Barbarossa, with his dreams of a universal empire, might have private designs on Byzantium. Last but not least, Isaac had been trying to seize the sultanate of Iconium, and to that end had formed an alliance with Saladin, who had hinted that he would respect Isaac's claim to the Holy Places if the Greeks did not engage in any hostilities against him. Unbeknown to Isaac, Saladin had also entered into negotiations with Iconium, pointing out that he was their only real ally against both Western and Eastern infidels.

Barbarossa was, perhaps, not greatly surprised by Isaac's attitude, for he must have known that the Greeks had little love for his people. But since it had never been his plan to conquer Byzantium—least of all now that all his energies were bent on reaching the Holy Land—he decided that he would not be disturbed by Isaac's intrigues and that he would press straight on to the Holy Land.

On 16 August, he ordered his troops to take Trajan's pass by assault, and eight days later he entered Philippopolis, captured several nearby fortresses and seized vast stocks of provisions. Next day envoys arrived from Isaac, who informed the emperor that, if he wanted to continue unmolested, he must provide hostages for his good conduct and guarantee Isaac a share in all his future conquests. Frederick sent a conciliatory reply, but when he heard that Isaac had thrown the imperial ambassadors into prison, he ordered his army, now recovered from the worst of their earlier hardships, to march on Constantinople, and to destroy everything in their path. In his first flush of anger, he even thought of annexing the Greek empire, instructing Henry VI, on 16 November, to assemble a fleet and to get the Pope's sanction for a crusade against the Greeks. But at the end of October, when the crusaders took Hadrianople, Isaac, dreading an attack on his capital, decided to sue for peace and on 21 January 1190, signed a treaty with the emperor. In it, he promised that if the crusaders would by-pass Constantinople and proceed via Gallipoli, he would provide the extra provisions and boats to cross the Dardanelles. The German army then rested for two months, and, towards the end of March, crossed into Asia Minor.

Meanwhile bad news kept reaching Frederick from the West. Upon the death of William II of Sicily on 18 November 1189, Henry VI and Constance had found it extremely difficult to assert their claim to the throne against Tancred, Count of Lecce, the bastard son of Roger II, who enjoyed the support of the Norman nobility. For a moment, Frederick may have been tempted to go to his son's rescue, but after brief reflection he must have decided that, since Germany and Northern Italy were at peace, the Sicilian problem, no less than the difficulties young Otto was experiencing in Burgundy, could be safely ignored until after the successful conclusion of the Crusade.

He accordingly decided to make straight for his next objectives—Iconium and Armenia—but once again ran into unexpected difficulties: Saladin had helped to oust the pro-German sultan of Iconium with his son, who now refused to honour his father's promise of provisions. It was only after great hardships and severe losses, that Frederick finally reached

Iconium on 18 May, taking it by storm and forcing the new sultan to guarantee him safe passage and to provide the promised supplies. Then the Crusaders proceeded to tiny Armenia, where they were well received.

It was here that the great emperor met his tragic end on 10 June 1190: while trying to cross the river Salef on his way to Seleucia, his horse shied and Frederick disappeared at once beneath the swift waters. His body was drawn lifeless from the river.

Frederick's sudden death cast a deep shadow over the crusaders. Many of his princes returned home, and there might easily have been a rout had Frederick of Swabia not restored order and discipline, before leading the army on to Antioch. Soon afterwards, however, an epidemic carried off many of the knights, among them young Frederick himself, and in the end the remnant of the great German expedition went to swell the ranks of the Anglo-French contingents before St. John of Acre. What was intended to be the glorious apotheosis of empire, had come to a sad conclusion.

But Barbarossa's own story did not end there. He had fallen upon the road to Jerusalem, at the height of his glory, after pledging his empire to the cause of Christianity. He had died, it could be said, for Christ. No wonder then that this great ruler, who had so wondrously restored the empire to all its former honour and glory, retained a unique and permanent place in the hearts of his people.

In the centuries to come, his memory became suffused with legend, and this contributed in no small measure to the myth of the universal emperor that was built on the ventures and struggles of his grandson Frederick II.

Our hero's life became a basic theme of German literature and mythology—even in his own lifetime an anonymous bard presented the Abbot of Tegernsee with a long poem entitled *Ludus de Antichristo*. This poem, written in about 1160, to

Frederick's glory, proclaimed that, on Judgment Day, when all good men would assemble against Antichrist, their extraordinary gathering would be led by another German emperor, another Frederick. In later years, the Minnesänger, who lived at the Hohenstaufen court, loudly sang the praises of Barbarossa and his chivalrous companions. Their glorious deeds were listed in the poems of Heinrich von Waldeck, Walter von der Vogelweide, Frederick von Hausen, who died during the Crusade, and a little later by Wolfram von Eschenbach. It was at about the same time that the Ring of the Nibelungs was written—in about 1160–70, an anonymous Austrian poet penned the second part, the epic *Das Ende des Nibelungen*, and in 1200–10 another Austrian combined this poem with two ancient Teutonic sagas and gave it its final form, brilliantly adapted to the taste of courtly society. It, too, exalted Germany and her ancient myths; it showed the Germanic hero, complete with every martial virtue, accepting and accomplishing his destiny, but not allowing himself to be a blind instrument of fate, as he strives with all his might to wrest the *Horst*, that treasured symbol of power and domination, from the enemy. "The Rhine will guard the gold of the warriors," Gunther says, "its rapids will preserve the treasure of the Nibelungs."

Behind all this lay pride in Barbarossa's accomplishments and exaltation of a life at once glorious and tragic. And yet the Frederick legend, woven round him even in his lifetime, fell into desuetude during the thirteenth century, when Barbarossa's own glory was overshadowed by the memory of Frederick II. It was out of the mortal and spiritual confusion that followed the latter's death in 1250 that there grew up "the vision of that ultimate emperor, who was persecutor and defender of Christianity in one".* This vision was born in Italy, the scene of a bitter struggle between the Guelphs and the Ghibellines. Their struggle culminated in the bloody battle of Monteaperti

R. Folz, *L'idée d'Empire en Occident au 5ème et au 14ème siècle* (Paris, 1953), p. 178.

in 1260, the very year that also saw the rise of the Flagellant sect in Perugia and the death of Conradin, the last of the Hohenstaufen. It was then that the legend arose that Barbarossa lived on in the fires of Etna, and also the myth that a Hohenstaufen would rise up to force the Pope to live a life of Christian humility and poverty.

Prophecies continued into the fifteenth and sixteenth centuries, when there also appeared the rival legend that a descendant of Charlemagne would free the church of all lay domination, not least by the German emperors. This was countered, in about 1420, by a famous prophecy, attributed to Gamalion, that "the Germans would elect an emperor from *Almania Alta*, that is from the upper Rhine valley, who would summon a lay council at Aix and install a patriarch in Mainz and himself be crowned pope; he would meet the Roman pontiff in combat and put him to death, whereupon Rome would cede her place as capital of Christianity to Mainz".*

Clinging to this legend, the Germans hoped for a brief period that the Emperor Sigismund (1361–1437), having put an end to the Great Schism by setting aside all three contending popes, might prove to be the emperor-saviour; next they placed their hopes in Frederick III of Habsburg, only to be cruelly disappointed again. And then, returning to the old thirteenth-century myth, which they now fused with ballads of an earlier period, they set their hopes on "an emperor both universal and German, who would bestow on his country all the blessings of the golden age".† His first name would be Frederick and he would come out from his mountains. But wounded national pride now prevented them from settling once more on Frederick II, who was more Italian than German. And thus the dream, the myth and the legend all united in the person of Barbarossa, the great *German* sovereign, who had imposed the *German* will on Italy and the Pope, and who had

* *Ibid.*, p. 183.
† *Ibid.* p. 183.

died, on the road to Jerusalem, at the head of a *German* crusade.

"He is not dead," one of the legends tell us, "but, seated between six knights at a table of stone, he sleeps in the Thuringian mountains, until the day when, at last, he will deliver Germany from slavery and make her leader of the whole world."

All this helps to explain the genesis and success, in 1520, of Martin Luther's *Appeal to the Christian Nobility of the German Nation for the Restoration of Christian Society*.

For a long time, the legend of Frederick Barbarossa, the emperor who sleeps an enchanted sleep but will surely arise as the saviour of Germany and, through her, with her, and in her, of the whole of Christianity, was to be a constant source of inspiration to his nation. Later, it was played down and even derided as unbefitting to a rational and cosmopolitan age, only to return again in the wake of nineteenth-century romanticism, with its love of exalted epics and all things medieval. And with the resurgence of German nationalism, *der alte Barbarossa*, as Friedrich-Johann Rückert (died 1866) called him, became enshrined in the hearts and collective memory of the people: a giant among giants and, as a typical German, greater even than Charlemagne. And so myth endowed the emperor, whose tragic death in a foreign river added a poignant note to a life of great achievement, with the greater glory that had eluded him in his lifetime. This is precisely what Victor Hugo, after his journey down the Rhine, tried to convey in *Les Burgraves*.

History, representing the intelligence of the ages, and legend, which is their poetry, were here united in one man, a man who during the thirty-eight years of his reign clung firmly and unflinchingly to the dreams of his youth.

Conclusion

FOR a real assessment of the life of Frederick Barbarossa we must leave the realms of legend and myth, and return to history.

At Barbarossa's coronation in 1152, his empire was weak, his princes divided, and Germany under the thumb of the Holy See. In Italy, the authority of the empire was fast vanishing and the imperial principle had ceased to govern the political organization of society. But by the time Frederick had done, the power of the monarchy was fully restored in Germany, the Welfs were on the run and most princes anxious to show their loyalty to the crown. In Italy, cities and nobles alike had come to accept the authority of Frederick's agents and officials; the Pope's sphere of influence and authority had been greatly reduced and his property rights circumscribed, and Sicily was ruled by Frederick's son Henry VI.

In short, within less than forty years, the empire had recovered "all its splendour"; never before had its "honour" shone so brightly; never before had it been so venerated and feared. No emperor, since Charlemagne and Otto the Great, had been so brilliantly successful, none so admired and revered. For although Otto had consolidated the power of the crown and of his own House in Germany, he had been quite unable to make his presence felt in Italy. Charlemagne's achievements, too, although on a grander scale, had proved far more transitory than Barbarossa's—his sons, unlike Frederick's, were unfit to step into their father's shoes.

But then Barbarossa, unlike his glorious predecessor, did not seek control of the entire West. Thus, on the highest level,

Charlemagne may, perhaps, be said to have been the greater of the two, one who by spreading and deepening the Christian faith, by lending new vigour to the concept of the state, and by resurrecting the Roman Empire, had helped to found those very institutions which, although changed by time, still form the basis of Western civilization. For all that, his work was dwarfed by the very size of the stage on which it was set— Charlemagne lacked a clear "geographical perspective" of the great area over which he ruled.

Barbarossa, by contrast, had a clear vision of his empire. His realism was the fundamental trait of his genius, though at times, in Lombardy for example, he was slow to face up to the facts. Realism explains his increasing caution towards Southern Italy, the relinquishment of all direct designs on the Kingdom of Sicily, his disinterest in the east, and his early tolerance of, and later sternness to, Henry the Lion. The area to which he restricted his activities was one he knew well—it extended in the north to just beyond the Lahn; in the east to Lusatia and Austria; in the west it took in the Moselle valley, modern Lorraine, Alsace and Franche-Comté, and in the south it ran as far as the southern borders of the Duchy of Spoleto and the March, that is to the confines of Rome. He was able to leave his mark on all these parts, and to bind them closely to the empire. And it is precisely because Charlemagne overstepped these narrow limits that Barbarossa must be considered the most illustrious ruler to have come out of medieval Germany.

But despite all his successes and the glory that attached to his name, Barbarossa's reign fell far short of perfection. Thus more than any other German he fostered the feudalization of social and political life, by greatly increasing the power of the princes. Possibly he could see no alternative, perhaps none even existed. But maintaining the authority of the crown by relying on the support of increasingly powerful princes called for enormous personal exertion, indefatigable energy, and, above all, for peace, both at home and abroad. Only by renouncing his major ambitions in Italy could Frederick have hoped to prevent abuses at home. As it was, the nobility raised ever-new territorial demands, and insisted that Barbarossa apply his own principle of obligatory reinfeoffment; nor had the breach between the Welfs and the Hohenstaufen ever been completely healed. And, in the game of feudal power politics, local interests tended quite naturally to take precedence over the good of the nation.

In Italy, though Barbarossa, after more than twenty years of fighting, eventually came to terms with the urban phenomenon, the Lombard cities continued to oppose his plans of empire. Moreover, he realized that if he pursued his "conservative" policy in Central Italy, the Tuscans, at least, would rise up against him just as the Lombards had done in 1167. And so Frederick was increasingly forced to reduce his sovereign claims, to refrain from running every city and county with the help of his own men or of loyal supporters—from 1183 onwards, he readily granted rights and privileges to anyone who would help him. From Head of State, the emperor had shrunk to the head of a party: the leader of the Ghibellines, who opposed the Guelphs out of personal conviction no less than for private advantage. German might thus introduced a deep and lasting split into Italy.

When all is said and done, therefore, we are left with Barbarossa's glory and undeniable qualities, with the unflinching resolve with which he tackled his life's work, but also with his profound failure to grasp certain essentials, and a number of decisions that, however skilful and realistic they may have appeared to be at the time, in the long run helped to blight his dreams of empire. On balance, Frederick's was no mean achievement; a memorial great enough for any man— in the rough and tumble of human history there is no one who is entirely without flaw, no one who is without error. This truism, which helps us to set limits upon the actions of all individuals, is no mere platitude in Barbarossa's case. For here we find an intelligent, energetic and respected leader grappling with overpowering political, social and psychological situations—among them the urban phenomenon in Italy and the feudal phenomenon in Germany. His very greatness was that he tried to come to terms with them, perhaps against his will; that he tried not to swim against the stream, while yet making resolutely for the shore he had set out to reach.

Frederick Barbarossa was a great man in his day, but one whose ambitions were strictly circumscribed by the limitations of his age.

Bibliography

1. *Narrative sources*

Annales Marbacenses, ed. Hermann Bloch: MG. SS. rer. Germ. in us. schol., Hanover-Leipzig, 1908.

Arnold von Lübeck: *Chronica Slavorum*, ed. Johann Martin Lappenberg: MG. SS. XXI (1869) pp. 101-250 and sep. SS. rer. Germ. in us. schol., Hanover, 1868 (New ed., 1930).

Boso: *Vita Alexandri III*, in: Liber Pontificalis, ed. Louis Duchesne, Vol. II (Paris, 1955) pp. 397-446.

Burchard von Ursperg: *Chronicon*, ed. Oswald Holder-Egger and Bernhard v. Simson: MG. SS. rer. Germ. in us. schol., Hanover-Leipzig, 1916.

Carmen de gestis Frederici I imperatoris in Lombardia, ed. Irene Schmale-Ott: MG. SS. rer. Germ. in us. schol., Hanover, 1965.

Chronica regia Coloniensis: ed. George Waitz: MG. SS. rer. Germ. in us. schol., Hanover, 1880.

Gesta Frederici I imperatoris in Lombardia auctore cive Mediolanensi, ed. Oswald Holder-Egger: MG. SS. rer. Germ. in us. schol., Hanover, 1892.

Gesta Treverorum, Cont. III., ed. Georg Waitz: MG. SS. XXIV (1879) pp. 380-9.

Gottfried von Viterbo: *Gesta Frederici I et Heinrici VI imperatorum metrice scripta*, ed. Georg Waitz: MG. SS. XXII (1872) pp. 306-34 and sep. MG. SS. rer. Germ. in us. schol., Hanover, 1872.

Helmold von Bosau: *Chronica Slavorum*, ed. Bernhard Schmeider: MG. SS. rer. Germ. in us. schol., Hanover, 1937. (Eng. trans. *Chronicle of the Slavs* trans. Tschan, F.J. 1935 Columbia University Press, N.Y.)

Historia Welforum, ed. Erich König in *Schwäbische Chroniken der Stauferzeit*, Vol. I, Stuttgart—Berlin, 1938.

Otto von Freising: *Chronica sive Historia de duabus civitatibus*, ed. Adolf Hofmeister: MG. SS. rer. Germ. in us. schol., Hanover, 1912. (Eng. trans. *Two Cities—A Chronicle of Universal History to the year 1146 A.D.* ed. Mierow, C.C. 1966 n.e. Octagon Press, U.S.A.).

Otto von Freising und Rahewin: *Gesta Frederici I imperatoris*, ed. Georg Waitz and Bernhard v. Simson: MG. SS. rer. Germ. in us. schol., Hanover, 1912. (Eng. trans. *Deeds of Frederick Barbarossa* trans. Mierow, C.C. 1966 n.e. Norton, U.S.A.).

Otto von Freising *Gesta Frederici* ed. Adolf Schmidt and Franz-Josef Schmale (Berlin 1965)

Otto and Acerbus Morena: *Historia Frederici I. Das Geschichtswerk des Otto Morena und seine Fortsetzer uber die Taten Friedrichs I in der Lombardei*, ed. Ferdinand Güterbock: MG. SS. rer. Germ. N. S. Vol. 7, Berlin, 1930 (New ed. 1964).

Otto von St. Blasien: *Chronica*, ed. Adolf Hofmeister; MG. SS. rer. Germ. in us. schol., Hanover-Leipzig, 1912.

Relatio de pace Veneta a. 1177, ed. Wilhelm Arndt: MG. SS. XIX (1866) pp. 461-3; ed. Ugo Balzani in Bull. Dell'Ist. Stor. Ital. 10 (1891) pp. 11-16.

Vincenz von Prag: *Annales*, ed. Wilhelm Wattenbach: MG. SS. XVII (1861) pp. 658-83.

Wibald von Stablo und Corvey: *Briefe*, ed. Philipp Jaffé in: *Monumenta Corbeiensia*, Berlin, 1864 (New. ed. Aalen, 1964) (Bibliotheca rerum Germanicarum, Vol, I) pp. 76-616.

Bibliography

2. Documents

Johann Friedrich Böhmer: *Acta Imperii Selecta. Urkunden deutscher Könige und Kaiser mit einem Anhange von Reichssachen.* Innsbruck, 1870 (New ed. Aalen, 1967), Sp. Nr. 93-167, 884-97.

Constitutiones et Acta publica (MG. Legum Sectio IV), Vol. I, ed. Ludwig Weiland (Hanover, 1893, New ed. 1963) Sp. Nr. 137-324, 403-10, 413-15, 455.

Julius Ficker: *Forschungen zur Reichs- und Rechtsgeschichte Italiens,* Vol. IV, Innsbruck, 1874 (New ed. Aalen, 1961), Sp. Nr. 122-78.

Cesare Manaresi: *Gli atti del Comune di Milano fino all'anno 1216.* Milan, 1919.

Karl Friedrich Stumpf-Brentano: *Die Reichskanzler vornehmlich des X., XI. und XII. Jahrhunderts. Nebst einem Beitrag zu den Regenten und zur Kritik der Kaiserurkunden dieser Zeit,* Vol. II; Chronologisches Verzeichnis der Kaiser-Urkunden. Innsbruck, 1865 (New ed. Aalen, 1964); Vol. III (In 5 sections): Acta imperii adhuc inedita. Innsbruck, 1865-82 (New ed. Aalen, 1964), Sp. Nr. 118-176.

Cesare Vignati: *Storia diplomatica della Lega Lombarda.* Milan, 1867 (New ed. with bibliogr. addendum by Raoul Manselli, Turin, 1966).

3. General Works

Appelt, Heinrich: *Die Kaiseridee Friedrich Barbarossas.* Vienna, 1967 (Österr. Akademie d. Wiss., philos.—histor.—Klasse, Sitzungsberichte, Vol. 252/4).

Böhm, Franz: *Das Bild Friedrich Barbarossas und seines Kaisertums in den ausländischen Quellen seiner Zeit.* Berlin, 1936. (New ed. Vaduz, 1965). (Historische Studien Ebering, Vol. 289).

Brühl, Carlrichard: *Fodrum, Gistum, Servitium regis. Studien zu den wirtschaftlichen Grundlagen des Königtums im Frankenreich und in den fränkischen Nachfolgestaaten Deutschland, Frankreich und Italien vom 6. bis zur Mitte des 14. Jahrhunderts.* 2 Vols. Cologne-Graz, 1968 (Kölner Historische Abhandlungen, Vol. 14), Sp. Vol. I S. 578ff.

Büttner, Heinrich: *Staufer und Zähringer im politischen Kräftespiel zwischen Bodensee und Genfersee während des 12. Jahrhunderts.* Zürich, 1961 (Mitteilungen der Antiquar. Gesellschaft in Zürich).

Fein, Hella: *Die staufischen Städtegründungen im Elsass.* Frankfurt, 1939.

Fichtenau, Heinrich: *Von der Mark zum Herzogtum. Grundlagen und Sinn des "Privilegium minus" für Österreich.* Munich, 1958 (Österreich Archiv).

Ficker, Julius: *Forschungen zur Reichs- und Rechtsgeschichte Italiens,* Vols. I-III, Innsbruck, 1868-72 (New ed. Aalen, 1961).

Ficker, Julius and Paul Puntschart: *Vom Reichsfürstenstand. Forschungen zur Geschichte der Reichsverfassung zunächst im XII. und XIII. Jahrhundert,* Vol. I, Innsbruck, 1861 (New ed. 1932); Vol. II/1: Innsbruck, 1911; Vol. II/2-3: Graz-Leipzig, 1921-3 (New ed. of entire work: Aalen, 1961).

Fliche, Augustin, Raymonde Foréville and Jean Rousset: *Du premier Concile du Latran à l'avènement d'Innocent III* (1123-1198), Vol. II, Paris, 1953 (Historie de l'Eglise, Vol. 9).

Fournier, Paul: *Le royaume d'Arles et de Vienne* (1138-1378). *Etude sur la formation territoriale de la France dans l'Est et dans le Sud-Est.* Paris, 1891.

Grundmann, Herbert: *Der Cappenberger Barbarossakopf und die Anfänge des Stiftes Cappenberg.* Cologne-Graz, 1959 (Münstersche Forschungen, Vol. 12).

Haller, Johannes: *Das Papsttum. Idee und Wirklichkeit,.* Vol. III: *Die Vollendung* (Darmstadt, 1962. First published in 1952) pp. 116ff.

Hampe, Karl: *Herrschergestalten des deutschen Mittelalters.* Sixth ed. amended by Hellmut Kämpf: Heidelberg, 1955, pp. 147-193-215 (*Friedrich I, Heinrich der Löwe*).

Bibliography

Hampe, Karl: *Das Hochmittelalter. Geschichte des Abendlandes von 900 bis 1250.* Fourth ed. Münster-Cologne, 1953 (New ed. Darmstadt, 1963) pp. 240-97.

Hampe, Karl: *Deutsche Kaisergeschichte in der Zeit der Salier und Staufer.* 11th ed. ed. by Friedrich Baethgen: Darmstadt, 1963, pp. 142-220.

Hauck, Albert: *Kirchengeschichte Deutschlands,* Vol. IV: Leipzig, 1913, 3 + 4 (many reprints) pp. 196ff.

Jordan, Edouard: *L'Allemagne et l'Italie aux XIIe et XIIIe siècles,* Paris, 1939 (Histoire générale, Histoire du Moyen-âge, Vol. IV/1).

Jordan, Karl: *Friedrich Barbarossa. Kaiser des christlichen Abendlandes.* Göttingen, 1959 (*Persönlichkeit und Geschichte,* Vol. 13).

Jordan, Karl: *Lothar III, und die frühe Stauferzeit,* in: Bruno Gebhardt: *Handbuch der deutschen Geschichte,* Vol. I: *Frühzeit und Mittelalter;* 8th ed. by Herbert Grundmann, Stuttgart, 1954 (several amended reprints) SS. 111-22.

Jordan R.: *Die Stellung des deutschen Episkopats im Kampfe um die Universalmacht unter Friedrich I. bis zum Frieden von Venedig 1177.* Würzburg, 1939 (Thesis).

Kauffmann, Heinz: *Die italienische Politik Kaiser Friedrichs I. nach dem Frieden von Constanz (1183-1189). Beiträge zur Geschichte der Reichspolitik und Reichsverwaltung der Staufer in Italien.* Greifswald, 1933 (Greifswalder Abhandlungen zur Geschichte des Mittelalters, Vol. 3).

Kienast, Walther: *Deutschland und Frankreich in der Kaiserzeit. Leipzig,* 1943.

Lamma, Paolo: *Comneni e Staufer. Ricerche sui rapporti fra Bisanzio e l'occidente nel secolo XII.* 2 Vols. Rome, 1955-7 (Instituto Storico Italiano per il Medio Evo, fasc. 14-18, 22-5).

Mariotte, Jean-Yves: *Le comté de Bourgogne sous les Hohenstaufen 1156-1208.* Paris, 1963 (Cahiers d'Etudes Comtoises, Vol. 4 (Annales Littéraires de l'Université de Besançon, Vol. 36).

Meyer, Hans: *Die Militärpolitik Friedrich Barbarossas im Zusammenhang mit seiner Italienpolitik.* Berlin, 1930 (New ed. Vaduz, 1965. (Historische Studien Ebering, Vol. 200).

Mitteis, Heinrich: *Der Staat des hohen Mittelalters.* Weimar, 1959 (many reprints) —253ff.

Otto, Eberhard: *Friedrich Barbarossa* in *Deutsche Könige und Kaiser,* Potsdam, 1940.

Pelzer, H.: *Friedrichs I von Hohenstaufen Politik gegenüber Dänemark Polen und Ungarn.* Thesis, Münster, 1906.

Rassow, Peter: *Honor imperii. Die neue Politik Friedrich Barbarossas.* Darmstadt, 1961.

Rassow, Peter: *Der Prinzgemahl. Ein Pactum Matrimoniale aus dem Jahre 1188.* Weimar, 1950 (Quellen und Studien zur Verfassungsgeschichte des Deutschen Reiches im Mittelalter und Neuzeit, Vol. VIII/1).

Rauch, Günter: *Die Bündnisse deutscher Herrscher mit Reichsangehörigen vom Regierungsantritt Friedrich Barbarossas.* Aalen, 1966 (Untersuchungen z. deutschen Staats- und Rechtsgeschichte, NF. Vol. 5) pp. 1-36.

Schmid, Karl: *Graf Rudolf von Pfullendorf und Kaiser Friedrich I. Freiburg,* 1954 (Forschungen zur oberrhein. Landesgesch:, Vol. 1).

Simonsfeld, Henry: *Jahrbücher des Deutschen Reiches unter Friedrich I.* Vol. 1: Leipzig, 1908 (Jahrbücher der Deutschen Geschichte).

Vollmer, Franz Xaver: *Reichs- und Territorialpolitik Kaiser Friedrichs I.* Thesis, Freiburg, 1951.

Index

N.B. Emperors, Popes and some Cardinals appear under their first names: other rulers and prelates under their territorial designations, unless otherwise indicated.

Acre, 48, 196, 205

Adelaide of Vohburg (F.B.'s first wife), marriage, 48; divorce, 58-9, 61

Agnes (daughter of Emperor Henry IV), marriages of, 41

Aix-la-Chapelle, F.B.'s coronation at, 46, 57; Diet of (1165), 118-20; inauguration of annual fairs at, 133-4; coronation of Henry VI at, 134

Aix-la-Chapelle, Philip of Hohenstaufen, Provost of, 201

Alba, 159; Benzo, Bishop of, 15

Albenga, 159

Albert the Bear, Margrave of Brandenburg 1136-70 (Duke of Saxony 1138-42), 22, 44, 106, 134, 135, 153, 154, 171

Albert of Morra see Gregory VIII

Albigensian heresy, 186

Alessandria (new city of), 137, 147, 148, 150, 151, 153, 155, 163, 178

Alexander the Great, 11

Alexander III, Pope 1159-81, election of, 94; excommunicates F.B., 96-7; goes to France, 102-3; enlists French support, 104-7, and secures allies in Germany, 108-9; beginnings of the struggle in North Italy and general improvement of position of, 109-13, 114, 115; F.B.'s continued opposition to, 116-17; returns to Italy but is driven by F.B. from Rome, 120-3; gives his support to Lombard rebels, 125 and again strengthens his position, 129, 132; becomes patron of Lombard League and enjoys their support, 137-46, 149, 150, 151, 152-6; finally comes to terms with F.B., 156-7; death of, 176-7; mentioned, 118, 175, 183, 185, 195

Alphandéry, Louis, quoted, 198

Alsace, 53, 131, 201, 210

Anacletus, anti-Pope 1130-8, 38, 94

Anagni, 92; Treaty of (1176), 156-8, 159, 160, 164, 177

Anastasius IV, Pope 1153-4, 64, 66

Ancona, 37, 70, 110, 121, 122, 140, 146, 147

Anhalt, Bernard III, Count of (Duke of Saxony 1180-1212), 171, 172, 192, 200

Annona, 168

Anselm of Dovaria, 149

Antioch, 195, 196, 198

Apulia, 38, 73, 75, 102, 110, 113, 153, 154

Aquila, Bishop of, 95

Aquileia, Ulrich, Patriarch of, 159, 188

Aragon, 97

Archipoeta, 98

Arles, 39; F.B.'s coronation at, 168; Archbishop of, 95

Armenia, 202, 204, 205

Arnold of Brescia, 36, 67, 68

Arnold of Lübeck, 198

Ascania, House of see Albert the Bear and Anhalt, Bernard III of:

Asti, 87, 136, 137, 147, 159, 168; Bishop of, 99, 161, 178

Augsburg, 25, 83, 121, 183; Bishop of (Hartwig of Lierheim), 132

Augustus, Emperor, 15

Austria, 21, 41-2, 52, 70, 114, 171, 173, 210

Dukes and Margraves of (House of Babenberg):—

Agnes, Margravine of, 41

Conrad see Salzburg, Archbishop of

Gertrude, Margravine of, 42; see also Bavaria

Henry II (Jasomirgott) Margrave (1141), Duke (1156)—also Duke of Bavaria 1141-54—died 1171, 42, 48, 60, 65, 70

Leopold III, Margrave of 1102-36, 41

Leopold IV, Margrave of 1136-41 (also Duke of Bavaria 1139), 41-2

Otto *see* Freising, Bishop of

Theodora (Comnena), Duchess of, 10

Babenberg, House of *see* Austria

Ballenstädt, Albert of *see* Albert the Bear

Bamberg, 41, 76, 131; Bishops of (Eberhard), 141, 143, 175, 199; Diet of (1168), 134

Barcelona, Counts of, 39; Raymond Berengar IV, 103, 104

Basle, 25; Bishop of, 157

Bavaria,
Dukes and Duchesses of:—
Gertrude, 42 *see also* Austria
Henry Jasomargott 1141-54 *see* Austria
Henry the Lion 1154-80 (also Duke of Saxony 1142-80) *see* Henry the Lion
Henry the Proud 1126-38 (also Duke of Saxony 1136-8), 42, 45, 46
Leopold IV 1139-41 *see* Austria
Matilda Plantagenet, 135
Otto I 1180-3 *see* Wittelsbach, Otto of

Beatrix (of Burgundy), Empress, second wife of F.B., 71, 120, 123, 186, 201

Beauvais, Bishop of (Henry of France), 104; Synod of (1160), 97

Becket, Thomas, Archbishop of Canterbury, 115, 129

Bellinzona, 154

Belluno, 179

Belmonte, 164

Benevento, 67, 73, 74, 123, 139; *see also* Concordat of Benevento

Berchtesgaden, Provost of, 95, 96

Bergamo, 89, 126, 127, 128, 148, 163, 178; Bishop of, 95

Bernard, Cardinal, 80, 94

Besançon, 39, 168; Archbishop of, 28, 95; Diet of (1157), 77-83, 94, 118, 156

Beuren, 41, 131; Frederick of, 41

Biandrate, Count of, 86, 89, 99, 127, 136, 144, 148, 159

Biandrate, Guido of *see* Ravenna, Archbishop of

Bobbio, 148, 164, 178

Bohemia, 19, 21, 25, 28, 48, 77, 83, 97, 106, 171, 172
Adalbert of *see* Salzburg, Archbishop of
Conrad of *see* Moravia
Frederick, Duke of (1173, 1177-89), 172
Henry of *see* Prague, Bishop of
Sobieslav I, Duke of (1173-7), 172
Vladislav II, Duke 1140 (King 1158-75), 45, 48, 77, 106, 172

Bologna, 68, 74, 85, 86, 90, 97, 127, 128, 148, 160, 164, 178; Bishop of, 103

Boso, Cardinal, 66, 75, 111, 138

Bouvines, battle of, 145

Brabant, 22, 147, 148, 171; Henry I, Duke of, 191

Brandenburg, 22, 171; *see also* Albert the Bear; Bishop of, 157

Bremen, 20, 25; Archbishop of, 66, 95, 132, 176, 200

Brescia, 88, 89, 100, 126, 127, 128, 148, 151, 155, 163, 177, 178; Bishop of, 103; *see also* Arnold

Breslau, 77, 109

Brixen, 21, 97, 176

Brunswick, 135, 171, 172

Buch, Christian of *see* Mainz, Archbishop of

Burgundy, 14, 15, 17, 22, 28, 39, 52, 59, 77 *et seq*, 95, 97, 103 *et seq*, 108, 109, 129, 168, 201, 204
Otto (of Hohenstaufen), Count of, 201, 204
Rainald III, Count of, 59, 71
Rudolf III, King of, 39

Busco, Marquis of, 99, 136

Byzantine Empire, 12, 16, 32, 33, 37, 38, 48, 62, 63, 75, 89, 121, 137 *et seq*, 183-4, 202-4
Isaac II (Angelos), Emperor 1185-95, 1203-4, 202, 203, 204
Manuel I (Comnenos), Emperor 1143-80, 38, 48, 70, 71, 73, 89, 90, 112, 121, 122, 137-9, 145, 146, 156, 183, 184
Sophia *see* Sicily
Theodora *see* Austria

Caesaria, new city of, 178

Calabria, 38, 75, 110

Calixtus III, anti-Pope 1168-78, 140, 152, 156, 157, 159, 167

Campagna, The, 94, 111, 176

Campo Grasso, F.B.'s meeting with Hadrian IV at, 68
Capua, 38, 75
Carinthia, 21, 25, 45, 171
Cassino, 163
Castille, 97; Alfonso VIII King of, 1158-1214, 201; Berengaria of, 201
Celestine II, Pope 1143-4, 36
Ceprano, 67
Cesena, 159
Chalon, 103, 105
Champagne, Henry I (the Liberal), Count of, 103, 104, 105, 106, 117, 192, 193
Charlemagne, 12-14, 15, 16, 32, 36, 38, 69, 98, 118, 119, 124, 207, 208, 209, 210
Charles II the Bald, Emperor, 22
Chiaravella, Abbot of, 62
Chiavenna, meeting between F.B. and Henry the Lion at, 153, 169
Chioggia, 163
Cîteaux, Abbot of, 94, 141
Clairvaux, Abbot of 94, 141
Clement III, Pope 1187-91, 193, 194, 198, 199-200
Cluny, 103, 105; Odo, Abbot of, *quoted*, 16
Cologne, 20, 25, 28, 134, 171; Archbishops of:—
    Arnold of Wied, 45, 58, 72
    Philip of Heinsberg, 132, 151, 153, 155, 157, 169, 171, 189, 190, 191, 192, 193, 194, 198, 200
    Rainald of Dassel, 72, 76, 80-1, 82, 83, 89, 95, 98, 105, 106, 107, 110, 111, 113, 114, 115, 117, 118, 119, 122, 124, 132
Como, 84, 88, 99, 136, 154, 158, 163, 178
Concordat of Benevento (1156), 73, 75-6, 78, 82, 89
Concordat of Worms (1122), 53, 60, 108, 184, 189
Conrad II, Emperor, 39
Conrad III (Hohenstaufen), Emperor, 11, 15, 41, 42, 44, 45, 47, 48, 49, 57, 58, 60, 127, 157, 195, 198, 201
Constance, Bishops of, 62; (Otto of Habsburg), 118, 176; Diet and Treaty of (1153), 62-3, 66, 74, 76, 78, 82, 90, 96, 98; Diet of (1182), 179, 181
Constitutions of Clarendon, 115

Corvey, Abbot of, 47
Crema, 88, 92, 94, 95, 150, 106, 107, 190
Cremona, 34, 84, 87, 99, 101, 103, 111, 125, 126, 127, 128, 145, 146, 147, 148, 150, 151, 152, 155, 158, 159, 161, 162, 163, 181, 186, 187, 190, 191
Crusades (Second), 48, 49, 198
Crusades (Third), 49, 186, 195-205, 206, 208

Dahn, fortress of, 131
Damascus, 48, 195
Dassel, Rainald of *see* Cologne, Archbishop of
Denmark, 20, 22, 97; Kings of:—
    Knut VI 1182-1202, 172, 192
    Svend III (V) 1147-57, 59, 77
    Waldemar I 1157-82, 77, 106, 134, 171
Diets *see* Aix-la-Chapelle, Bamberg, Besançon, Constance, Erfurt, Fulda, Gelnhausen, Goslar, Mainz, Merseburg, Nuremberg, Parma, Ratisbon, Roncaglia, and Würzburg
Dole, council meeting at (1162), 106-7, 108
Dortmund, 20, 25
Dorylaeum, battle of (1147), 48
Duisburg, fairs at, 133-4

Edward the Confessor, King of England 1042-66, 118
Eichstadt, Bishops of (Egilolf), 132; 176
Eicke of Repgau, 173
Emilia, 159
England, Kings of *see* Edward the Confessor and Henry II
Eppingen, castle of, 131
Erfurt, Diets of (1160), 99; (1181), 172; (1188), 193
Eschenbach, Wolfram von, 205
Este, Obizzo d', 182
Eugenius III, Pope 1145-53, 36, 57-9, 61-4, 74
Ezelino (consul of Treviso), 149

Faenza, 159, 178; Bishop of, 95
Feltre, 179
Fermo, Bishop of, 95
Ferrara, 91, 112, 127, 128, 148, 160, 163, 178
Florence, 111, 139, 145, 187

Folmar, 184-5, 188, 189, 190, 191, 192, 193, 199
Folz, Robert, 118-19
Forcalquier, Counts of, 39, 103
Forli, 159
Forlimpopoli, 159
France, Kings of *see* Louis VII and Philip Augustus
Franconia, 23, 131, 175, 201
Frederick I (Barbarossa) Emperor (1125/6-90)
  (1) *His Personal Life and Character*
  ancestry and background, 41-2; early life, 46-7; first marriage, 47-8; character and aims, 48-56; divorce, 58-9, 61; second marriage, 71; family, 120, 134, 180; death of Empress Beatrix, 186; takes the Cross, 194 *et seq*; last will and testament, 201
  (2) *Activities in Germany*
  policy and aims there, 52-4; proclamation of *Landfrieden*, 59-61, 71; relations with Henry the Lion, 64-5; relations with neighbouring countries, 76-7, 97, 108; identifies himself with Charlemagne, 118-20; consolidates his position, 130-6; takes Bavaria and Saxony from Henry the Lion, 168-76; proceeds against Archbishop of Cologne, 191-2, 194; makes final arrangements in, 199-201; his posthumous reputation in, 205-8
  (3) *Quarrel with Papacy*
    (a) *The Opening Phase* (1152-4), relations with Eugenius III, 57-9, 61, leading to Treaty of Constance, 62-4; relations with Anastasius IV, 64-6
    (b) *Pontificate of Hadrian IV* (1154-9), F.B.'s early relations with, 66-7; his occupation of Rome and coronation, 68-70; his attitude to Concordat of Benevento, 75 *et seq*; resentful of Papal claims at Diet of Besançon, 78-83; his actions in Lombardy and at Diet of Roncaglia provoke opposition, 83-8; his relations with Pope steadily deteriorate till death of Hadrian IV, 88-92
    (c) *Struggle with Alexander III*

(1159-81), F.B. champions anti-Pope Victor IV in disputed Papal election, 93-6, and is excommunicated by Alexander III, 96-7; plans to crush Lombard cities and install Victor in Rome, 98 *et seq*; tries vainly to enlist French support against Alexander, 103-7; makes further preparations and again invades North Italy, 107-13; engages in fresh diplomatic activities against Alexander and on behalf of Victor IV (successor Paschal III), 114 *et seq*; again invades Italy and drives Alexander from Rome, 122-4; obliged to quit Rome because of plague, F.B. is faced with revolt of Lombard cities, 124-9; tries unsuccessfully to divide Alexander from Lombard League, 137-46; takes military action against Lombard League and again tries to separate them from Pope, 147 *et seq*, reaches agreement with Alexander at Anagni, 156 *et seq*, and signs Treaty of Venice, 163-5; death of Alexander III, 176
    (d) *Pontificates of Lucius III, Urban III, Gregory VIII and Clement III* (1181-91), F.B. continues to negotiate on outstanding differences with Pope, 176 *et seq*, but these reach a deadlock at Verona, 182, 184-6; F.B.'s open quarrel with Urban III, 188 *et seq*, only terminates with Pope's death, 192; F.B. enjoys better relations with Gregory VIII, 193, and comes to terms with Clement III, 193-4
  (4) *The Last Phase* (1188-90), F.B. takes the Cross, 195, makes his final arrangements, 199-201, departs on Third Crusade, 202, is drowned in Armenia, 205
  (5) *The Final Assessment*, 209-12
Frederick II (Hohenstaufen), Emperor, 205, 206, 207

Frederick III (Habsburg), Emperor, 207

Freising, Otto, Bishop of (died 1158), 15, 30, 32, 33, 34, 42, 45, 46, 48, 76, 84, 88, 97, 109, 111, 127, 137

Fulda, Diet of (1157), 76

Gaeta, 32, 38, 102

Gamalion, 207

Ganbara, Albert, 151

Gelasius I, Pope 496-502, 57

Gelnhausen, 131; Diets of (1180), 171, (1186), 190-1

Geneva, 39, 71

Genoa, 33, 34, 87, 101, 102, 110, 112, 122, 137, 145, 159, 168, 199, 201

Germany, 19-29, 52-4, 55, 56, 59-61, 64-5, 70-1, 76-7, 88, 106, 107, 108-9, 113, 114, 116-17, 118-20, 130-6, 146, 147, 149, 153-4, 157, 168-76, 182, 189, 190-1, 199-201, 206-8, 209, 210, 211

Ghibellines, 42, 126, 136, 140, 145, 187, 206, 211

Goslar, 20, 25, 131; Diets of (1154), 64, (1188), 200-201

Grande Chartreuse, Prior of, 141

Gregory VIII, Pope 1187, 192

Guastalla, 158, 190

Gubbio, 110

Guelders, Count of (Otto I), 199

Guelphs, 42, 126, 136, 140, 145, 148, 150, 159, 165, 181, 188, 206, 211

Guido of Santa Pudenziana, Cardinal, 67

Gurk, Bishop of, 97

Habsburg *see* Constance, Otto, Bishop of and Frederick III, Emperor

Hadrian IV Pope 1154-9, 11, 66-70, 73-6, 78-83, 88-92, 96, 193

Hadrianople, 204

Hagenau, 131

Hainault, Baldwin, Count of, 193

Halberstadt, Gero, Bishop of, 157, 168; Ulrich, Bishop of, 117, 168, 175

Haller, Johannes, 52

Hampe, K, *quoted*, 134

Hausen, Frederick von, 205

Hauteville, Tancred of, 37

Havelberg, Bishop of, 62

Henry II, King of England 1154-89, 95, 97, 103, 104, 107, 115, 116, 120, 129, 135, 145, 171, 198

Henry III, Emperor, 28

Henry IV, Emperor, 15, 26, 28, 41, 42, 161, 165

Henry VI, Emperor (F.B.'s son), 120, 134, 180, 181, 183, 185, 186, 188, 190, 191, 193, 194, 199, 200, 201, 204, 209

Henry the Lion (Duke of Bavaria and Saxony), 42, 44, 49, 56, 60, 64, 70, 84, 106, 108-9, 110, 116, 120, 121, 134-6, 153-4, 168-72, 173, 174, 182, 192, 200, 210

Herfeld, Abbot of, 199

Hildesheim, 25, 72

Hohenstaufen, House of, 19, 41 *et seq*, 54, 126, 131, 134, 169, 173-4, 190, 201, 211

relationship to F.B. indicated:—
Conrad III, Emperor (1092-1153) —uncle—*see* Conrad III
Conrad (1135-95)—half-brother —*see* Rhine, Count Palatine of
Conrad (1172-96)—son—*see* Rothenburg, Count of
Conradin (1252-68)—great great grandson, 206
Frederick I (Barbarossa) *see* Frederick I
Frederick II (1194-1250)—grandson—*see* Frederick II
Frederick of Beuren—great grandfather *see* Beuren
Frederick of Rothenburg (1145-67)—cousin—*see* Rothenburg
Frederick I of Swabia (1050-1105) —grandfather—*see* Swabia
Frederick V of Swabia (1164-91) —son—*see* Swabia
Henry VI, Emperor (1165-97)—son—*see* Henry VI
Henry (son of Conrad III) (1137-50)—cousin, 45
Otto, Count of Burgundy (1167-1200)—son—*see* Burgundy
Philip (1176-1208) *see* Aix-la-Chapelle, Provost of

Holstein, Adolf II of Schauenberg, Count of, 44-5, 108, 153, 172, 191

Hugo, Victor, 208

Hungary, 83, 97, 203
Kings of:—
Bela III 1173-96, 172, 201, 202, 204
Geza II 1141-61, 77

Iconium, 201, 202, 203, 204

Imola, 159, 178

Innocent II, Pope 1130-43, 36, 38

Index

Innocent III, anti-Pope 1178-80, 176
Investiture Dispute, 24, 34, 36, 174
Italy, 30-9, 54-6, 61 *et seq*, 73-6, 83-92, 93-7, 98-103, 109-13, 120-9, 136-46, 147-66, 167-8, 176-81, 182-94, 206-7, 210, 211-12
Ivrea, 159, 168, 190

Jerusalem, 97, 153, 170, 183-4, 195 *et seq*
Kings of:—
    Amauri I 1163-74, 195, 196
    Baldwin IV 1174-85, 196
    Baldwin V 1185-6, 196
Jordan (Byzantine envoy), 137-8
Jordan, Cardinal, 199
Justinian, Emperor, 85, 118

Kaiserslautern, 131
Kinammos, John, 139

Landfrieden (Land Peace), 26, 59-60, 71, 169
Landsberg, Dietrich of, 170
Lateran Comal (Third), 176, 177, 184, 186
Lecce, Tancred, Count of, 203
Legnano, battle of, 154-5
Lewis II, Emperor, 22, 36, 38
Liège, Raoul, Bishop of, 132
Lodi, 66, 84, 87, 88, 99, 100, 103, 111, 122, 125, 127, 128, 136, 137, 148, 163, 178, 186
Lombard League, 127-9, 136-7, 139-46, 147-66, 177-81
Lorraine, 21, 22, 23, 25, 45, 171, 191, 192, 200, 209
Lothar III, Emperor, 36, 41, 42, 45, 46, 57, 58, 82, 127, 157, 165
Louis the Pious, Emperor, 118
Louis VII, King of France 1137-80, 95, 97, 103, 104, 105, 106, 107, 115, 117, 137, 145, 146
Lübeck, 108, 135, 171, 175; *see also* Arnold of Lübeck
Lucca, 110, 113, 145, 187
Lucius II, Pope 1144-5, 36
Lucius III, Pope 1181-5, 177, 182, 183-6, 187, 195
Ludus de Antichristo, 98, 205-6
Lund, 66; Eskil, Bishop of, 79, 80
Lüneburg, 20, 172
Lusatia, 21, 22, 45, 175, 200
Luther, Martin, 207
Lützelhard, Conrad of, 140
Lyons, 39, 168; Archbishops of, 78,

95; (Guichard de Pontigny), 109, 129

Mâcon, 103; William II, Count of, 59, 71
Magdeburg, 20, 25, 170; Archbishops of:—
    Frederick of Wettin, 61
    Wichmann, 61, 64, 82, 95, 109, 156, 190-1
Maguelonne, 102, 104
Mainz, 25, 76; Archbishops of, 28, 82, 95, 108;
    Christian of Buch, 108, 114, 117, 121, 122, 145, 147, 153, 154, 155, 156, 157, 159-60, 161, 163, 165, 167, 176, 177
    Conrad of Wittelsbach, 108, 109, 117, 123, 157, 176, 177, 184, 186, 188
    Diets of (1184), 181, 182; (1188), 194, 195
Mantua, 112, 126, 127, 148, 163, 177, 178; Bishop of, 95, 157
Manuel I *see* Byzantine Empire
Matilda, Countess, estates of, 37, 60, 91, 136, 140, 157, 162, 176, 177, 181, 187, 190, 200
Maxey-sur-Vaise, F.B. meets Louis VII at, 145
Mecklenburg, Pribislaw, Prince of, 135
Merseburg, Bishop of (Eberhard of Seeburg), 132: Diet of (1152), 59; Provost of (Christian of Buch), 114; *see also* Mainz, Archbishop of
Metz, Bishops of, 109; (Frederick), 132
Milan, 34, 49, 66, 70, 74, 76, 83-4, 86-8, 89, 92, 96, 98, 99-100, 101, 102, 111, 113, 121, 126, 127, 128, 139, 147, 148, 149, 154, 163, 178, 182, 186, 187, 188, 190, 191
    Archbishops of—Galdin, 103, 121, 125, 136
    Hubert Crivelli *see* Urban III
Misnia, 21, 22, 45
Mitteis, Heinrich, 173
Modena, 127, 128, 148, 160, 164
Monaco, 32, 102
Mondovi, 159
Monteaperti, battle of (1260), 206
Montebello, truce of, 149
Montferrat, Margraves of—Conrad, 176; William, 87, 99, 127, 136, 137, 144

Moravia, 21; Conrad of Bohemia, Duke of, 172
Morena, Acerbo of, 87, 111, 136; Otto of, 115
Mouzon, Synod of (1186), 192; F.B.'s meeting with Philip Augustus near, 193
Munich, 109, 171
Münster, Ludwig of Tecklenburg, Bishop of, 132

Namur, succession in, 192, 193-4
Naples, 38, 102
Napoleon I, 11
Narni, 189, 199
Newmarket, synod of (1160), 97
Non est dubium (Papal Bull 1170), 142-5
Norway, 103
Novara, 136, 148, 163, 178; Bishop of, 99
Nur-ed-Din, Sultan, 195, 196
Nuremberg, 108, 131; Diets of (1166), 117; (1186), 192

Octavian of Monticello, Cardinal, 90-1, 92, 94, 95, 96; thereafter *see* Victor IV
Orleans, Manasse, Bishop of, 103
Orta, 199
Orvieto, 190, 199
Ostia, 123, 139; Ubaldo, Cardinal, Archbishop of, 103, 152, 160, 161, 177; thereafter *see* Lucius III
Otto I, Emperor, 14, 15, 24-5, 29, 32, 36, 67, 85, 98, 165, 209
Otto III, Emperor, 16, 17
Otto IV (Welf), Emperor, 145

Paderborn, 171; Bishop of, 176
Padua, 112, 127, 128, 148, 163, 178; Bishop of, 103
Palermo, 38, 54, 102, 121, 123, 183, 184, 187
Palestrina, Paul Scolari, Bishop of *see* Clement III
Papal States, 14, 32, 36-7, 55, 88, 89, 91, 92, 98, 190, 189, 199
Parma, 125, 127, 128, 148, 164, 178, 187
Paschal III (Guy of Crema), anti-Pope 1164-8, 113 *et seq*, 119, 120, 121, 122, 123, 137, 139, 140, 156
Passau, see of, 118; Conrad, Bishop of *see* Salzburg
Pavia, 34, 66, 67-8, 84, 87, 96, 111, 125, 126, 127, 148, 149, 152, 154, 155,

159, 160, 161, 163, 187; Archbishop of, 141; Cardinal William, 90
Pavia, synod of (1160), 94-6, 103, 108
Perrin, Charles E., *quoted*, 23
Perugia, 189, 207
Pesta, Gerard, 149, 151, 161, 178
Peter, Cardinal, 199
Pfullendorf, 175, 201
Philip, Augustus, King of France 1180-1223, 145, 174, 192, 193, 198
Philippopolis, 203
Piacenza, 65, 84, 87, 100, 127, 128, 148, 164, 178, 179, 190; Bishop of, 103
Piedmont, 34, 65, 147, 168, 182
Pierleone family, 94
Pisa, 33, 34, 101-2, 110, 122, 123, 145, 168, 193, 199
Poland, 23, 77, 83, 172
    Kings of:—
    Boleslav IV 1142-73, 77, 109
    Vladislav II 1139-42, 77
Pomposa, 161, 163
Pontida, 126
Pontremoli, 125
Porto Venere, 101, 102
Prague, Henry of Bohemia, Bishop of, 172
Provence, 22, 39, 103, 104, 168
Prüm, Abbot of, 61

Rainald of Dassel *see* Cologne, Archbishop of
Rainier, Cardinal, 160
Ratisbon, 20, 202; Bishop of (Henry), 48, 118, 175; Diets of (1152), 60
Ratzeburg, Henry, Count of, 44
Ravenna, 91, 101, 140, 148, 158, 159, 160, 161; Archbishops of (Anselm), 88; (Guido of Biandrate), 89, 95
Ravensburg, 20
Reggio, 148, 164, 178, 187
Reichersberg, Gero, Provost of, 117
Reims, Henry of France, Archbishop of, 104
Rhine, Counts Palatine of:—
    Conrad of Hohenstaufen, 47, 71
    Herman of Stahleck, 45, 71
Rimini, 148, 158, 159
Roland (Bandinelli), Cardinal, 74, 78, 80, 92 *see* thereafter Alexander III
Romagna, 37, 110, 122, 159, 187, 200

Rome, city of, 16, 17, 36, 61, 62, 63, 64, 66-7, 68-70, 74, 76, 88, 89, 90, 91, 92, 93-4, 98, 102, 107, 109, 110, 112, 114, 120, 121, 122-4, 139, 140, 141, 142, 149, 156, 157, 167, 176, 177, 182, 183, 193, 194, 199, 210

Roncaglia, Diet of (1158), 65, 86, 87, 88, 101, 102, 110, 112, 130, 131, 149, 161, 165

Rothenburg, Conrad of Hohenstaufen, Count of, 201
    Frederick of Hohenstaufen, Count of, Frederick IV, Duke of *see* Swabia

Rouen, talks at, 115, 129; *see also* Stephen of Rouen

Rügen, 134

St. Jean de Losne, proposed conference at, 104, 115, 118

Saladin, 196, 203, 204

Salef, River, F.B. drowned in, 205

Salerno, 33, 102; Romuald, Archbishop of, 162

Salzano, 99

Salzburg, Archbishops of:—
    Adalbert of Bohemia, 132, 146, 157, 175, 176
    Conrad of Austria (previously Bishop of Passau), 45, 114, 117, 132
    Conrad of Wittelsbach, 175
    Eberhard, 92, 95, 97, 99, 108, 109, 114

San Miniato, fortress of, 111

Sardinia, 60, 91; Oristano, King of, 112

Savona, 159

Savoy, 39, 129

Saxony, 12, 23, 25, 28, 42, 119, 135, 154, 169-72, 175, 201
    Dukes of:—
    Albert 1140-2 *see* Albert the Bear
    Bernard 1180-1212 *see* Anhalt, Bernard III of
    Henry the Lion 1142-80 *see* Henry the Lion
    Henry the Proud 1136-8 *see* Bavaria, Henry, Duke of

Schiltach, 131

Schramberg, 131

Schwerin, 135

Selestat, 131

Sens, meeting between Alexander III and Becket at, 115

Serbia, 202, 203

Serravalle, 178

Sicily, 32, 37-8, 39, 54, 55, 62, 63, 64, 67, 70, 73-6, 78, 89, 90, 92, 93, 94, 96, 98-9, 101, 102, 103, 107, 110, 111-12, 114, 121, 123, 124, 128, 137, 138, 139, 140, 141, 143, 153, 156, 157, 161, 162, 163, 165, 183, 204, 210
    Constance of (wife of Henry VI), 183, 188, 204
    Margaret (of Navarre), Queen of, 121
    Roger II, King of 1130-54, 37, 38, 62, 64
    Sophia, Queen of, 145, 146
    William I, King of 1154-66, 64, 67, 73, 74-6, 89, 90, 92, 96, 112, 121, 137
    William II, King of 1166-89, 121, 145, 146, 156, 161, 162, 163, 165, 183

Siena, 74, 97, 139, 187, 189

Sigismund, Emperor, 207

Silesia, 22, 109

Soissons, Hugh of Champfleury, Bishop of, 104

Spires, 25, 108; Bishops of, 118; (Rapodo), 132, 176; Diet of (1178), 169

Spoleto, 32, 37, 60, 70, 91, 110, 168, 177, 210; Bidulf, Duke of, 140

Stablo, Wibald, Abbot of, 47, 58, 88

Stade, 171

Stahleck, Herman of *see* Rhine, Count Palatine of

Staufenberg, castle of, 131

Stephen of Rouen, 15

Strasbourg, Bishop of, 157; Diets of (1187), 192
    Treaty of (1189), 199-200, 201

Styria, 21, 171

Susa, 108, 129, 147

Sutri, 68, 189

Swabia, 23, 25, 28, 41-2, 47, 53, 60, 131, 171, 175, 201
    Dukes of:—
    Frederick I 1079-1105 (F.B.'s grandfather), 41
    Frederick II (the One-Eyed) 1105-47 (F.B.'s father), 41, 47
    Frederick III 1147-52 *see* Frederick I, Emperor
    Frederick IV (of Rothenberg) 1152-67 (F.B.'s cousin), 41, 60, 124, 201
    Frederick V 1191 (F.B.'s son), 120, 181, 201, 205

Swabia (*contd.*)
Judith (Welf), Duchess of, 46
Syracuse, 102

Tegernsee, Abbot of, 98, 205
Terracina, 102, 199
Thuringia, 53, 131, 175; Landgraves of, 135, 153; (Louis III), 191
Tivoli, 69, 91, 199
Tortona, 68, 137, 148, 158, 159, 178
Toul, Bishop of, 192, 193
Tours, council of (1163), 107, 108
Treves, 21; Archbishops of (*see also* Folmar):—
 Arnold, 132, 184
 Hillin, 45, 58, 60, 95, 109
 John, 199
 Rudolf of Wied, 184, 185, 189, 199; Synod of, 107
Treviso, 112, 127, 128, 148, 149, 158, 163, 178
Trifels, fortress of, 131
Tripoli, 195, 196, 197
Turin, 108, 149, 159, 168; Bishop of, 161
Tuscany, 34, 60, 88, 89, 90, 91, 93, 108, 110, 111, 121, 145, 168, 187, 190,
Tusculum, 122, 177, 199

Urban III, Pope 1185-7, 188 *et seq*, 192
Utrecht, Bishop of, 198

Valentinian, Emperor, 118
Vasto, Marquis of, 32, 99, 136
Venice, 32, 33, 37, 38-9, 52, 65, 111-12, 125, 127, 128, 140, 148, 160 *et seq*, 178
Venice, Treaty of (1177), 161-6, 167, 168, 176, 177, 183, 184, 190, 195
Ventimiglia, 159
Vercelli, 136, 148, 163, 178; Bishop of, 99
Verdun, bishop of, 109, 192, 193
Verdun, Treaty of (843), 22
Veroli, 141, 145
Verona, 44, 65, 122, 128, 147, 148, 151, 163, 177, 178, 182, 184, 185,
186, 189, 195; Bishop of, 103
Verona, League of, 112, 125, 127
Vicenza, 112, 127, 128, 148, 163, 178; Bishop of, 157
Victor IV, anti-Pope 1159-64, 94, 96-7, 98, 103, 104, 105, 106, 107, 108, 110, 112, 113, 114, 116, 156
Viterbo, 68, 121, 189, 200
Viviers, Bishop of, 103
Vogelweide, Walter von der, 205
Voghera, 148

Waiblingen Castle, 42, 126, 131
Waldeck, Heinrich von, 206
Weinsberg, castles in 131
Welf, House of, 19, 42, 45-6, 53, 60, 145, 168 *et seq*, 193, 211
 Welf VI
 (died 1191), 42, 46, 48, 60, 110, 136, 140, 154, 169, 175, 201
 Welf VII (died 1167), 124, 136 *see also* Bavaria, Henry the Lion, Otto IV; Swabia, Judith, Duchess of
Westphalia, 119, 171, 189
Wettin, House of, 22, 45; *see also* Magdeburg, Frederick, Archbishop of
Wittelsbach, House of—Conrad *see* Mainz, Archbishop of; Otto (Count Palatine of the Rhine), 44, 81, 82, 83, 89, 91, 93, 94, 106, 108, 171
Worms, 25, 53, 192; Conrad of Steinberg, Bishop of, 132, 156; *see also* Concordat of
Wortwin, Protonotary, 153, 156
Würzburg, 25, 71; Bishops of:—
 Harold of Hocheim, 118
 Reinhard of Abensberg, 132, 134, 198
 Diet of (1165), 116-18, 129, 149, 152, 165, 171

Zähringen, Dukes of:—
 Berthold IV, 42, 44, 59, 71, 107
 Conrad I, 47
 Rudolf, 108